TOWARD PROSPERITY

The Transformation of
Atlantic Canada's Economy

DON MILLS & DAVID CAMPBELL

NIMBUS
PUBLISHING
NIMBUS.CA

PRAISE FOR
TOWARD PROSPERITY

Toward Prosperity constitutes a valuable contribution to the debate about how best to understand and manage our region, its economy, and its communities. Not all of the authors' recommendations will be broadly accepted, but their sense of optimism, based on their research and experience, is welcome. Atlantic Canada has had enough economic doom and gloom when, actually, as Campbell and Mills point out, a lot of good things are happening.

– Dan Leger, author, *Stephen McNeil: Principle and Politics*

Copyright © 2025, Don Mills & David Campbell

All rights reserved. No part of this book may be reproduced, stored in a retrieval system or transmitted in any form or by any means without the prior written permission from the publisher, or, in the case of photocopying or other reprographic copying, permission from Access Copyright, 1 Yonge Street, Suite 1900, Toronto, Ontario M5E 1E5. No part of this book may be used in the training of generative artificial intelligence technologies or systems.

Nimbus Publishing Limited
3660 Strawberry Hill Street, Halifax, NS, B3K 5A9
(902) 455-4286 nimbus.ca

Nimbus Publishing is based in Kjipuktuk, Mi'kma'ki, the traditional territory of the Mi'kmaq People.

No part of this book may be used in the training of generative artificial intelligence technologies or systems.

Printed and bound in Canada
NB1731

Developmental editor: Dan Leger
Design: Jenn Embree

Library and Archives Canada Cataloguing in Publication

Title: Toward prosperity : the transformation of Atlantic Canada's economy / Don Mills & David Campbell.
Names: Mills, Don (Social scientist), author. | Campbell, David (Economist), author.
Identifiers: Canadiana (print) 20240523636 | Canadiana (ebook) 2024052439X | ISBN 9781774714256 (softcover) | ISBN 9781774714263 (EPUB)
Subjects: LCSH: Economic development—Atlantic Provinces. | LCSH: Industries—Atlantic Provinces. | LCSH: Entrepreneurship—Atlantic Provinces. | LCSH: Clean energy industries—Atlantic Provinces. | LCSH: Sustainable development—Atlantic Provinces. | LCSH: Education, Higher—Economic aspects—Atlantic Provinces. | LCSH: Technological innovations—Economic aspects—Atlantic Provinces. | LCSH: Atlantic Provinces—Economic conditions.
Classification: LCC HC117.A8 M55 2025 | DDC 338.09715—dc23

Nimbus Publishing acknowledges the financial support for its publishing activities from the Government of Canada, the Canada Council for the Arts, and from the Province of Nova Scotia. We are pleased to work in partnership with the Province of Nova Scotia to develop and promote our creative industries for the benefit of all Nova Scotians.

CONTENTS

Foreword. . . . . *vii*
Preface: A Note from the Authors . . . . *x*
Introduction . . . . *xiv*

PART ONE
ATLANTIC CANADA'S HISTORY OF ECONOMIC UNDERPERFORMANCE

CHAPTER 1: *The Underperforming Economy* 2
CHAPTER 2: *The Demographic Tsunami*. 16
CHAPTER 3: *The Impact of Limited Immigration* 29
CHAPTER 4: *Structural Growth Challenges*. 37
CHAPTER 5: *Too Many Workers, Too Few Jobs* 45
CHAPTER 6: *An Aging Workforce* 60
CHAPTER 7: *The Employment Insurance Conundrum*. 73
CHAPTER 8: *Overreliance on Government* 81
CHAPTER 9: *The Private-Sector Investment Gap*. 89
CHAPTER 10: *The Challenge of Accessing Capital* 91
CHAPTER 11: *The Weak Entrepreneurial Environment*. 98

PART TWO
THE TURNAROUND: IS ATLANTIC CANADA POISED FOR GROWTH?

CHAPTER 12: *Immigration as an Economic Driver* 106
CHAPTER 13: *Post-Secondary Education: A Catalyst for Growth* . 118
CHAPTER 14: *The Downside of High Population Growth*. 125
CHAPTER 15: *Regional Incubators and Accelerators*. 132
CHAPTER 16: *Renewed Entrepreneurship and Economic Growth*. . 138
CHAPTER 17: *Becoming a More Innovative Place* 144
CHAPTER 18: *The Prosperity Disparity* 152
CHAPTER 19: *Expanding the Definition of Economic Development*. 158

PART THREE
A PRESCRIPTION FOR FUTURE PROSPERITY

CHAPTER 20: *The Role of Economic Hubs* **168**
CHAPTER 21: *The Importance of Economic Clusters.* **178**
CHAPTER 22: *A More Competitive Tax Environment* **182**
CHAPTER 23: *Developing the Export Economy* **191**
CHAPTER 24: *The Green Economy and New Energy Alternatives* **198**
CHAPTER 25: *Seizing the Green Opportunity* **205**
CHAPTER 26: *Emulating Entrepreneurial Success* **210**
CHAPTER 27: *First Nations in Regional Economic Development* **222**
CHAPTER 28: *The Risk of Backsliding* **226**
CHAPTER 29: *Measuring Economic Momentum* **231**
CHAPTER 30: *10 Ways to Maintain the Momentum* **236**
CHAPTER 31: *Toward Prosperity.* **245**

Acknowledgements **247**
Endnotes. **248**
Bibliography. **251**
About the Authors. **256**

FOREWORD

"GROW OR GO" HAS BEEN ATLANTIC CANADA'S MAIN ECONOMIC NARRATIVE since the late nineteenth century. Out-migration has been the preferred path to prosperity for many, especially the most mobile. We have had growth—just not enough. By times, we've defaulted to calling ourselves "have-nots."

With *Toward Prosperity: The Transformation of Atlantic Canada's Economy*, Don Mills and David Campbell tell a different story. They offer a current account of how Atlantic Canada is prospering. They envisage a future that is even more prosperous based on proffered directions, commitments, and policies.

The foundation of this work is storytelling, something Atlantic Canadians have always been good at. Campbell and Mills have spent their careers analyzing development in the region. Their *Insights* podcast series, launched in 2021, has resulted in more than two hundred episodes that feature business and community leaders. Based on their podcasts and the authors' in-depth analysis, this volume is peppered with examples and stories of real prosperity and leadership.

The overriding outlook is one of optimism. The underlying characteristic is confidence, something that has frequently been lacking in Atlantic Canada. The prescriptions presented by Campbell and Mills have a boldness and clarity that will generate debate.

Those debates will need to be informed by good data and analyses, which are leading features of *Toward Prosperity*. This work digs deep to offer comparative insights among the four Atlantic provinces and between the region and Canada as a whole. The central focus is economic, while the illuminating framework is demographic. The authors analyze the four decades between 1981 and 2021, corresponding to the entry into the workforce and retirement of the baby boomer generation. Their overall conclusions echo the observation of nineteenth-century French sociologist and mathematician Auguste Comte: "Demography is destiny."

The authors make a compelling case that population growth is essential to economic growth. They point with urgency to the reality that, over the next decade, nearly 150,000 baby boom–aged workers in the region will leave the workplace. They describe a coming "demographic tsunami" with workforce shortages, rising health-care costs, and perilous fiscal challenges.

They underline the transformational impact of enhanced immigration for Atlantic Canada, notably during the most recent decade. They make the case that, contrary to general assumptions that newcomers will take jobs from current residents, there is a direct correlation between population growth and increased employment.

A rigorous decade-by-decade study of the period 1981–2021 reveals uneven results, with the Atlantic region falling further behind Canada by 33 percent while Prince Edward Island's growth exceeded that of Canada by 5 percent. The authors point to PEI's performance in population growth. All four provinces now have population strategies, building on collaborative efforts to create the Atlantic Immigration Pilot and the Atlantic Growth Strategy.

To understand PEI's growth from 1981 to 2021, it is useful to know about the 1970s. During that decade, PEI had the third-strongest economic growth in Canada, after Alberta and British Columbia. The province had an unprecedented turn to net in-migration for seven consecutive years from 1972 to 1978. A mix of housing programs, with the lion's share of funding coming from the federal government, saw new construction and upgrades affecting one-fifth of the province's housing stock. Not least, PEI created a single provincial university and a new community college.

This background helps to explain how PEI outpaced the region during the subsequent four decades. Bear in mind when analyzing comparative growth that it is an advantage to start out behind. PEI's per capita GDP in 1960 was one-half that of Canada. Growth is more impressive when compared with modest baselines. But modesty doesn't get you far in the world of growth. PEI's other advantages during the years 1981 to 2021 included the construction of the Confederation Bridge, which led to a takeoff in export-oriented industries and manufacturing, and an intentional approach to immigration.

PEI also benefitted from a couple of shocks. The closure of the Summerside air base produced an outcry that led to a new focus on industrial development, notably in aerospace. When the Atlantic Investment Partnership (AIP) was revealed in 2000, PEI was mainly left on the sidelines. We resolved to fight back based on competitive excellence, not by crying for our fair share. This led to a rigorous process to identify clusters of strength and competitive advantage or aspiration, pointing to bioscience, aerospace, information technology, and renewable energy. The analysis pointed later to "food" as a competitive cluster, including a significant part of PEI's growth in manufacturing and exports. Competitive excellence lifts all boats; it's not about winners and losers. After an initial decade of experience with the AIP and its Atlantic Innovation Fund, there were complaints from other provinces that PEI was getting too much.

While the main message of *Toward Prosperity* is one of confidence, this work includes a warning about tendencies to resist change. The discussion around attitudes toward immigration is the most disturbing. While Atlantic Canada is not the only place in the world that defaults to pulling up the drawbridge in the face of change, we don't admire it in others. We should resist it among ourselves. That will take leadership at all levels, including the thought leadership offered by Don Mills and David Campbell. Perhaps a shock would help. As is plainly evident in the pages of this book, attracting and retaining talent is globally competitive. So too is the urgency to upgrade skills and productivity across the board.

There are three lessons, among others, about Atlantic Canada that emerge from the pages of this book. One is that we fare better when we work together, including collaborations beyond the region. Collaboration matters; leadership matters. A second lesson, one that we tend to have in mind only cyclically, is that our region has a competitive advantage in higher education. Our universities and colleges are a clear strength. If they did not exist, we would have to create them.

The third lesson is that geography is changing. For most of the twentieth century, we treated ourselves, or allowed ourselves to be treated, as if Atlantic Canada were the hinterland. The metropolis was elsewhere. This is no longer the case. Ironically, it took the shock of the COVID-19 pandemic and the success of the Atlantic Bubble to drive this point home. The world is more connected than ever. Remote work is possible. Digital opportunities are ascendant. Our populations are growing. Atlantic Canada combines a special quality of life and sense of community with unlimited opportunities to be metropolitan. The most important geography to change may be in our own minds.

Toward Prosperity is a stride in the right direction.

H. Wade MacLauchlan, CM, OPEI
Chancellor, University of New Brunswick
President emeritus, UPEI
32nd premier, Prince Edward Island
West Covehead, PEI

PREFACE
A NOTE FROM THE AUTHORS

DON MILLS: AFTER SELLING CORPORATE RESEARCH ASSOCIATES INC. (NOW Narrative Research)—a company I had co-founded and led for forty years—at the end of 2018, I started to write a book to chronicle my learnings and theories about why Atlantic Canada chronically underperformed the rest of the country economically. Over the years, I had uncovered a number of systemic issues that were contributing to our economic underperformance, including having a smaller private sector relative to the rest of the country and twice as many people living in rural communities than elsewhere in Canada. Turns out these were the consequences of a slow-growing and aging population. Atlantic Canada's population was simply not developing in the same way as the rest of the country's. The lack of population growth over a long period of time meant that the urbanization process did not proceed at the same pace as elsewhere.

One of the findings of my research over the years was that our six largest urban communities generally performed well relative to their counterparts in other regions of the country. It was evident that the region did not have an economic problem with its urban communities, but the disproportionately higher percentage of those living in rural communities did not have access to full-time, year-round jobs and was too dependent on seasonal work and Employment Insurance. This reality contributed significantly to the region's chronic economic underperformance.

I spent a good part of my career speaking out about the economic issues facing our region and advocating for the types of changes needed to alter our economic future. Chief among those changes was the need to address our stagnant and aging population, to rebuild our labour force, and to attract immigrants to the region. I have had the opportunity to present fact-based information that underscored the need to change our region's demographics to the largest organizations in the region. I have also had the opportunity to present our findings and recommendations to nearly every premier and provincial government in Atlantic Canada across several decades, as well as most opposition parties. I've presented data to the Nova Scotia Commission on Building Our New Economy regarding the need to address our demographic decline. I would like to think I had some impact in alerting governments in the region to our population and labour force challenges long before they became apparent to the public.

I have to admit, for a long time I did not think governments would act on the recommendations I had been advocating. Governments tend to have a short-term election-cycle focus and are more concerned about getting re-elected than making good policy decisions for the long term. Frankly, there are no excuses for the current labour force issues in Canada. The demographics and direction of the labour force have been known for decades. Governments and government departments have ignored the warning signs.

After I sold my business, I actually started to write a book. In fact, I drafted the first four chapters, then I stopped writing. At the time—in early 2019—I was frankly discouraged about whether Atlantic Canada would ever realize its full potential. I thought no one would be interested in what I had learned about the region, the reasons for its economic underperformance, and what needed to be done to change our economic future.

Around that time, I started writing a regular column for both the Saltwire Network and Brunswick News, which allowed me an outlet to continue to highlight what was happening in the region economically and to continue to advocate for the kind of change needed to address this underperformance. Then in 2021, David Campbell and I launched the *Insights* podcast to focus on the positive economic stories and opportunities in the region. The podcast also provided us with an opportunity to continue to advocate for policy changes needed to improve economic prosperity in the region. After doing about a hundred podcasts, David and I became increasingly optimistic about the economic direction of Atlantic Canada, mainly because of population growth. That optimism led to the decision to write this book to provide a better understanding of what got the region to its current economic situation, what has changed that is leading to an economic renaissance across Atlantic Canada, and how we can ensure that the momentum can be maintained—even increased. I hope the book will provide readers with a better understanding of both the generational shift in economic opportunity that is currently under way, and the need to take full advantage of that opportunity.

Halifax, Nova Scotia
April 2025

DAVID CAMPBELL: IN THE FALL OF 1992, MY FIRST CAREER-RELATED JOB OUT of university was on a team mandated to attract industry to New Brunswick. I was hired to help the New Brunswick Department of Economic Development and Tourism devise the business case for attracting companies to the province. Since then, much of my career has been focussed on answering a simple question: what can jurisdictions such as New Brunswick and Nova Scotia do to foster a prosperous economy?

Over my three-decade career since, economic development in Atlantic Canada can be segmented into three phases. The first phase ran from the early 1990s to around 2007 and was overwhelmingly focussed on creating jobs for the surplus of young people graduating from the region's high schools, colleges, and universities. I call this the "jobs, jobs, jobs" phase. This was a time when we had too many people and not enough jobs for them across the region—although as will be shown in chapter 5, the real story was not quite as simple.

The second phase ran from about 2007 to 2016. I call this the "lost decade" because, in much of the region, the population stagnated, GDP growth was substantially curtailed, exports declined, and the number of people in the workforce actually started to drop. I say "much of the region" because Prince Edward Island had a much better "lost decade" than the other three Atlantic provinces. This was a period where I felt the region was at a tipping point. In the 2010 to 2012 time frame I made speeches to various audiences across the region, trying to get people interested, but I felt like the prophet Jeremiah beating my head against a wall. Finally, with the Ivany Report from the Nova Scotia Commission on Building Our New Economy in 2013, Nova Scotia started to realize that a structural shift in the region's demography was under way. The aging workforce across Atlantic Canada was becoming a main cause of the region's economic malaise.

When I was asked to join the New Brunswick government as chief economist in early 2015, my number one priority was the development of a population growth plan with real substance.

As of 2025, we are now in a third phase. I call this the "people, people, people" phase. The story of this phase is currently being written. All four Atlantic provinces have population growth and immigration targets. All four provincial governments know they need a workforce renewal and that they need an expansion of entrepreneurs across the region. As will be developed in detail in this book, attracting people and ensuring the region has the workforce needed to meet labour market demand is only one part of the puzzle. It is a fundamental piece, but we also will need new export industries, a focus on competitiveness, reform of labour market policies, investment in economic development–enabling infrastructure, and top-notch public service delivery.

My motivation for collaborating with Don Mills on this book is to shine a light on what we need to do to ensure that the next thirty years in this region will be a time of prosperity and economic renewal across urban and rural Atlantic Canada.

A thriving economy is not an end in itself, but it is a foundation on which individuals, families, municipalities, and provinces can advance broader personal, social, and community goals. A structurally weak economy leads to personal and family insecurity, endless battles about where to allocate scarce tax dollars, and infighting between successful and struggling communities, creating an environment where few can truly succeed. A thriving jurisdiction is one with a strong economic foundation where few are left behind and where all citizens have the potential to achieve their goals in life.

Economic development helps set the table. Don and I want this book to help make sure the table is set for this and subsequent generations in our region.

Cocagne, New Brunswick
April 2025

INTRODUCTION

WE HAVE BOTH SPENT MOST OF OUR CAREERS TRYING TO UNDERSTAND WHY Atlantic Canada has not enjoyed the same level of economic prosperity as the rest of the country and why the region has led the country in unemployment for decades. We have examined and studied the social, economic, and political trends over a long period of time to better understand the root causes of an underperforming economy across the region.

There is little debate that the region has for too long relied on the generosity of other Canadians to maintain a standard of living in keeping with the rest of Canada through transfer plans and Employment Insurance programs. We believe that dependency has led to attitudinal issues which have hurt the region over time. We have a higher propensity to resist change and to fight the development of our natural resources. We seem to support change as long as nothing really changes.

Atlantic Canada has underperformed the rest of Canada economically since the 1950s. As a consequence, our population has not grown materially since the 1990s—a pattern that has only changed recently. This has led to Atlantic Canada having the highest taxation in the country, and has delayed the urbanization of the region that has happened everywhere else in the country. Having twice as many residents living in less economically advantageous rural communities has hurt economic growth across the region. The good news is that recent population growth has driven new economic growth. What is now apparent is that the lack of population growth over the past three decades in particular has been a drag on economic growth in the region. We have simply not benefitted from the population growth dividend the rest of the country has enjoyed.

This book attempts to explain why Atlantic Canada has trailed the rest of the country economically for decades, how the economy is finally transitioning to higher growth, and what must be done to maintain the current momentum across the region.

Over the past four years, as we have co-hosted the *Insights* podcast, we have focussed most on economic development issues and opportunities within the region and have recorded more than two hundred episodes to date. We have had the opportunity to better understand all segments of the economy across the region, including emerging sectors like bioscience, green energy, and the blue (ocean) economy. We have talked with political leaders both provincially and federally, as well as leaders and entrepreneurs in the private sector, and those involved in economic development at every level. We have come away from those conversations with a heightened level of optimism about the future for this region and that has been a primary motivation to write this book together. We believe the future has never been brighter for Atlantic Canada. Now, instead of managing the problems of decline, we are challenged by managing the problems of growth.

We are confident in the region's ability to address the problems of growth, especially with regard to current housing shortages, the increasing demands on health care, and the challenges in public education. A growing population provides the opportunity to fund the investments needed to grow our economy responsibly and equitably, as well as to address the uncompetitive tax environment within the region. We have the opportunity to lead the country in the production of hydrogen and to become an energy superpower through offshore wind. We need to think big and seize the opportunities that are presenting themselves. Both hydrogen and wind energy present enormous export opportunities for our region.

With more immigration and population growth, we are becoming more entrepreneurial in the region. This will help rebalance our workforce to be less dependent on government jobs and to benefit from the prosperity that private-sector jobs generate.

Atlantic Canada is in the early stage of an economic renaissance that needs to be managed and nurtured to ensure that everyone shares in the prosperity being created. We offer ten recommendations in chapter 30 to ensure we do not squander this opportunity. In the end, we need to shift our attitudes in Atlantic Canada to be less reliant on government and more ambitious than we have in the past and to have a bigger vision of what is possible for our future.

PART ONE

ATLANTIC CANADA'S HISTORY OF ECONOMIC UNDERPERFORMANCE

CHAPTER 1

THE UNDERPERFORMING ECONOMY

FOR DECADES, ATLANTIC CANADA HAS, ON AVERAGE, UNDERPERFORMED THE country overall in terms of economic growth. Every year—until only recently—the region had become a smaller part of the Canadian economy and arguably less important politically. For years, we have been independently trying to understand why this is the case. Why does Atlantic Canada have to lead the country in unemployment rates year after year? Are Atlantic Canadians less educated, less motivated to do well, less entrepreneurial? What is wrong with our economic base? Do we have fewer natural resources or less manufacturing? Have we become too dependent on federal transfers and social programs?

Considerable effort and numerous resources have been devoted to economic development across the region over the last half-century. A plethora of economic development agencies exist at the federal, provincial, and municipal levels across the region, with little to show for their efforts. We conservatively estimate that more than a billion dollars are spent annually on those efforts, with little evidence of a significant impact on economic development, as measured by GDP and job growth.

Donald Savoie, in his 2017 book on economic development in the Maritimes, *Looking for Bootstraps*, looked at some of the federal policy decisions that put the region at a competitive disadvantage with the rest of the country. Savoie is often credited as the father of the Atlantic Canada Opportunities Agency (ACOA), tasked with leading economic development in the region, although he now feels that the agency has grown far too big and bureaucratic. As he stated in our 2022 *Insights* podcast with him, "I don't want to be cynical here, because I'm not the cynical type, but a chap not too long ago in Moncton told me that ACOA's main contribution was the three hundred well-paying head office jobs in Moncton. Great pension plans and so on. That's the main contribution. But frankly, that's not good enough. That's not what economic development should be about." When the main benefit of economic agencies is the employment created by these agencies, perhaps there is a need to rethink the economic development strategy in the region.

When we suggested that more than a billion dollars were being spent on economic development in the region by the multitude of agencies involved in economic development without much to show for it, he said, "I couldn't agree more—and I think a billion is probably on the low end. It's a lot more than that. In Moncton, we have agencies coming out of our ears. We have one from Moncton, we have one for Dieppe, we have one in Riverview, we have ACOA. We have the provincial government and on it goes. There's a lack of coordination…so there is a need to streamline."

Nonetheless, when asked about the future prospects for the region he added, "There is no question that I am ten times more optimistic than in the past. I see the light. I really do. I see a class of young entrepreneurs pursuing new markets in Asia and the United States and the Eastern Seaboard. I see a number of young John Braggs emerging. We are seeing the population grow. Halifax is like a mini-Boston. So something is going on in this region. It is very encouraging."

LOOKING BACK

Let's begin by looking back. We have chosen to focus on the forty-year period between the early 1980s and early 2020s for most of the data used in this book for our historic review. We have chosen the early 1980s as the baseline for this analysis, as this coincides closely with full entry of the baby boomer generation into the workforce, while the early 2020s coincides closely with the exit of the baby boomers from the workforce. The role of the baby boomers over the last four decades in the economy will be a common theme throughout this book; it helps inform many of the current economic challenges facing Canada. It is also a period with the availability of the most consistent and comparable economic data.

As people who have studied trends and data for a living, it took us some time to formulate a theory for the chronic underperformance of the economy in the region. Understanding cause and effect has been a big part of our business careers, especially as it relates to economic development and growth, social change, and consumer behaviour. Economic cause and effect are as complex as consumer behaviour cause and effect and involve many factors and considerations.

STRUCTURAL CHALLENGES

Two structural problems have at least partially contributed to an underperforming economy in Atlantic Canada, although neither is the cause of our economic underperformance in the region, but rather symptoms of the problem. One is related to the composition of the workforce in the region, and one is related to the distribution of the population. We will deal with both of these structural issues in more detail later, but can summarize the issues as follows: compared to the rest of the country, the region has proportionately 1) too many people working for the public sector and too few working for the private sector; and 2) twice as many people living in small rural communities that lack a sufficient economic base to provide year-round employment to residents. This latter point has led to a higher dependence on seasonal work and a greater reliance on Employment Insurance across the region, which will be further discussed in a later chapter. The impact of these two realities is that the region has proportionately fewer full-time workers to contribute to growing the economy year-round. This conclusion is premised on our belief that it is largely the private sector that is responsible for economic prosperity and growth and the creation of wealth in the country. The role of the public sector is largely the use and redistribution of that wealth for the well-being of all citizens.

ECONOMIC GROWTH OVER TIME

Let's review the economic performance of the four Atlantic provinces relative to Canada's performance over the last four decades or so. We will use real GDP as compiled by Statistics Canada as a measure of comparison of economic performance between our region and the rest of the country. This data is only available in comparable form since 1982. Real GDP accounts for the removal of inflation in determining economic growth and is a truer measure, in our view, of economic progress over time. Over the past four decades, the Atlantic provinces have rarely achieved economic growth at the national average for the country. We would argue that it is not possible to achieve average economic growth due to the two structural problems identified earlier.

We would like to look at each of the last four decades of economic performance in some detail. Real GDP growth for Canada between 1983 and 2023 was 160 percent. This compares to real GDP growth in Atlantic Canada of 102 percent. The region overall has been, on average, growing nearly 1 percent slower per year for the last four decades. In simple terms, had the region been growing at the average rate of economic growth for the country, Atlantic Canada's economy would be 36 percent larger than it is today if it had grown as fast as the rest of the country. Our collective capacity to fund public services would be nearly 40 percent larger, and our public debt would likely be significantly smaller.

DECLINING ECONOMIC RELEVANCE

Atlantic Canada has been shrinking in economic importance relative to the rest of the country for a long time. In 1983, Atlantic Canada represented 6.8 percent of the Canadian economy. By 2023, this had shrunk to 5.3 percent of the Canadian economy. The good news is that it now appears that the economy within the region is no longer shrinking thanks to improved economic growth led by recent population growth.

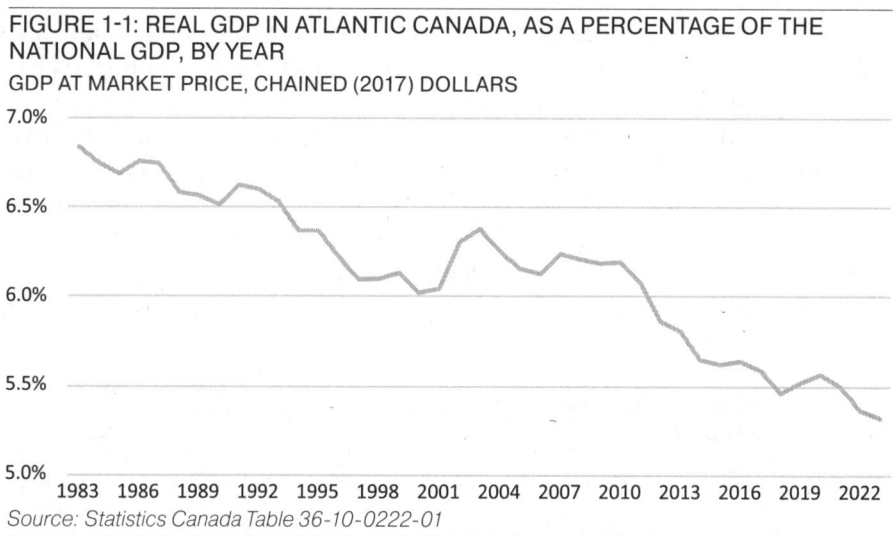

FIGURE 1-1: REAL GDP IN ATLANTIC CANADA, AS A PERCENTAGE OF THE NATIONAL GDP, BY YEAR
GDP AT MARKET PRICE, CHAINED (2017) DOLLARS

Source: Statistics Canada Table 36-10-0222-01

With the exception of Prince Edward Island, the story is the same for all the remaining Atlantic provinces—all less economically important in Canada than four decades earlier. And this trend was poised to continue, barring a significant change in direction for the region. The underperformance in economic growth over many decades has left the economy in the region much smaller and weaker than if Atlantic Canada had experienced growth at the national average. Aspiring to be average seems like a low benchmark, but being below average is not where we need to be.

While the trend in Atlantic Canada indicates a significant gap in economic growth for the region overall in comparison to Canada as a whole, this masks some important differences by individual provinces within the region, particularly Prince Edward Island, which has largely maintained its proportion (although small) of the overall economy since the early 1980s and has nearly kept pace with Canada's economic performance over the past four decades, with real GDP growth of 152 percent between 1983 and 2023 compared with a national growth rate of 160 percent.

CHAINED DOLLARS
"Chained dollars" is a method of adjusting real dollar amounts for inflation over time; it allows for the comparison of data from different years.

Since 1983, New Brunswick has become a smaller part of the Canadian economy and now represents only 1.6 percent of the national GDP. Over the past four decades, New Brunswick has had the slowest overall GDP growth in Atlantic Canada, growing 41 percent slower than the Canadian economy over that period.

Nova Scotia has also declined proportionately as a share of the Canadian economy and now represents 2 percent of the national GDP. Nova Scotia has grown 35 percent slower over the last four decades than the country overall.

Newfoundland and Labrador has declined to 1.3 percent of the Canadian economy and, like Nova Scotia, has grown 39 percent more slowly than the country overall since 1983. This despite the significant economic benefits of the oil and gas industry that developed in the province over this period

Table 1-1 shows real GDP in dollar terms (chained 2017 dollars) over the forty-year period in Atlantic Canada compared to the country overall.

TABLE 1-1: REAL GDP BY YEAR, CHAINED (2017) DOLLARS, $BILLIONS
GDP AT MARKET PRICES

Year	Canada	Newfoundland and Labrador	Prince Edward Island	Nova Scotia	New Brunswick	Atlantic Canada	Atlantic Canada (% of national GDP)
1983	$918.8	$15.9	$3.2	$23.9	$19.8	$62.9	6.8%
1993	$1,176.0	$19.1	$3.8	$29.5	$24.4	$76.9	6.5%
2003	$1,641.6	$29.3	$5.3	$37.9	$32.3	$104.8	6.4%
2013	$1,985.9	$33.5	$6.3	$41.2	$34.4	$115.3	5.8%
2023	$2,385.4	$31.4	$8.1	$48.8	$38.6	$126.9	5.3%

Source: Statistics Canada Table 36-10-0222-01

THE WIDENING ECONOMIC GAP

An *Insights* podcast with Niels Veldhuis, CEO of the Fraser Institute in 2022, underscores Atlantic Canada's economic challenges. In 2019, the Fraser Institute merged with the Atlantic Institute of Market Studies, the long-time think tank focussed on economic issues within Atlantic Canada. After the merger, the Fraser Institute initiated the Atlantic Canada Prosperity Initiative to focus attention on the region's economic gap compared to the rest of the country. As Veldhuis noted in our conversation, the goal in Atlantic Canada is for the region to catch up with the rest of Canada.

One of the most concerning trends over the last four decades is that the gap in economic growth has widened significantly, paralleling the population trends in the region, which started to stagnate in the 1990s. The economic performance gap has been accelerating since, to the point that the economy in the region in the most recent decade grew at only half the rate of the country overall. This trend is expected to reverse itself in the next decade with the recent growth in the population as the key stimulus.

Figure 1-2 shows the relative change in real GDP by time frame in Atlantic Canada compared to the country overall. Between 1983 and 1993, real GDP in the four Atlantic provinces combined increased more slowly than in the rest of the country, but not by much. (New Brunswick and Prince Edward Island outperformed the national growth rate during this period.) This period coincided with population growth across the region that closely matched that of the country overall.

The next decade (1993 to 2003) resulted in a widening gap in growth rates and coincided with a decrease in population growth compared with the rest of the country. Even though Atlantic Canada witnessed a 36 percent GDP growth rate over the decade, it was still 8 percent slower than the country overall. Part of the growth in the region during this decade was attributed to the launch of the offshore oil and gas sector in Newfoundland and Labrador, which masked much slower economic growth in the rest of the region.

Between 2003 and 2013, the gap in real GDP growth between Atlantic Canada and the rest of the country widened further. Across the country, real GDP increased by 21 percent while only growing by 10 percent in Atlantic Canada. New Brunswick and Nova Scotia were particular laggards as economic growth in those two provinces was only half the rate of growth across the country.

The most recent decade, 2013 to 2023, saw the GDP gap widen further. Atlantic Canada's GDP expanded 50 percent more slowly than the country's overall (10 percent growth over the decade versus 20 percent across Canada). Prince Edward Island continued to outperform the rest of Atlantic Canada during this period as a result of its rapid population growth relative to the rest of the region. Newfoundland and Labrador's real GDP decreased by 6 percent over the full decade.

FIGURE 1-2: RELATIVE DIFFERENCE IN REAL GDP GROWTH IN ATLANTIC CANADA COMPARED TO THE NATIONAL GROWTH RATE, BY DECADE
GDP AT MARKET PRICES, CHAINED (2017) DOLLARS

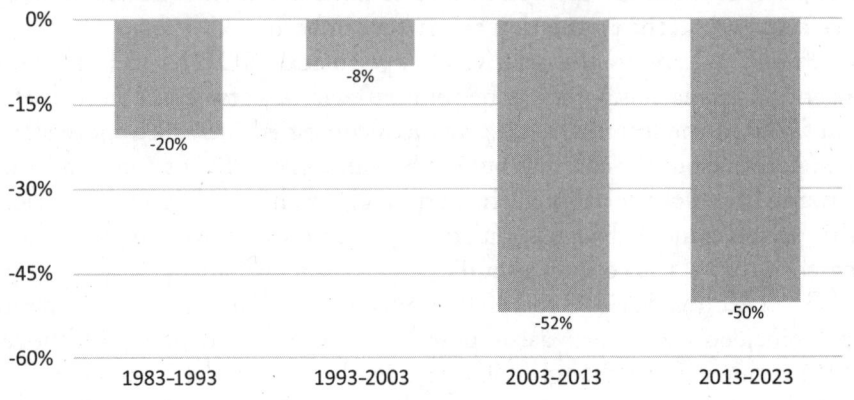

Source: Statistics Canada Table 36-10-0222-01

As table 1-2 illustrates, there is significant variability in real GDP growth by individual provinces in the region between 1983 and 2023 for each of the past four decades. This is especially the case for Prince Edward Island over the past decade. PEI's unprecedented economic growth over the past decade has mirrored the unprecedented growth in its population, which has outpaced the rest of the region over this period of time. Newfoundland and Labrador's outperformance during the 1990s was driven by robust growth in the oil and gas industry.

TABLE 1-2: CUMULATIVE REAL GDP GROWTH IN ATLANTIC CANADA COMPARED TO THE NATIONAL GROWTH RATE
GDP AT MARKET PRICES, CHAINED (2017) DOLLARS

Year	Canada	Newfoundland and Labrador	Prince Edward Island	Nova Scotia	New Brunswick	Atlantic Canada
1983–1993	28%	20%	20%	23%	23%	22%
1993–2003	40%	54%	37%	29%	32%	36%
2003–2013	21%	14%	19%	9%	7%	10%
2013–2023	20%	-6%	29%	19%	12%	10%

Source: Statistics Canada Table 36-10-0222-01

Interestingly, while PEI's economic performance relative to the country has generally outperformed the rest of Atlantic Canada since the early 1980s, the province's economic performance in the last decade has outperformed the country. How is that possible? What changed in that period to cause this improvement in economic performance? The answer is relatively simple: steady population growth in PEI, while population in the rest of the region stagnated. PEI has led the country in population growth for much of the last decade. Most of the population growth in PEI has been the result of immigration, and PEI is now the model for the rest of the region in terms of economic growth. One thing that is apparent: population growth is essential to economic growth. Without population growth, Atlantic Canada will not be able to consistently perform at the national average for economic growth.

EMPLOYMENT TRENDS

One important measure of economic growth is the number of new jobs created over time. Between 1983 and 2023, the number of people working in Canada increased by 83 percent. This compares to only 50 percent in Atlantic Canada. Among the four Atlantic provinces, Prince Edward Island has not only led Atlantic Canada in the growth of jobs, with an increase of slightly more than 82 percent, but also has kept pace with the country overall.

The other important measure is the size of the labour force that provides the capacity of an economy to grow over time, which has been a public policy challenge in the last few years and has led to a significant increase in immigration to address labour shortages in practically every profession. Since 1982, the Canadian labour force has grown by over 70 percent, paralleling the growth in employment over that period. Over the same period of time, growth in the labour force across Atlantic Canada has lagged significantly, only growing 38 percent. This is largely the consequence of weak or stagnant population growth and a rapidly aging workforce, particularly since the early 1990s.

As the following employment graphs demonstrate, weak periods of job growth coincide with weak periods of population growth. Growth in employment since 2000 provides a good snapshot of what has been happening in Atlantic Canada over the most recent time period. As table 1-3 indicates, PEI was the first to benefit in job growth that coincided with earlier population growth on the Island. Nova Scotia and New Brunswick experienced job growth later, again coinciding with population growth in these provinces. Newfoundland's slower population growth has yet to have an impact on job growth in that province.

Proportionately, the share of jobs in Atlantic Canada compared to all the jobs in the country has been in decline for the last four decades, consistent with the decline in the share of the national GDP.

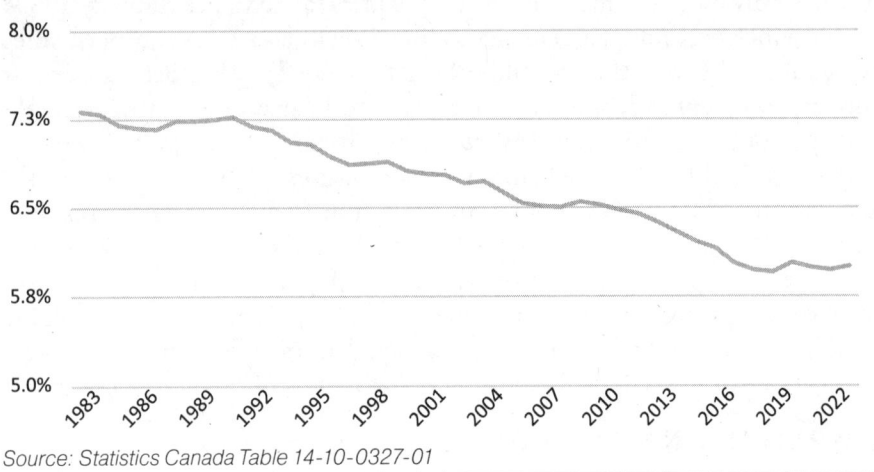

FIGURE 1-3: EMPLOYMENT IN ATLANTIC CANADA, AS A PERCENTAGE OF NATIONAL EMPLOYMENT, BY YEAR

Source: Statistics Canada Table 14-10-0327-01

Only Prince Edward Island kept pace with job growth in Canada between 1983 and 2023. Employment in the other three provinces significantly underperformed the national economy.

TABLE 1-3: EMPLOYMENT IN ATLANTIC CANADA, SELECTED YEARS (000S)

Year	Canada	Newfoundland and Labrador	Prince Edward Island	Nova Scotia	New Brunswick	Atlantic Canada	Atlantic Canada % of national employment
1983	11,022.0	180.8	48.8	324.8	251.3	805.7	7.3%
1993	12,792.7	193.8	54.6	366.5	299.9	914.8	7.2%
2003	15,660.8	210.7	66.1	431.3	341.7	1,049.8	6.7%
2013	17,712.2	241.9	73.8	455.3	357.6	1,128.6	6.4%
2023	20,170.9	236.7	89.0	497.8	386.5	1,210.0	6.0%
% change 1983–2023	83%	31%	82%	53%	54%	50%	

Source: Statistics Canada Table 14-10-0327-01

The number of jobs in the region, in proportion to the number of jobs nationally, has been decreasing over time, as the following graph demonstrates, with the number of jobs in the region growing 48 percent more slowly in the last decade than in the rest of the country.

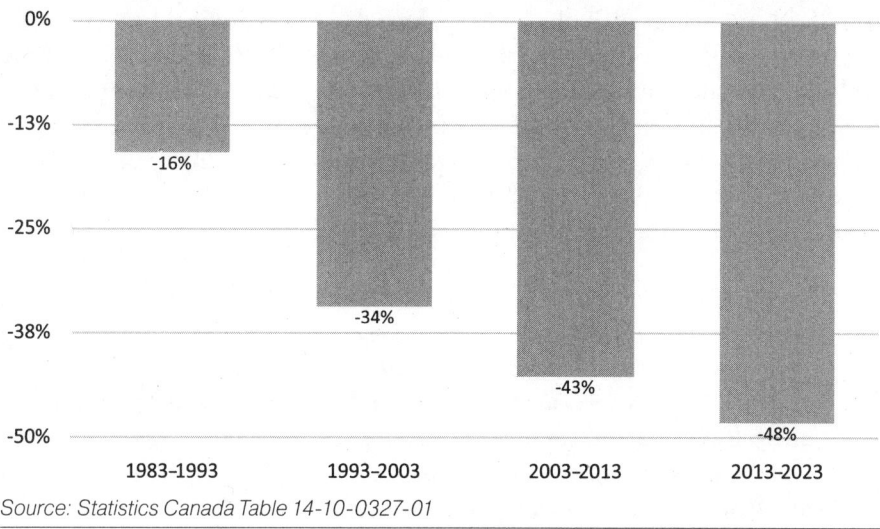

FIGURE 1-4: RELATIVE DIFFERENCE IN EMPLOYMENT GROWTH IN ATLANTIC CANADA COMPARED TO THE NATIONAL GROWTH RATE, BY TIME FRAME

Source: Statistics Canada Table 14-10-0327-01

Employment growth in Newfoundland and Labrador has been a rocky road since the collapse of the cod fishery in the 1990s, through the boom of oil and gas that began after the great recession and the downturn that coincided with the pandemic. The employment situation in Newfoundland and Labrador is much more difficult given the out-migration of the population following the cod moratorium in mid-1992, when thirty thousand jobs disappeared virtually overnight. The province has not yet fully recovered the population lost during that period and continues to struggle to attract newcomers to the province. It was the last province in the region to fully embrace immigration as a labour force and population-growth strategy. There are positive signs related to full-time job growth in the last couple of years, but the province remains below the peak number of jobs it had in 2013 and is just now returning to a similar employment level of a decade ago.

One of the most notable observations about employment growth in Prince Edward Island over the past four decades has been the steady increase in the number of jobs on the Island. This has coincided with the steady growth in the Island's population over the same period of time, which has recently accelerated in concert with rapidly increasing population growth that has led the country.

Nova Scotia endured nearly a decade of stagnant employment growth that only began to increase with increasing population growth that began in earnest just prior to the pandemic.

In New Brunswick, employment growth was also stagnant for a decade and only began to increase with the increasing population growth that started just prior to the pandemic.

One of the best examples of the impact of population growth, especially from entrepreneurial immigrants, is that of the Hadhad family, originally from Syria, who had their chocolate factory destroyed during the civil war in that country. The family ended up in Antigonish, NS, of all places and were embraced by the community, eventually building a new chocolate manufacturing facility in that town and creating dozens of new local jobs. Peace by Chocolate is a shining example of the value immigrants bring to our communities. As Tareq Hadhad, the founder and CEO of Peace by Chocolate, told us in a very compelling two-part podcast in 2022:

> *Our family wouldn't be where we are today without the people of Nova Scotia. If we had ended up in a large centre and not in the little town of Antigonish our journey would have likely taken much longer. We didn't come here to take jobs; we came here to rebuild our lives and have now created job opportunities for many others from our community. Our family is so grateful to have made the right decision to choose Canada. While there is a lot of learning [when] rebuilding a business in a new place, we have received tremendous support from Nova Scotians. We have a lot of gratitude for the kindness they have shown us as they champion us along the way.*

TABLE 1-4: CUMULATIVE EMPLOYMENT GROWTH BY TIME FRAME AND JURISDICTION

	Canada	Newfoundland and Labrador	Prince Edward Island	Nova Scotia	New Brunswick	Atlantic Canada
1983–1993	16%	7%	12%	13%	19%	14%
1993–2003	22%	9%	21%	18%	14%	15%
2003–2013	13%	15%	12%	6%	5%	8%
2013–2023	14%	-2%	21%	9%	8%	7%
1983–2023	83%	31%	82%	53%	54%	50%

Source: Statistics Canada Table 14-10-0327-01

TABLE 1-5: CUMULATIVE EMPLOYMENT GROWTH IN ATLANTIC CANADA COMPARED TO THE NATIONAL GROWTH RATE, PERCENTAGE DIFFERENCE IN GROWTH BY DECADE

	Newfoundland and Labrador	Prince Edward Island	Nova Scotia	New Brunswick	Atlantic Canada
1983–1993	-55%	-26%	-20%	20%	-16%
1993–2003	-61%	-6%	-21%	-38%	-34%
2003–2013	13%	-11%	-58%	-64%	-43%
2013–2023	n/a*	48%	-33%	-42%	-48%
1983–2023	-63%	-1%	-36%	-35%	-40%

*TOTAL EMPLOYMENT DECLINED OVER THE DECADE
Source: Statistics Canada Table 14-10-0327-01

UNEMPLOYMENT TRENDS

For decades, the unemployment rate in Atlantic Canada has been higher than the rest of the country, at least partially related to the higher proportion of the population living in rural communities where there are fewer economic opportunities than elsewhere in Canada. At the same time, in Atlantic Canada's six largest urban communities, unemployment rates were much more in line with those elsewhere in Canada. Having twice as many people living in rural communities has been one of the key economic limitations challenging the region. Atlantic Canada has simply not urbanized at the same pace as the rest of the country because population growth has been so anemic for so long.

Unemployment rates have been trending downwards in the region over the last five years or so—particularly in PEI, which now has the lowest unemployment rate in nearly fifty years. Having more workers on the sidelines than any other province on a year in, year out basis has hurt our economic performance because we simply have proportionately fewer workers available to grow the economy.

In looking at unemployment rates, it is useful to look at these rates for Atlantic Canada's largest urban communities. Generally speaking, unemployment rates of these larger urban communities are in line with those in the major cities in Canada, suggesting that rural, rather than urban, communities are the issue when it comes to employment. Unfortunately for the region, we are the least urbanized part of the country. We have, as a result, a higher proportion of the labour force dependent on seasonal work than elsewhere in the country. Population growth in line with national trends will eventually balance the urbanized population within the region, although it will take many decades as most of the growth in populations occurs in urban communities where more economic opportunities exist.

UNEMPLOYMENT RATES

Historically, Prince Edward Island and Newfoundland and Labrador have had the highest rates of unemployment in Canada. Ironically, the lack of population growth has contributed to our higher rates of unemployment mainly due to the much less vibrant construction sector where demand for housing, in particular, has been much lower than elsewhere in Canada.

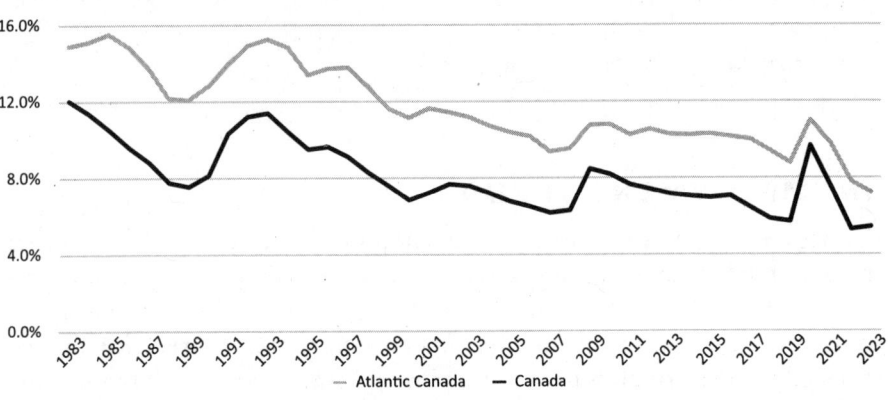

FIGURE 1-5: UNEMPLOYMENT RATE IN ATLANTIC CANADA VS. THE NATIONAL AVERAGE, 1983–2023

Source: Statistics Canada Table 14-10-0327-01

Recent population growth has been accompanied by robust job growth and lower levels of unemployment. In addition, the exit from the workplace of baby boomers is creating many job opportunities for younger workers and will continue to do so over the next decade or so. Our unemployment rates will decline over time even without any job growth. That is because over the next decade, nearly 150,000 baby boom–aged workers will be leaving the workplace. As the labour force shrinks (at least without significant population growth), the base of workers upon which unemployment rates are calculated will decrease, causing rates to decline. This trend is increasing job opportunities for young people and leading to higher rates of youth retention in the region. The need to "go down the road" is slowly declining.

This will, however, create an even bigger problem: too few workers available to fill all the existing jobs, let alone any new jobs being created. Furthermore, the switch from an economy with too many workers and too few jobs to an economy with too few workers and too many jobs will see a rapid increase in the cost of wages and competition for talent within the region. This is already occurring. Employers need to begin preparing for this inevitable circumstance now. In some job categories and professions, wages and compensation are already at national levels. For decades, Atlantic Canadian employers have enjoyed a discount advantage in terms of employee compensation. With tightening labour markets, this gap is quickly disappearing. The competition for talent will be extra challenging for the four Atlantic provinces because the region has the highest personal income taxes in the country. High-priced talent will want to be compensated for these high tax rates and will likely expect a premium in their compensation packages for this purpose.

Even if unemployment rates fall to near–national averages due to declining numbers in the labour force alone, this will not address the underperforming economies in most of Atlantic Canada (excepting PEI). Without population growth at or near population growth for Canada (3 percent between July 1, 2023, and June 30, 2024, in Canada; the highest in sixty-five years), the region can expect to fall further behind the rest of the country economically. At the same time, solutions are needed across the region in the short term to provide greater economic opportunities for the high percentage of the population living in smaller rural communities. More on this later.

The good news is that governments have finally recognized both the population issue and the coming labour shortage. The government of Prince Edward Island was the first in the region to recognize and address these issues when it launched the Provincial Nominee Program in 2001 to attract and retain more immigrants under then premier Pat Binns. There were problems with the initial Provincial Nominee Program, which should be noted. Later, PEI premier Wade MacLauchlan was a key player in getting the Atlantic Immigration Pilot Program launched in 2017, as we will discuss later in the book. It is interesting to note that the Island's population growth in 2024 was 2.8 percent, similar to the national rate (3 percent).

CHAPTER 2
THE DEMOGRAPHIC TSUNAMI

DON MILLS: I DEVOTED A GOOD PORTION OF MY WORKING CAREER TO STUDYING population trends and demographics and advising both clients and governments about the challenges related to aging populations and stagnant population growth, particularly related to impacts on labour availability and the ability to fund social programs. It was clear decades ago that Canada was facing a demographic tsunami that is now impacting the economy in significant and challenging ways. David Foot's book *Boom, Bust, & Echo*, co-authored by Daniel Stoffman and published in 1996, foresaw many impacts the baby boomer generation would have on the job market, real estate, education, and health care over time. It helped inform my work and that of my former company, Corporate Research Associates Inc. (now Narrative Research).

Over the years, I had the opportunity to present the pending demographic challenges to most of the premiers and their cabinets across Atlantic Canada, and to advocate for the need to focus on population growth and immigration to address the negative impacts on the labour force that were completely predictable at the time. In addition, I frequently presented my findings publicly over the years, as well as privately to my clients, most of whom represented the largest companies in the region. For example, as recently as in 2015, it was well understood that there were going to be 250,000 more people sixty-five or older in 2030 than there were in 2015 in Atlantic Canada. Based on labour market participation rates (the percentage of those of working age that work), this translated to a loss of more than 150,000 from the workforce over that time period. Those numbers will have a huge impact on the job market and the health care system.

THE IVANY REPORT

One of the most important reports in the last decade was the Ivany Report: *Now or Never: An Urgent Call to Action for Nova Scotians*, which was prepared by the Nova Scotia Commission on Building Our New Economy for the province of Nova Scotia. It led to a series of recommendations to the then government under Premier Darrell Dexter to improve the economic future for the province. The report was not only an important milestone for Nova Scotia, but for the rest of the Atlantic region, providing a blueprint of actions that were clearly applicable to the other provinces in the region.

In my capacity as President and CEO of Corporate Research Inc., I presented my findings on the economic challenges facing the province and my recommendations for ways to address these economic challenges to the Ivany commission during its consultation process, indicating that the province faced a shortfall of workers of more than sixty thousand by 2030 without immediate remedial action. One of my recommendations to the committee was that Nova Scotia needed to commit to net population growth of seven thousand people per year to address the expected labour shortfall. Among my recommendations were the following three devoted to immigration specifically:

- challenge current public misconceptions regarding immigrants;
- target nationalities where Nova Scotia already has critical mass;
- establish an expedited process to fast-track foreign students interested in living in Canada.

Ivany's report was released in February 2014 and established ambitious targets to strive for by 2024, including increasing immigration, growing the number of start-ups, doubling tourism revenues, and increasing exports. One of the key recommendations in the report addressed concerns about an aging population and workforce in the province and called for a population growth strategy that focussed on increasing net interprovincial migration to one thousand people per year (at that time it was averaging negative eight hundred in out-migration), realizing Nova Scotia's proportionate share of international immigrants (2.7 percent) and the retention of 10 percent of foreign students as permanent residents that would net seven thousand new residents to the province, the same number I recommended.

To be clear, successive governments in each of the four Atlantic provinces had long been aware of the population and demographic challenges facing their provinces but had not acted on those warnings until it became evident that labour shortages were beginning to occur. Short-term thinking in four-year cycles has always been a problem for governments at all levels, as the parties in power focus too much attention on getting re-elected, rather than getting things done. Many of the labour shortages today are a result of this short-term focus.

POPULATION TRENDS

The trend in population growth in Canada has been remarkably consistent until very recently. Over the last five decades, the population in Canada has grown on average about 1 percent per year as the graph below illustrates. Over this period of time, Canada urbanized to the point that more than 80 percent of the population lives in urban communities. The growth of the population at such a consistent rate has allowed that growth to be absorbed into the economy without any real disruption. More importantly, the steady growth of the population has provided the needed growth in the labour force to allow the economy to continue to grow. In our view, population growth is essential to economic growth. The pace of population growth has recently increased to address a rapidly aging workforce in Canada and is now more than double the previous historic growth rate. There are now growing concerns about the pace of immigration and the strain it has been placing on the housing market. Population growth is now almost completely accounted for through immigration, as birth rates in Canada continue below the replacement rate needed to maintain the population.

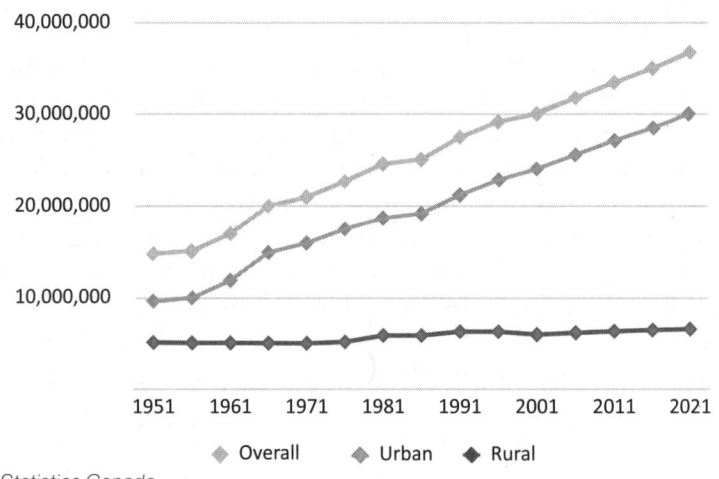

FIGURE 2-1: URBAN AND RURAL POPULATION GROWTH BY CENSUS PERIOD, CANADA, 1951–2021

Source: Statistics Canada

POPULATION GROWTH OVER TIME

Unfortunately, over the same period of time, Atlantic Canada became (until only very recently) a proportionately smaller part of Canada in terms of the size of its population. According to census numbers, in 1971 there were 21.5 million people living in Canada, of which 2.1 million lived in Atlantic Canada. At that time, the population in the region represented 9.5 percent of the total Canadian population. In the most recent census, the population in Canada had increased by 72 percent to 37 million, while the population in Atlantic Canada had increased to 2.4 million, an increase of only 17 percent over a fifty-year period. Now the region represents only 6.5 percent of the total Canadian population. With decreasing population relative to the rest of the country comes decreasing political influence, as more federal seats are created in faster-growing areas of the country. In 1971, Atlantic Canada had 12 percent of all Members of Parliament. Now the region has 9.5 percent of the total MPs, still proportionately higher than its share of the population.

The region's share of the national population has now stabilized as a consequence of recent growth in population that has matched the growth of the population across the country.

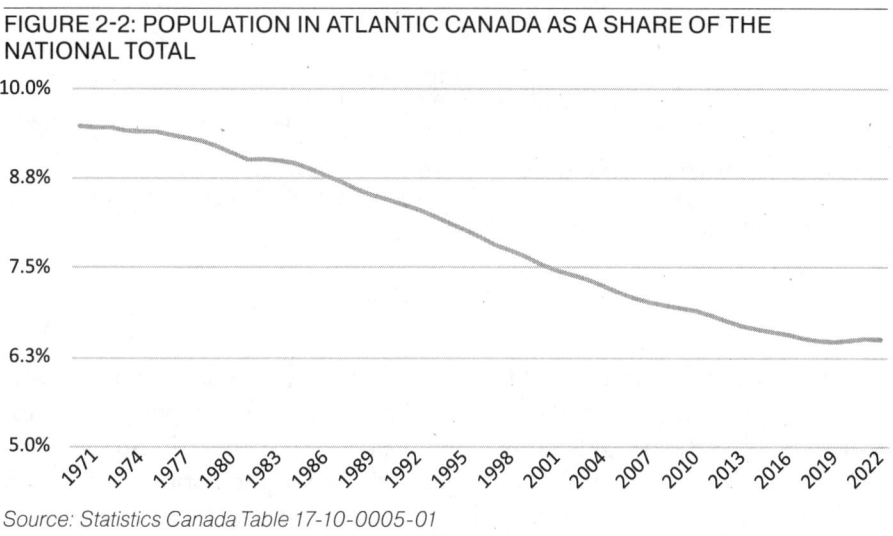

FIGURE 2-2: POPULATION IN ATLANTIC CANADA AS A SHARE OF THE NATIONAL TOTAL

Source: Statistics Canada Table 17-10-0005-01

AN AGING POPULATION

The consequence of a population that is growing much more slowly than the rest of the country's is an aging population relative to the rest of Canada. The four Atlantic provinces have the oldest populations in the country, as measured by the median average (median age is the point where half the population is above that age and half are below that age). Of note, Newfoundland and Labrador now has the oldest population in Canada but had the youngest population in 1971. Recently, the median age in Canada has plateaued and has begun to decrease as a consequence of population growth driven by much younger immigrant families coming to Canada. This same trend is now evident in PEI.

FIGURE 2-3: RELATIVE SHARE OF THE POPULATION BY AGE GROUP IN NEWFOUNDLAND AND LABRADOR COMPARED TO THE COUNTRY OVERALL, 2024*

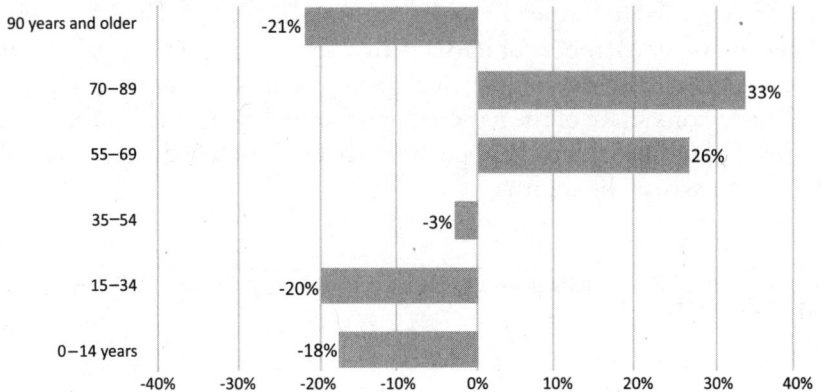

*EXAMPLE: COMPARED TO THE NATIONAL POPULATION, NEWFOUNDLAND AND LABRADOR HAS 26 PERCENT MORE PEOPLE IN THE 55-69 AGE GROUP AND 20 PERCENT FEWER IN THE 15-34 AGE GROUP.

Source: Statistics Canada Table 17-10-0005-01 (formerly CANSIM 051-0001)

A more graphical means of looking at the aging populations in Atlantic Canada is by comparing each of the four province's age pyramids with Canada's. These pyramids clearly demonstrate that there is currently an insufficient younger population to replace the older population within each of the four Atlantic provinces and Canada as a whole. This helps explain the federal government's recent push to significantly increase immigration to address this population gap.

FIGURE 2-4: POPULATION ESTIMATES ON JULY 1, BY AGE AND GENDER

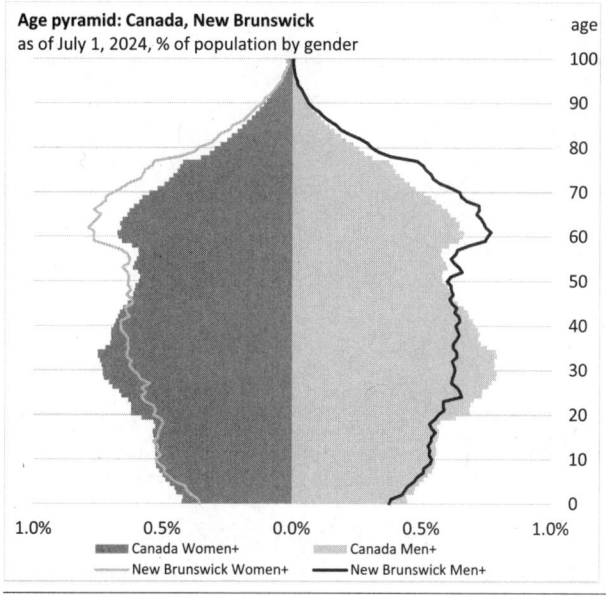

Newfoundland and Labrador has a much higher percentage of its population that is older and a much low percentage of its population that is younger relative to Canada overall and the rest of Atlantic Canada.

FIGURE 2-5: POPULATION ESTIMATES ON JULY 1, BY AGE AND GENDER

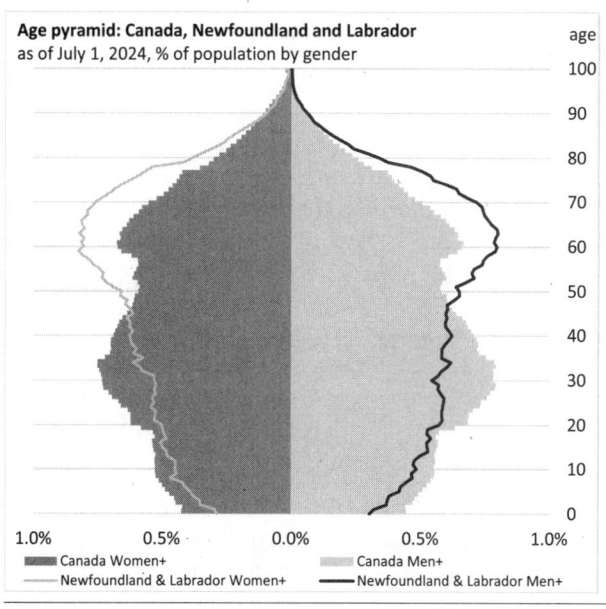

THE DEMOGRAPHIC TSUNAMI 21

FIGURE 2-6: POPULATION ESTIMATES ON JULY 1, BY AGE AND GENDER

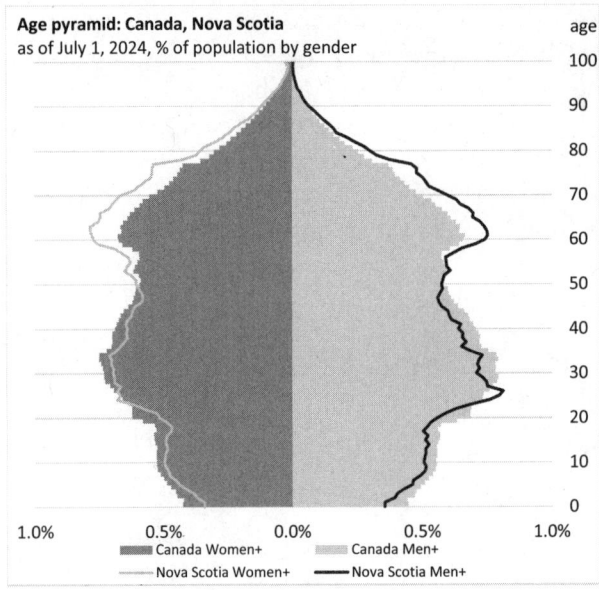

PEI's age pyramid is closest to the one for Canada overall but has a much higher number of those aged twenty to twenty-five in its population relative to either Canada or the other three Atlantic provinces. This is good news for the Island in terms of its long-term labour needs.

FIGURE 2-7: POPULATION ESTIMATES ON JULY 1, BY AGE AND GENDER

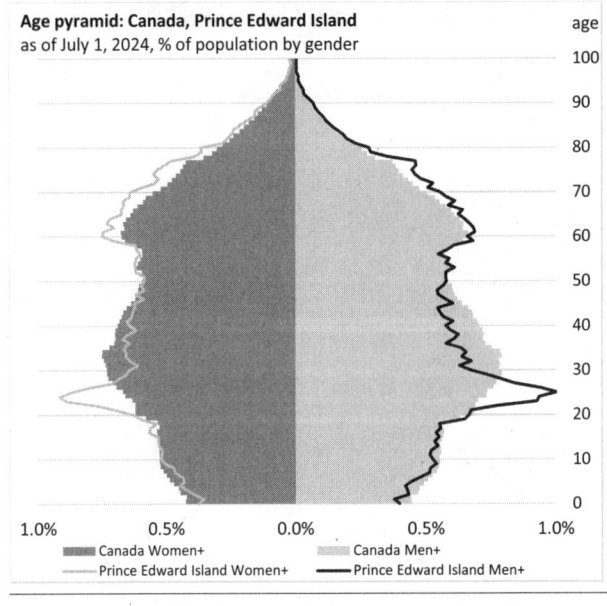

The median age in Canada in 1971 was twenty-six years. The median age in Canada is now forty-one, according to the 2021 Census. Much of the increase in median age in Canada is driven by the baby boom bubble and declining birth rates over a long period of time. Baby boomers are defined as those born between 1946 and 1964. The sheer size of the baby boomers led to an echo boom of births that included Gen-Xers (those born between 1965 and 1980) and some of the early millennials (those born between 1981 and 1996).

The median age in Canada appears to have peaked, and there are signs that the median age will decline in the next few years due to the influx of much younger immigrants. This is a consequence of increasing immigration numbers and Canada's aggressive policy of significantly increasing the numbers of immigrants allowed into the country. It should be noted that the federal government moved in 2024 to reduce the number of immigrants and temporary workers to address concerns related to overheated population growth. Across the region, median age is significantly higher, led by Newfoundland and Labrador with a median age of 48.4 in the 2021 Census, followed by New Brunswick (46.8), Nova Scotia (45.6), and Prince Edward Island (44.0). The median age in PEI has been declining recently due to rapid population growth led by immigration.

With the exception of Prince Edward Island, the population in Atlantic Canada has been largely stagnant since the 1990s until relatively recently. The limited population growth up to that time was largely driven by baby boomers having children when birth rates were higher than today's. Recently, much of Atlantic Canada has experienced more deaths than births. This has been particularly problematic for rural communities. This phenomenon is largely the result of an aging population base, which has not been supplemented by immigrants to keep the median age of the population in line with the rest of the country.

TABLE 2-1: POPULATION GROWTH RATES BY TIME FRAME, 1971–2023

	Newfoundland and Labrador	Prince Edward Island	Nova Scotia	New Brunswick	Canada
1971–1981	8.4%	9.7%	7.2%	10.0%	13.0%
1981–1991	0.8%	5.5%	7.0%	5.5%	13.0%
1991–2001	-9.9%	4.8%	1.9%	0.6%	10.6%
2001–2011	0.6%	5.3%	1.2%	0.8%	10.7%
2011–2019	0.5%	8.3%	3.4%	2.9%	9.5%
2019–2023	2.1%	11.6%	8.5%	7.4%	6.6%
Cumulative (1971–2023)	1.5%	54.4%	32.8%	29.9%	82.6%

Source: Statistics Canada Table 17-10-0005-01

Looking at the four Atlantic provinces individually over the last five decades, population growth peaked in the 1990s. This corresponded to the end of the baby boomers having children. Since that time, Prince Edward Island had the highest population growth, while Newfoundland and Labrador has not recovered from the out-migration of its population following the moratorium on the cod fishery in 1992 (which was partially lifted in June of 2024). Its current population is still lower now than in 1992. Between 1971 and 2023, PEI led population growth in the Atlantic region, growing by over 54 percent. This compares to growth of nearly 83 percent for Canada overall during the same period. In comparison, Nova Scotia grew nearly 33 percent, while New Brunswick grew nearly 30 percent over the same period. Meanwhile, the population of Newfoundland and Labrador remained virtually static over that period with growth of about 1.5 percent, which helps explain why Newfoundland and Labrador has the oldest population in the country.

Interestingly, in recent years, about 0.7 percent of the 1 percent in annual population growth for the country overall has come through immigration, and that proportion is expected to increase over the next few years at least, even if the pace of immigration returns to its previous levels. Recent increases in the number of immigrants being allowed in the country are an acknowledgement by the federal government of the need to further increase its workforce to accommodate continuing economic growth and an aging population. The federal government increased the number of immigrants from 250,000 in 2001 to 500,000 in 2023, although there are increasing concerns about Canada's ability to absorb such a large number. This concern has been acknowledged by the federal government's 2024 decision to reduce the number of immigrants entering the country, although the problem is more directly related to the number of international students and foreign temporary workers that have been allowed in the country over the past couple of years, which has placed such an enormous strain on the housing market.

Therein lies the problem that is now finally coming to a head for most of Atlantic Canada. The lack of population growth has not only been a drag on economic growth for the region but has now led to a growing labour shortage as literally hundreds of thousands of baby boomers begin to leave the workplace. There are simply too few people coming along to replace all those retiring baby boomers over the next ten years or so. It is imperative that Atlantic Canada dramatically increase its population to deal with this growing labour shortage, which is already apparent across virtually all job categories. Doctors and nurses are a prime example, and just ask those in the trucking industry about their difficulty in recruiting new drivers. One company, JDI-owned Midland Transport, has been actively recruiting drivers in Eastern Europe for some time already. J. D. Irving has been recruiting foresters from Brazil for its woodland operations and, according to Jim Irving, even provides housing to these newcomers. In a 2020 *Insights* podcast, he said, "We say one of the biggest issues is housing. You know there are not enough houses...so someplace like Chipman [NB], for example, we worked with the community and provincial government. We've put up some houses and are adding more. This is about people having a good place to live, particularly if they're going to bring their families."

Irving went on to talk about the challenges related to building housing in rural communities, especially with regard to financing those new houses from a developer perspective. But employers like J. D. Irving and Cooke Aquaculture are interested in taking some risk out of building houses in rural areas by "putting some effort and some money" into housing to ensure all the risk is not loaded on government. He added, "If you're running businesses in rural New Brunswick, housing becomes a challenge pretty quickly and so we need to be a bit more creative in partnership with the government to do that."

DECLINING BIRTH RATES

As is the case in most of the developed world, Canada's birth rates have been declining for some time. The same is true for Atlantic Canada. A recent book, *Empty Planet: The Shock of Global Population Decline* by Darrell Bricker and John Ibbitson, makes a strong case that has upended the thinking about the world's population by suggesting that, contrary to most current thought, world population will likely peak by mid-century before slowly declining. This is already happening in some countries, including China and Japan, which coincidentally have little or no immigration.

Bricker, the global president for public affairs for Ipsos, one of the largest market research firms in the world, made an interesting observation on an *Insights* episode with us. "Both John and I are realistic about immigration," he said, "and if Canadians understood what was really going on, they'd understand the necessity of immigration. Our population is rapidly aging. In fact, the reason our population continues to grow is mostly from two things: one of them is people not dying as fast as they used to, and the second thing is immigration. Our birth rates are now down...so the only way that you can keep things going is immigration."

There is a major potential downside for Canada's immigration strategy if the world's population peaks by mid-century. One of Canada's largest sources of immigrants, China, already has a declining population, mostly as a result of its one-child policy, which recently changed to a three-child policy to try to reverse the population decline. Says Bricker:

> *The three largest sources of immigrants to Canada today are India, China, and the Philippines. Our three major sources of immigrants are losing that group of young people, particularly the group with the skills we've been*

> looking for—because it's not just a numbers game. It's not just to say, "We're going to bring in a million immigrants."
>
> To bring in a million dependents is probably not what we want to do. We want to bring in people who can contribute fairly early because that's what immigration does. It plugs holes fast. It's a short- to medium-term solution to what our [population] issue is going to be, but we're going to be on the same trajectory as Japan, just a bit later."

The implication from Bricker is that the competition for talent globally is likely to tighten considerably, as traditional markets for immigrants face declining populations and the loss of some of their most talented people resources. There are already efforts by China to repatriate their citizens from around the world. If that were to occur, Canada's immigration strategy, which is focussed on talent recruitment from foreign countries, would be considerably more challenging.

CANADA'S POPULATION TARGET

Canada is likely to approach a population of 100 million by the end of the century, based on current population growth rates. There is actually an organization called the Century Initiative devoted to this effort. On an *Insights* episode, their CEO, Lisa Lalande, stated that one of the key benefits of growing the population to this size would increase Canada's voice and influence in the world. But this is predicated on the assumption that such growth will be largely driven by immigration, and this drive will likely become less necessary as populations decline elsewhere—especially countries that are important sources of immigration to Canada. China's population is already in decline, and India has overtaken China as the most populous country in the world. China has also eliminated the one-child-per-family restriction and is encouraging larger families—to little effect so far.

Declining birth rates in the developed world have been concurrent with rising education levels for females and with the increased economic independence that results from higher levels of education. These same factors are now impacting most other countries in the world.

In Atlantic Canada, there are now more deaths than births. The birth rate required to maintain a stable population is 2.1 children per female. In Canada, the current birth rate is 1.4 per female. At the end of the baby boom generation (1965) the birth rate was 3.1 per female. Across the region, New Brunswick has the highest birth rate at 1.4, but this is still well below replacement. Nova Scotia has the lowest current birth rate at 1.2 per female, while Newfoundland and Labrador's birth rate is 1.3 per female, and PEI's birth rate is 1.3. It is clear that the lack of population growth in the region relative to the rest of the country has had a negative impact on birth rates in Atlantic

Canada in general, as immigrants tend to have more children than people born in Canada.

POPULATION TRENDS ACROSS ATLANTIC CANADA

The major reason for the population growth discrepancy in Atlantic Canada has been the lack of immigration to the region. In the last census, population growth within the three Maritime provinces was closer to the Canadian average (5.2 percent between 2016 and 2021), with PEI's growth higher than the national average at 8 percent, followed by Nova Scotia at 5 percent, New Brunswick at 3.8 percent, and Newfoundland and Labrador at -1.8 percent (although the population in Newfoundland and Labrador has since grown).

It should be noted that it was in 2015, under the first year of former premier Wade MacLauchlan's mandate, that PEI adopted the most aggressive population strategy within Atlantic Canada in 2015, not only leading the region in population growth during his term in office but leading the country. As MacLauchlan told us on *Insights* in 2022:

> *In the first year of our mandate, we introduced a population action plan that sets out three pathways: to recruit, to retain, and to repatriate. And over that time period, 2015 to 2019, Prince Edward Island's population growth led that of other provinces in the country and was approximately double the growth that Canada as a whole had during that time.*
>
> *Happily, the economy grew even faster. Over that same period, Prince Edward Island's economy expanded by just under 15 percent, which again would be about double what was experienced by Canada as a whole. Quite unusual for Prince Edward Island to be growing at that pace, and we were very happy, of course, to have those results because that enabled the government to do a lot of other things in other program areas.*

His statement underscores the value of population growth to drive economic growth, which in turn allows for increased investment in government programs like health care.

One of the benefits of a rapidly aging population will be that Atlantic Canada's historically high unemployment will diminish over the next few years and will come more in line with the rest of the country. This will be the result of workers leaving the workplace, opening more job opportunities for those left behind seeking employment. This is already happening. A shrinking labour force will decrease the unemployment rate but will not necessarily lead to more people working unless the population increases on a steady and predictable basis.

POPULATION GROWTH AS PUBLIC POLICY

Provincial governments across Atlantic Canada have finally understood the implications of an aging population and the need for population growth: all four provinces in the region now have population-growth strategies, with immigration as a core focus of those strategies. Two provinces have aggressive population-growth goals, with Nova Scotia seeking to double the population to 2 million by 2060 and New Brunswick targeting a population of 1 million within the next decade or so. Most of the region's largest municipalities now have their own population growth strategies as well. All these population strategies acknowledge the critical role of immigration to drive labour force and population growth.

The recognition of the need for a population strategy is an important turning point for the region. It also recognizes the need for more cultural diversity in the population across Atlantic Canada—the least diverse region in the country—and the need for policies to help more successfully retain immigrants, particularly by helping integrate newcomers into their communities.

CHAPTER 3

THE IMPACT OF LIMITED IMMIGRATION

FOR DECADES, ATLANTIC CANADA HAD AN OVERSUPPLY OF LABOUR RELATIVE to the number of jobs available in the region and much higher unemployment than the rest of the country. There was little reason to attract workers from elsewhere. Even though Atlantic Canadians have a well-deserved reputation with visitors to our region as being friendly, they have not always been welcoming to newcomers to the region because they were too often considered competition for the few jobs available. That may help explain the low incidence of immigrants in the region relative to the rest of Canada, and it certainly explains the out-migration of Atlantic Canadians over many decades. For the most part, immigrants were not welcomed.

For decades, the proportion of immigrants coming to Atlantic Canada was well below our share of the population in Canada. As a consequence, the four Atlantic provinces have the lowest number of foreign-born residents than any other province in Canada. The average number of foreign-born Canadians according to the latest census is 23 percent, or roughly four times the average of Atlantic Canada. Simply put, our region has not received its share of immigrants which has negatively impacted our economies and economic growth. Newfoundland and Labrador has the smallest percentage of foreign-born residents in Canada.

FIGURE 3-1: PERCENTAGE OF FOREIGN-BORN RESIDENTS, CANADA VS. EACH OF THE FOUR ATLANTIC PROVINCES

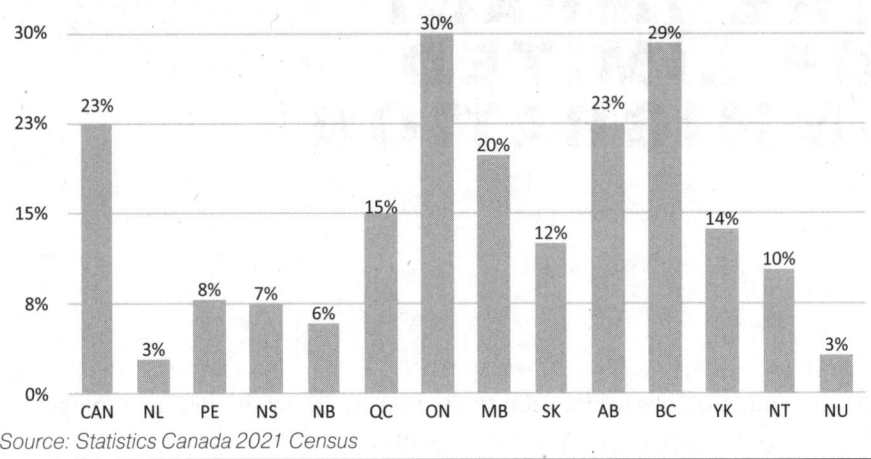

Source: Statistics Canada 2021 Census

For many Atlantic Canadians, the threat that newcomers (from other parts of Canada or other parts of the world) would take jobs away from locals has always been a concern, but also a myth. For proof of this misconception, one only has to look at Prince Edward Island. In the past decade, from 2011 to 2021, PEI has had the largest increase, percentage-wise, in population. It has also had the best performing economy in terms of real GDP growth, has created the most full-term jobs per capita in the region, and has reduced its unemployment rate to the lowest levels since the 1970s. (So much for newcomers taking jobs away from locals.) PEI's model for success has been emulated by the other Atlantic provinces—particularly Nova Scotia, and to a lesser extent New Brunswick.

Before examining current trends in each of the four Atlantic provinces in terms of immigration and population growth, the aging of the population needs to be better understood. In Atlantic Canada, there is expected to be an increase of more than a quarter of a million sixty-five-year-olds by 2030 relative to 2015. That represents an increase of 55 percent in the number of this age demographic in the population in less than a decade from now. There are two significant challenges with this aging demographic group.

One challenge is related to the issue of workplace replacement for the baby boom cohort, which is beginning to leave the workforce in growing numbers. In Atlantic Canada, we have the oldest population in Canada. Conversely, we also have the smallest population under fifteen years old. This age demographic represents the replacement labour force for those sixty-five or older. As the following chart indicates, Atlantic Canada has a deficit in terms of those in the under-fifteen category and a surplus of those in the sixty-five-and-over category relative to most of the rest of the country. This is known as the replacement ratio. This means that Atlantic Canada will have to attract and retain population from elsewhere to make up this deficit. The same situation holds true for the rest of the country, although to a lesser extent.

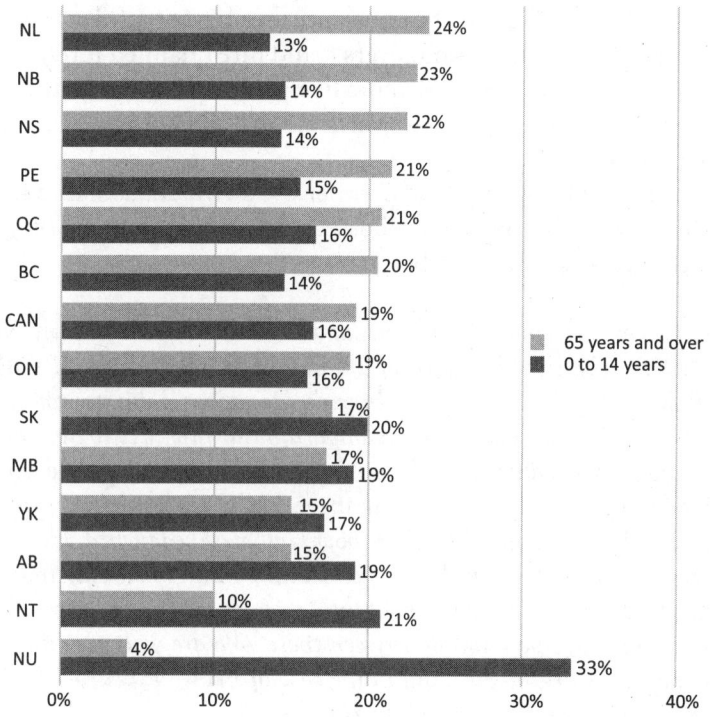

FIGURE 3-2: PROPORTION OF THE POPULATION AGED 0–14 AND 65+ BY PROVINCE, 2021

Source: Statistics Canada 2021 Census

INCREASE IN IMMIGRATION

As previously mentioned, birth rates have been in decline for decades across the Western world. In Canada, current birth rates are well below those needed to replace the population. This helps explain Canada's focus on immigration to address an aging workforce.

There has been a noticeable increase in immigration across the region in the last five years, but that progress was briefly interrupted by the pandemic. Prince Edward Island started on the immigration track earlier than the rest of the region and has benefitted the most from immigration as a result. Their provincial nominee programs, under the Joe Ghiz and Pat Binns governments, were the first of their kind in the region. The recognition of the need to grow the population and ensure the availability of a workforce to drive economic prosperity is now fully accepted in Atlantic Canada.

The importance of the Atlantic Immigration Pilot (AIP) strategy, an initiative supported by the Council of Atlantic Premiers which was implemented in 2017 as part of the Atlantic Growth Strategy, cannot be understated because it allowed employers the opportunity to directly recruit immigrants to fulfill job opportunities. This in turn has helped retention rates for newcomers to the region. The key feature of the Atlantic Immigration Pilot Program was that it was employer driven. Employers could hire qualified foreign workers, and participating employers were more likely to help foreign workers get settled in their jobs and communities, which led to higher retention rates among this cohort of foreign-born workers.

Former Prince Edward Island premier Wade MacLauchlan, a key driver behind the Atlantic Immigration Pilot Program, told us on our *Insights* podcast how that program came to be:

> *We had an election nationally in Canada in late October or early November of 2015. The new minister of Immigration, Refugees and Citizenship [IRCC] was John McCallum. In early December, I did my round of visits to the new cabinet ministers. It's important for premiers to do. On my visit with John McCallum—and I'd known him some in a previous life—one of the things I said to him was that the IRCC is run the way you'd run a library if you didn't want to let the books out, and he laughed. He said he was beginning to see that, and he hoped I didn't mind him using that analogy. We also spoke on that visit about the dependency ratio of the relationship of the working-age population between those who are younger and those who are beyond working age, and in the case of Prince Edward Island at that time it looked pretty scary out to 2065.*
>
> *John laughed, and he said it was the first time he'd seen a premier walking around with the dependency ratio, but he really took it to heart. Then the next summer he and his wife, Nancy, came on a personal vacation to Prince Edward Island. One of their main reasons to come was to visit with their friends Lawrence and Francis MacAulay, and there's always a personal story behind some of these big public policy developments. So, John and Nancy came to lunch at our place, and he asked if I had told him when we met in December about Royal Star Fisheries. It's a great story of a very successful fish processing and export operation and a fishing community that feeds a whole region. Indeed, there are spillover benefits throughout Prince Edward Island.*
>
> *If you look at the workforce at the fish plant, there's no question that the plant would not be operating were it not for immigrant workers—a very large number who've come from the Philippines over a period now of fifteen years; great people and they're happy there. But given the pathways open to*

> immigrant plant workers as recently as 2015, these workers were in a very tenuous situation, especially with their families back in the Philippines. If, for example, they had to go back if someone was sick, they had to start all over again. They might not even be able to return. So, John McCallum asked if I would invite some of those workers to the lunch. Francis Morrissey, who is the manager of that operation and a very effective business and community leader, came with four of the workers. There wasn't a trace of a grievance. It was simply storytelling, and storytelling is so important in this world. But John and Nancy, who herself started out originally, I believe in Singapore, took this all to heart, and by a year later, in July of 2017, the Atlantic Immigration Pilot Program had been put together.
>
> That pilot that has made life a lot more secure for those workers, and for many others, so they can bring their families and they can come and go. They've got what is now the fastest pathway in Canada to permanent residency. I do believe the example of Royal Star helped to inform the Atlantic Immigration Pilot in that sense—the integral role of employers in speaking up, putting their hand up, providing not just jobs but really becoming an effective part of the settlement process for people who come through the Atlantic Immigration Pilot.

And, of course, based on the success of the AIP, the program became permanent in January 2022. With at least six thousand admission spaces available yearly, the AIP complements the provincial nominee programs in each of the four Atlantic provinces.

Nevertheless, much more work needs to be done to ensure the long-term prosperity for Atlantic Canada. Newfoundland and Labrador continues to be the province most challenged by population growth, and the province's immigration targets have generally been below what is needed to drive its economy and address its aging workforce. But, again, there has been recent progress in Newfoundland and Labrador on the population growth front, driven in large part by increasing immigration numbers.

As the following charts demonstrate, with the exception of 2020, which was impacted by the pandemic, there has been an upward trend in immigration across Atlantic Canada. It is important to point out that, in the past two years, Newfoundland and Labrador has finally caught up with the rest of the region in terms of attracting immigrants to that province.

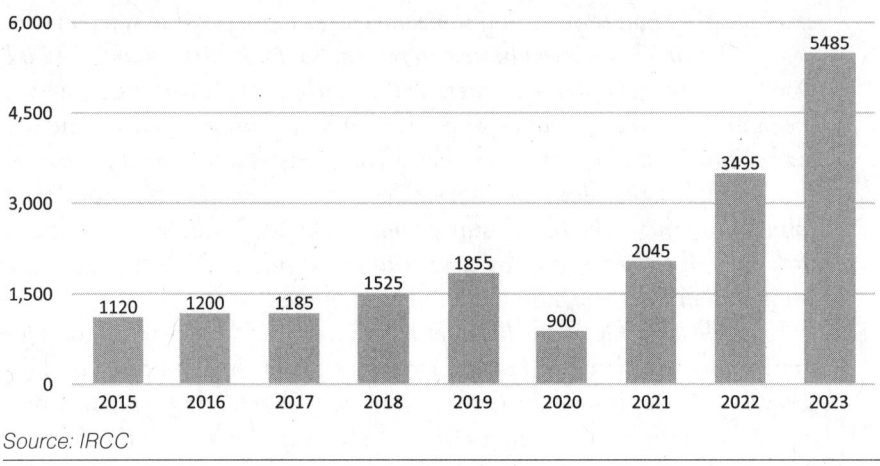

FIGURE 3-3: PERMANENT RESIDENT ADMISSIONS BY YEAR, NEWFOUNDLAND AND LABRADOR

Source: IRCC

On a per-capita basis, Prince Edward Island continues to attract the highest number of immigrants, with a dramatic increase in 2023 of about 2 percent of the population.

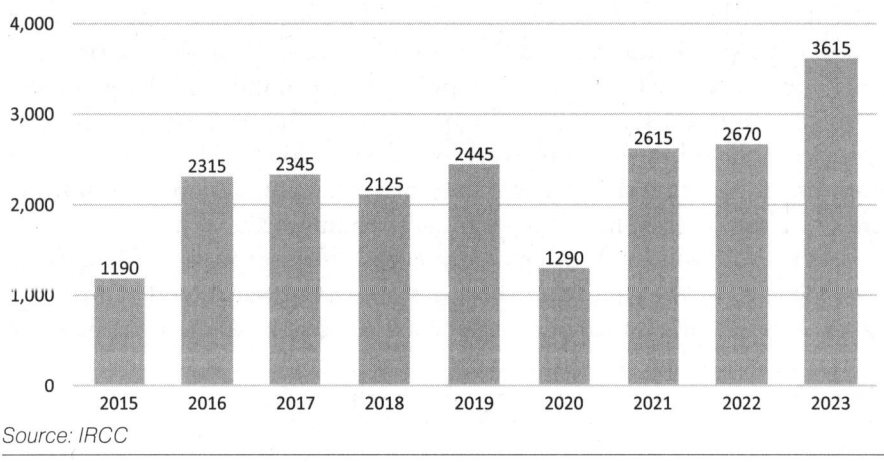

FIGURE 3-4: PERMANENT RESIDENT ADMISSIONS BY YEAR, PRINCE EDWARD ISLAND

Source: IRCC

Nova Scotia has more than tripled the number of immigrants to the province in the past decade, with the number now exceeding 1 percent of the population per year.

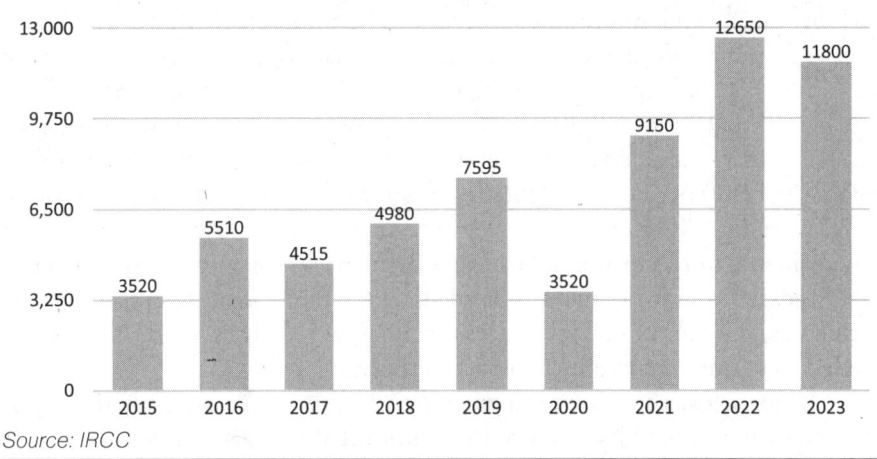

FIGURE 3-5: PERMANENT RESIDENT ADMISSIONS BY YEAR, NOVA SCOTIA

Source: IRCC

The growth in immigration in New Brunswick over the last decade is even more spectacular, with the number of immigrants more than quadrupling over that period. New Brunswick is now challenging Nova Scotia in terms of the absolute number of immigrants attracted to the province.

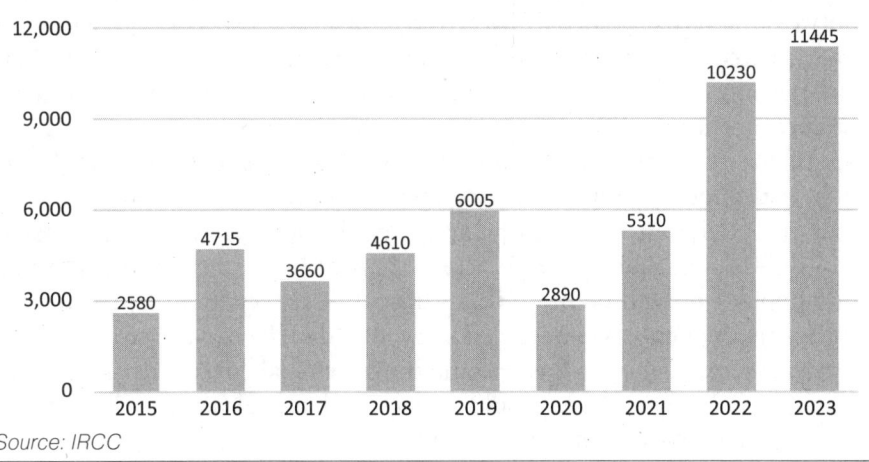

FIGURE 3-6: PERMANENT RESIDENT ADMISSIONS BY YEAR, NEW BRUNSWICK

Source: IRCC

Workforce demand as a result of an aging population and growing economies means that the Atlantic provinces must better understand their labour requirements over the next several decades and develop strategies to attract that workforce. The gap between the current workforce and that required to meet economic must be well understood. Given current participation rates, which will be discussed in more detail later in the book, about 60 percent of working-aged residents can be expected to be available to work. The Ivany Report from the Nova Scotia Commission on Building Our New Economy identified that this gap is the equivalent of 7,000 net new residents needed per year between 2015 and 2030 to maintain current economic levels. The province has greatly exceeded this number in recent years. The equivalent number for PEI is 1,000 net new residents to maintain the current level of economic activity. Again, PEI has had more than four times this target number of net new residents in recent years. For New Brunswick, the number is 5,700 net new residents, and for Newfoundland and Labrador the number is 3,000. In both cases, the number of net new residents now greatly exceeds the number needed to maintain current economic activity.

It is now clear that there is a growing labour force to not only maintain current economic activity but also to significantly grow that activity. Growth in full-time jobs across the region is providing evidence that growing the population and the workforce is also leading to economic growth across Atlantic Canada.

Given the current participation rates in the population among working-aged individuals, there will be nearly 150,000 jobs to be filled over the next decade or so as baby boomers leave the workplace in growing numbers. This does not account for new jobs generated through economic growth.

The second significant challenge related to an aging population relates to the impact on health care, especially the costs of health care and the availability of long-term care beds. Given that health-care costs rise with age, with an anticipated increase of 55 percent more sixty-five-year-olds by 2030 than 2015, the impact of this aging population is bound to be significant. Provincial governments across Atlantic Canada are already responding to increasing demand for long-term care by building new facilities across the region. This will have the added benefit of freeing up primary care beds in the region.

Further, without significantly increasing the number of those employed, the ability to fund the expected increase in health-care costs to tend to this aging population will be more than difficult—especially in a jurisdiction that has the highest taxes in the country already. The capacity to fund this expected increase in costs has become the provincial governments' greatest challenge in the region. One would anticipate that health care will continue to be the top public concern over the next decade or more.

CHAPTER 4
STRUCTURAL GROWTH CHALLENGES

TWO IMPORTANT STRUCTURAL CHALLENGES HAVE DISADVANTAGED THE region economically for decades in comparison to the rest of Canada, and they help explain Atlantic Canada's chronic economic underperformance.

The first is that Atlantic Canada has a disproportionate reliance on government jobs relative to the rest of the country. This is best reflected in the composition of the workforce in each of the four Atlantic provinces. In Canada, about one in five of those in the workforce work in the public sector. In Atlantic Canada, that number is at least one in four or more across the region. This higher percentage of public-sector workers is in reality a structural economic issue that needs to be addressed. It is really the consequence of a slower-growing economy relative to the rest of the country over an extended period of time. It is a barrier to economic growth and one of the reasons Atlantic Canada has trailed economic growth in the country for literally decades. It also contributes to higher levels of taxation in the region.

The second relates to the distribution of the population within Atlantic Canada. More than twice as many residents live in rural communities compared to the rest of Canada, leading to weaker economic performance and service delivery issues.

A PROPORTIONATELY SMALLER PRIVATE SECTOR

Having a proportionately smaller private sector simply means that our capacity to grow the economy is relatively weaker. Having fewer private-sector workers who can build prosperity through the creation of goods and services for sale has led the region to underperform the national economy for decades by about 1 percent annually. That may not seem like a lot, but compounded over decades it has meant that the regional economy has become a smaller and smaller part of the Canadian economy over the last fifty years. That means the capacity to fund public services has been compromised by a slower-growing economy in the region. It means that the level of taxation has risen to the highest in the country to offset the rise in the cost of public services, which has outpaced the growth in the economy for many years. It means that the growth in new jobs (and new taxpayers) has not kept pace with the growth in the cost of government.

COMPARISON OF PUBLIC-SECTOR WORKERS

The ratio of public-sector workers has risen over the past decade or so. The ratio peaked following the Great Recession across the region and continued to be higher than prior to 2008. Currently, Newfoundland and Labrador and Prince Edward Island have the distinction of having the highest proportion of public-sector workers in Canada, but the rest of the region has disproportionately higher numbers of public-sector workers than the Canadian average. This means that the region also has fewer private-sector workers to grow the economy.

The higher-than-average ratio of public-sector workers in the economy can, at least in part, be attributed to weak economic growth over a sustained period of time, which has made the creation of private-sector jobs more challenging in the region.

One specific area of opportunity to rebalance the workforce in Atlantic Canada is the possible outsourcing of non-essential services to the private sector. Over the years, there has been considerable discussion regarding the privatization of liquor sales as has been done in other provinces. The regulation and control of liquor would remain a government function, while the distribution and sale would become a private-sector function. Governments would continue to benefit from the sale of liquor through taxation; proceeds could offset provincial debts and free up more public money for other services such as health and education. The public would benefit through a more competitive environment which might result in better pricing and more product choices. Having said that, there has been a considerable improvement in service by provincial liquor commissions in recent years. This is particularly the case in Nova Scotia.

Another area of opportunity is with the provincial registries which have been outsourced in other provinces. In Alberta, British Columbia, Ontario, Nova Scotia, and New Brunswick, provincial governments have outsourced the management of registries (land titles, personal property, corporate or vital statistics). One of the best examples at the federal level was the partnership between Service Canada and IBM to contract IT services to the department, including data centre operations and IT infrastructure management.

We are over-governed in Atlantic Canada. There are too many municipalities in Atlantic Canada to serve the relatively small population in the region. This leads to a lot of unnecessary duplication. There are many examples of this across the region. In Pictou County in Nova Scotia, there are six municipal units, all within a half-hour drive of one another, to serve a population of about forty thousand. While there are currently some shared services, the inefficiencies of delivering other services like policing lead to unnecessary costs to taxpayers.

There are other, larger, examples. In the greater Moncton area there are three side-by-side municipalities: the cities of Moncton, Riverview, and Dieppe. These municipalities should be amalgamated; research conducted by Narrative Research indicates that the majority of people living within the greater Moncton area actually favour such an amalgamation. In the greater Saint John area, the City of Saint John struggles to be financially sustainable; until just recently, it had a declining population, while communities such as Rothesay and Quispamsis continued to benefit from all the city's amenities and economic opportunities without paying their share of the costs. This is not right. The greater Saint John area needs to be amalgamated as well. There are many other examples across the region where the amalgamation of smaller municipalities would be of benefit to those living in these communities. It would result in more efficient delivery of public services and more sustainable taxes.

UNFAIR COMPETITION FOR WORKERS

The most sought-after jobs within Atlantic Canada are increasingly government jobs. Public-sector employers now have every advantage over their private-sector counterparts. At one time, public-sector jobs had the advantage on the basis of the benefits and pensions offered, while the private sector had an advantage on salary and wages. That is no longer the case.

Let's begin with pensions. In Canada, nearly 87 percent of public-sector workers have pensions, mostly defined-benefit plans and inflation-protected. Only 23 percent of private-sector workers have pensions, and the vast majority of those are defined-contribution benefits with no protection against inflation. In fact, more than 90 percent of public-sector pensions are defined benefits plans. This compares with only 40 percent of private sector plans that are defined-benefit plans. It is perhaps interesting to note that public-sector workers are able to retire about two and a half years earlier than their private-sector counterparts.

Why don't more private-sector employers offer pensions? It's a question of affordability and scale. In a competitive market, cost management is key to survival and success. It's also a question of size; only the largest companies have the scale to offer pensions. But even the country's largest financial organization, RBC, changed its pension from a defined-benefit program to a defined-contribution program due to cost issues. The vast majority of companies in Canada are small businesses that do not have the financial capacity to provide benefits to their employees. The vast majority of these businesses operate on thin margins.

In a recent *Insights* podcast, Dan Kelly, the CEO of the Canadian Federation of Independent Business, clearly defined the composition of businesses in Canada:

> There are 1.2 million small and medium-sized companies in Canada with paid staff. When you include the self-employed in that mix, there's about another 2.5 million businesses that are effectively businesses of one. Together, self-employed and small business owners with paid staff represent over half of the GDP in the country. Sixty percent of total employment in the country is in small and medium-sized firms. It is also often surprising: 99 percent of all businesses in Canada would be considered small or medium-sized. Typically, when we say small-sized, we usually use a headcount indicator of fifty employees or fewer, with medium-sized being fifty to five hundred, with large enterprises being five hundred-plus employees.

> In a defined-benefit pension plan, the employer promises to pay the employee a set amount of regular income after they retire. In a defined-contribution pension plan, the employee knows how much they'll pay into the plan, but they don't know how much they'll get when they retire.

In fact, 87 percent have fewer than twenty employees. Proportionately, Atlantic Canada has fewer large enterprises than the rest of the country. There are few small businesses that have the financial capacity to provide pensions. The best that can be done is to match their employees' contributions to an RRSP, but even then, that contribution is usually fairly modest.

Public pensions are funded by Canadian taxpayers, the vast majority of whom do not themselves have a pension and are left to their own devices to fund their retirements. It is time for Canada to ensure all Canadians have access to an adequate retirement by increasing the Canada Pension Plan for those without pensions. It is only fair that all Canadians have access to a reasonable pension upon retirement.

In terms of benefits, the Fraser Institute notes that public-sector employees in general have better sick time access, time off for personal reasons, health care, and drug coverage than their private-sector counterparts. Additionally, public-sector jobs offer better job security, with public-sector workers five times less likely to lose their jobs than those in the private sector. This might say something about performance management practices in both sectors.

POPULATION DISTRIBUTION CHALLENGES

Slow population growth over decades has had a lasting impact on the composition of the population across Atlantic Canada. Canada's population, until only very recently, has grown at a consistent rate of about 1 percent a year.

The majority of that growth has taken place in urban communities, consistent with what has happened elsewhere in Canada for much of the last century. In fact, in the most recent census, the population in urban communities grew by 6.3 percent, while rural communities grew by only 0.4 percent.

Recent population growth within the three Maritime provinces indicates that the process of urbanization is now under way within the region. It also demonstrates the particular challenges faced by Newfoundland and Labrador, which has had a noticeable decline in its rural population and only modest population growth overall.

Population growth in Prince Edward Island, while favouring urban communities, has also been strong in the rural population. This is mainly a result of its small geography. The Island is smaller in size than the Halifax Regional Municipality, which results in a greater ability to live in rural communities and still have access to full-time employment within reasonable commuting distances.

TABLE 4-1: GROWTH IN RURAL/URBAN POPULATION IN ATLANTIC CANADA, 2016–2021

	Rural Population		Rural Growth	Urban Growth
	2016	2021	2016–2021	2016–2021
Canada	6,575,373	6,601,982	+0.4%	+6.3%
Newfoundland	217,988	204,086	-6.4%	+1.6%
Prince Edward Island	78,498	83,350	+6.2%	+10.2%
Nova Scotia	393,629	398,776	+1.3%	+7.7%
New Brunswick	380,919	380,490	-0.1%	+7.9%

Source: Statistics Canada 2016 and 2021 Censuses

Slow or stagnant population growth in Atlantic Canada has meant that the region has not urbanized at the same pace as the remainder of the country. The result is that the region has twice as many people living in rural communities as the country as a whole. Prince Edward Island is the most rural province in Canada, although recent population growth has favoured urban communities. The relatively small geographic size of the Island mitigates the problem of a lack of urbanization relative to the rest of the country. It may surprise some that Newfoundland and Labrador, despite their large geography, has the highest proportion of urban population in the region. Part of this can be attributed to the closure of 250 outports by the government in that province between the mid-1950s and the mid-1970s.

TABLE 4-2: COMPARISON OF URBAN/RURAL SPLIT BETWEEN ATLANTIC CANADA AND CANADA

	Urban	Rural
Canada	82%	18%
Nova Scotia	59%	41%
New Brunswick	51%	49%
Prince Edward Island	46%	54%
Newfoundland and Labrador	60%	40%

Source: Statistics Canada 2021 Census

We know that many rural communities do not have a sufficient economic base to provide full-time employment opportunities to all the people in those communities; many rural residents are dependent on seasonal work and the support of Employment Insurance to support themselves. Intergenerational reliance on EI has led to attitudinal challenges related to willingness to work among some within the region. I (*Don Mills*) conducted specific research on this issue for the New Brunswick Department of Labour while I was the CEO and owner of Corporate Research Associates. This was an attempt at the time to try to understand why employers were having a hard time recruiting workers in areas of the province with high unemployment. The conclusion from the study at that time was that a proportion of the workers in those high unemployment areas were more interested in working the system than in actually working for a living.

The urbanization of Canada continues. Between the 2016 and 2021 Censuses, the urban population grew by 6.3 percent. The good news is that most of Atlantic Canada, except Newfoundland and Labrador, had their urban populations grow at a faster rate than the country overall.

COSTS OF SERVICE DELIVERY

Some of the challenges related to a disproportionately higher rural population are the cost of and access to service delivery. In a region where there are twice as many people living in rural areas compared to the rest of the country, the costs of service delivery will inevitably be higher and basic services such as municipal water and sewer are largely unavailable for many rural residents. Access to high-speed internet service is slowly improving but needs to be heavily subsidized. Other services such as garbage collection are more expensive to deliver due to greater distances in rural communities compared to urban communities. Access to public transportation is limited or non-existent in most rural communities. Health-care services are concentrated in more heavily populated urban areas.

SHARING THE TAX BURDEN

Another issue related to population distribution is sharing the tax burden equitably between those living in rural communities and those living in nearby urban communities.

In 1996, four municipalities were amalgamated to form the Halifax Regional Municipality in order to share the tax burden. In the case of Halifax, the shared costs of service delivery of a municipality that is bigger in geography than Prince Edward Island have been heavily subsidized by those living and doing business in the urban core.

New Brunswick recently introduced municipal reform within the province. One of the aims was to have a fairer system to share the costs of services. As an example, in the greater Saint John area there is a Regional Service Commission that has had its mandate expanded beyond regional garbage collection to include oversight for the sharing of capital costs across the region. The City of Saint John has long complained that nearby communities, such as Rothesay and Quispamsis, do not contribute their fair share toward the cost of services and major infrastructure used by those outside the city proper. The recent formation of Envision, the economic development agency for the greater Saint John region, has a shared funding model in place that addresses one area of shared interest: growing the economy.

Looking ahead, municipalities that provide amenities and job opportunities to those living in nearby communities are likely to seek more cost-sharing from those communities, as is happening in Saint John.

AN INVESTMENT GAP

One of the main reasons for the region's overall economic underperformance has been a relative lack of business investment. Business investment is important to help jurisdictions remain competitive and create jobs. It is also important in terms of research and development (R & D) to develop future opportunities for communities.

Statistics Canada tracks private-sector investment relative to GDP year by year on an inflation-adjusted basis. Business gross fixed capital formation (also known as business investment) in Atlantic Canada relative to GDP underperformed the country as a whole for forty-two of the forty-three years between 1981 and 2023. Even adjusting for residential housing investment, business gross fixed capital formation in Atlantic Canada relative to GDP underperformed for thirty-eight of the forty-three years. Business investment is a crucial indicator of the strength of an economy. If firms are investing in the region, they are making a bet they can make a good return on the invested capital into the future.

And the investment data in the region has not improved in recent years in either New Brunswick or Nova Scotia. As shown in table 4-3, between

2003 and 2012 business gross fixed capital formation (excluding residential structures) in Nova Scotia as a percentage of GDP averaged 9 percent per year, or 27 percent below the national investment level. Between 2014 and 2023, the annual business investment level in Nova Scotia dipped to 8 percent of GDP, or 34 percent below the national level.

In New Brunswick, the annual average business gross fixed capital formation (excluding residential structures) rate as a percentage of GDP dipped from 10 percent between 2003 and 2013 to 8 percent between 2014 and 2023—27 percent below the national level.

Prince Edward Island, which has few capital-intensive industries, saw its private-sector investment rate increase slightly in recent years. Newfoundland and Labrador, which has two very capital-intensive industries—oil and gas and mining—has been well above the national level of investment in recent years.

TABLE 4-3: AVERAGE ANNUAL BUSINESS GROSS FIXED CAPITAL FORMATION AS A PERCENTAGE OF GDP BY TIME FRAME, EXCLUDING RESIDENTIAL STRUCTURES, CHAINED (2017) DOLLARS

	2003–2013	CAN = 1.00	2014–2023	CAN = 1.00
Newfoundland and Labrador	14%	1.12	21%	1.84
Prince Edward Island	7%	0.59	7%	0.62
Nova Scotia	9%	0.71	8%	0.66
New Brunswick	10%	0.78	8%	0.73

Source: Statistics Canada Table 36-10-0222-01

CHAPTER 5

TOO MANY WORKERS, TOO FEW JOBS

DAVID CAMPBELL: MY FIRST JOB AFTER GRADUATING FROM UNIVERSITY WAS with the New Brunswick Department of Economic Development and Tourism. It was the early 1990s and a top priority of then premier Frank McKenna was finding jobs for all the young New Brunswickers graduating from high school or post-secondary education. At that time, the province had too many young people and not enough jobs. According to Statistics Canada, an average of 3,500 young people aged eighteen to twenty-four left New Brunswick every year during the 1980s. This meant that more than one out of every three young New Brunswickers left during the decade to further their aspirations elsewhere. The premier was determined to arrest this decline and give young people more career opportunities at home. Essentially, the same story was playing out in the other three Atlantic provinces.

Thirty years later, the number of young people leaving Atlantic Canada every year has dropped sharply. People still leave to pursue careers elsewhere, but they have more options at home than ever before. In fact, there are now more jobs in Atlantic Canada than young people, and that has necessitated efforts to bring young people to the region to meet workforce demand.

This chapter looks at the evolving workforce in Atlantic Canada and how that influences the region's economic growth and prosperity.

A WORKFORCE FOCUSSED ON NATURAL RESOURCES

The workforce in Atlantic Canada has evolved over time to meet the specific demands of industry. This is the case across the country, since each province has a different industrial structure. The Ontario economy ranks first among the thirteen provinces and territories for the share of economic output derived from service industries such as finance, legal services, publishing, and information and communications technology (ICT). The workforce has evolved to meet the demands of service industries.

Quebec has a large manufacturing sector and in recent years has developed its digital media and information technology services sectors; the workforce has evolved to meet the needs of these three industries. British Columbia has a highly diversified economy with the country's largest movie and television production sector along with important natural resources industries and tourism. Manitoba has leveraged its geographic position at the centre of Canada to develop the largest transportation and warehousing sector in Canada, relative to population size, while Saskatchewan generates a much larger share of its economic output from farming, specifically crop and animal production. In each case, the post-secondary education system and immigration programs are tuned to address workforce demand in sectors specific to those jurisdictions.

This is no different in Atlantic Canada, which has many strengths in both natural resource–based and services-based industries. The region relies far more on fishing and seafood processing than the rest of the country. Prince Edward Island, in particular, generates more economic activity from fishing and food production, ranking first among the provinces and territories for share of GDP from these two sectors. In recent years, the Island has seen the development of the largest biosciences cluster in the country relative to the size of the provincial economy. Nova Scotia has important fishing and food production sectors, but it is also the province with the largest plastics and rubber products manufacturing sector and generates more economic output than any other province or territory from its universities sector. The workforce has evolved to meet the demands of local industry.

New Brunswick has the distinction of generating more of its economic output from both wood products and paper products manufacturing than any other province or territory. The province also has the largest administrative services sector in the country due, in part, to its bilingual (French and English) workforce. Because several national trucking companies are headquartered in New Brunswick, the province also has the largest truck transportation sector in Canada, relative to the size of its economy. While historically there has been enough workers for these strategically important industries, these two sectors are now facing significant workforce challenges that could negatively impact the economic contribution in years ahead.

Newfoundland and Labrador is even more reliant on natural resources than the rest of Atlantic Canada. The province ranks second among the provinces and territories for the share of GDP from the oil and gas extraction sector and also produces iron ore, nickel, copper, cobalt, and gold. These industries pay high wages and have traditionally faced no real challenges in attracting workers. Now, even these industries are starting to face serious workforce challenges.

This varied mix of industries, combined with the region's larger rural economy, has influenced the structure and attributes of the regional workforce.

THE COMPOSITION OF ATLANTIC CANADA'S WORKFORCE

Until recently, Atlantic Canada attracted considerably fewer immigrants than the country overall. The post–Second World War baby boom led to strong growth in the size of the workforce in the 1970s through the early 1990s, but by the early 2000s there were not enough local people to support workforce growth.

To illustrate this, in the late 1970s and 1980s, the workforce in Atlantic Canada expanded each year almost as fast as that in the rest of the country. Between 1977 and 1984, the Canadian workforce expanded by 2.4 percent per year on average, and the Atlantic region workforce increased by 2.2 percent. This trend continued until the early 1990s. At that point, the workforce continued to grow across the country, but growth stalled in Atlantic Canada. Throughout the 1990s and early 2000s, the national workforce increased three times faster than in Atlantic Canada. Then, in the early 2010s, the size of the workforce across Atlantic Canada actually started to decline. Between 2010 and 2018, the national workforce swelled by 1.4 million people but, in Atlantic Canada, the size of the workforce declined by seven thousand.[1]

What happened? Put simply, the local workforce pipeline in the region started to shrink even as the number retiring from the workforce started to grow. In the 1970s, there were far more births than deaths across the region. As shown in figure 5-1, in 1972 there were 253 births for every 100 deaths across Atlantic Canada. What this meant in demographic terms is that the local population in Atlantic Canada was large enough to meet workforce demand without the need for much inward migration from elsewhere in Canada or from other countries. In fact, as discussed above, from the 1970s to the 1990s, with the exception of recession years, the Atlantic region mostly experienced negative interprovincial migration each year, meaning more people moved out than in. By 2024, there were only 61 births per 100 deaths across the region.

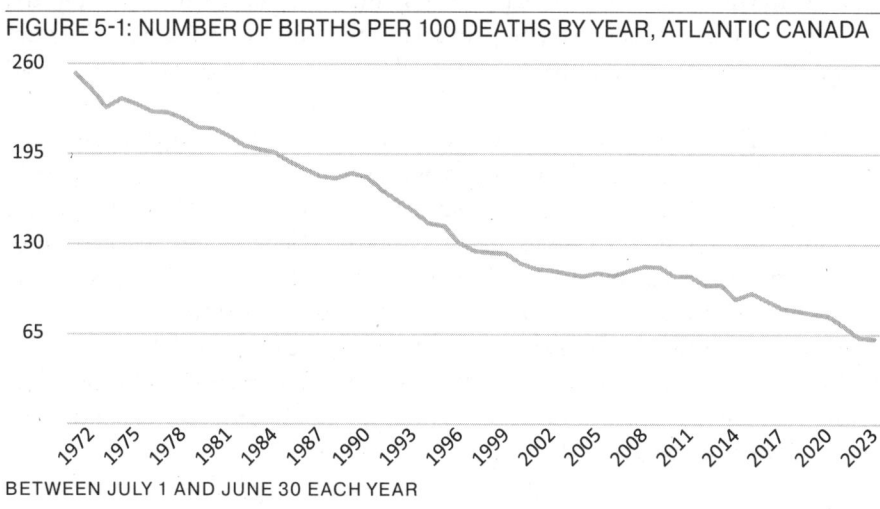

FIGURE 5-1: NUMBER OF BIRTHS PER 100 DEATHS BY YEAR, ATLANTIC CANADA

BETWEEN JULY 1 AND JUNE 30 EACH YEAR
Source: Statistics Canada Table 17-10-0008-01

By the time the recession hit in 2008, this demographic reality caught up with the region. While the rest of the country also faced an aging population, the level of immigration was rising to compensate. In the 1970s and 1980s, the average number of immigrants settling in Canada each year was 133,000 per year. From 1990 to 2013, the annual number increased by almost 77 percent to 235,000. By contrast, Atlantic Canada registered only a modest increase in immigration during that period. In fact, in the early 2000s, despite the increasingly obvious demographic challenge, the number of immigrants settling in the region each year actually declined.

IVANY REPORT SOUNDS THE ALARM

In 2014, the Ivany Report came out in Nova Scotia; it clearly indicated the need for a rapid expansion of immigration and population growth to address a structural shortage in the workforce.[2] By then, Prince Edward Island had already taken the challenge and was leading the country in annual immigrant inflows. In 2015, the New Brunswick government published a population growth strategy that also called for a substantial boost to immigration. This focus, combined with changes to federal immigration policies, led to a rise in population and to renewed growth in the workforce. Since the COVID-19 pandemic, workforce growth has paralleled the national growth rate once again.

PROVINCIAL WORKFORCE TRENDS

While there are many workforce similarities across Atlantic Canada, there are also many differences. Newfoundland and Labrador's workforce expanded strongly in the late 1970s and early 1980s, due in large part to growth in the mining and fishing sectors. The province saw another small growth spurt during the launch of the offshore oil and gas sector in the late 1990s and early 2000s.

Prince Edward Island has consistently featured faster workforce growth than the other three Atlantic provinces, with the most notable period of workforce growth in the past few years, from 2009 to 2023, when the Island's total workforce growth was 3.4 times faster than Nova Scotia's and nearly 6 times faster than New Brunswick's.

Nova Scotia and New Brunswick witnessed consistent workforce growth from the 1980s through to the early 2000s, but after the 2008 recession both provinces struggled. Along with Newfoundland and Labrador, New Brunswick had the worst workforce growth of all of the provinces and territories between 2009 and 2023.

HIGH UNEMPLOYMENT RATE

One of the curious workforce characteristics in Atlantic Canada is that the unemployment rate has remained relatively high even as it has become much harder to recruit people into many sectors of the economy.

The nominal unemployment rate across the region has been slowly declining for the past thirty years. In the early 1990s, it peaked at over 15 percent, and by 2023 it was down to a record low of 7.2 percent. However, relative to the national unemployment rate, it has remained stubbornly high. In 2023, the share of the workforce in the region defined as unemployed was 33 percent higher than in the country overall. The main reason there seems to be a structural gap between the unemployment rate in Atlantic Canada and the rest of the country is related to the seasonal nature of the workforce and the over-dependence on the Employment Insurance (EI) program. In an *Insights* interview, economist Richard Saillant described the challenges of seasonal industries and reliance on EI. He indicated these seasonal industries were critically important to the rural economy in the region, but also said the overuse of EI is having a distorting impact on the workforce picture in the region.

THE GENDER GAP

In addition to the large number of young people joining the workforce in Atlantic Canada in the 1970s and 1980s, women were entering the workforce at an unprecedented rate. By the 1970s, the workforce gender gap was already narrowing in Atlantic Canada and across the country, but in the next forty years it would essentially disappear. In 2022, there were ninety-nine women aged twenty-five to forty-four in the workforce across the Atlantic region for every one hundred men in the workforce—a ratio even higher than the country's overall (figure 5-2). To emphasize the importance of female workforce growth to the regional economy over the past four decades, consider the following statistic: between 1976 and 2022 the male workforce across Atlantic Canada increased by 127,000. Over the same period, the female workforce expanded by 329,000.

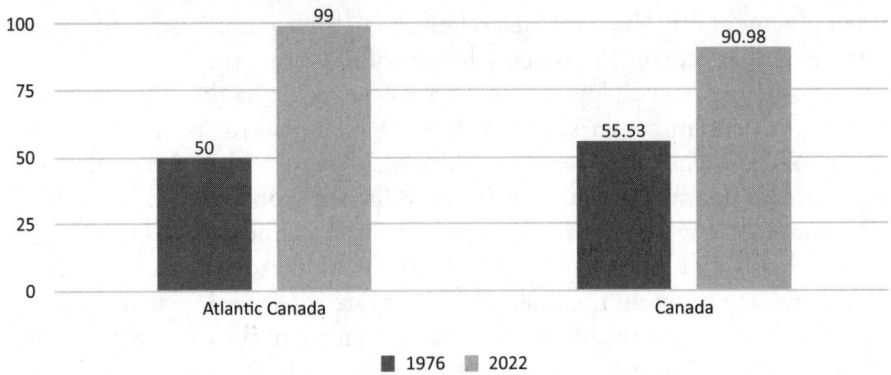

FIGURE 5-2: NUMBER OF WOMEN AGED 25–44 IN THE WORKFORCE PER 100 MEN, BY TIME FRAME AND LOCATION

Source: Statistics Canada Table 17-10-0008-01

Women still face many challenges in the workforce. They earn considerably less than men across the region and the share in senior management roles is still much lower, but there has been substantial progress. As of the 2021 Census, women accounted for 38 percent of all senior managers in the public and private sectors across Atlantic Canada, compared to only 30 percent in the rest of the country. However, men in these senior management roles still earned on average around 50 percent more than women.

ATLANTIC CANADA'S RURAL WORKFORCE

Another difference that sets Atlantic Canada apart from the rest of the country is the larger share of both the population and workforce that live in rural areas.[3] According to Statistics Canada, 51 percent of the workforce in Prince Edward Island lives in a rural area, 47 percent in New Brunswick, 37 percent in Nova Scotia, and 32 percent in Newfoundland and Labrador. Across Atlantic Canada, two out of every five workers live in a rural area, compared to only 15 percent across the country.

Figure 5-3 shows the share of the workforce living in rural areas of the province as of 2022. The implications of having a relatively large rural workforce will be developed further in chapter 6.

FIGURE 5-3: SHARE OF THE WORKFORCE LOCATED IN RURAL AREAS BY PROVINCE, 2022

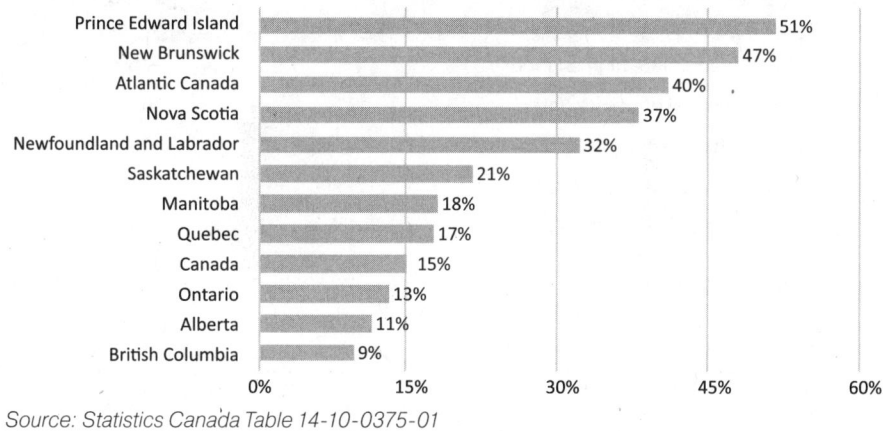

Source: Statistics Canada Table 14-10-0375-01

WORKFORCE BY EDUCATIONAL LEVEL

Like the rest of the country, the workforce in Atlantic Canada has become more educated in recent decades, but the structure of the economy discussed above means there are differences compared to the country overall.

There has been a significant decline in the share of the workforce without high school education. In 1992, 28 percent of Atlantic Canada's workforce had not completed high school. By 2022, only 7 percent had not. Thirty years ago, only 14 percent had completed university; as of 2022, 32 percent report having a university degree. Table 5-1 shows the education attainment rate of the workforce and how it compares to the country overall. In general, Atlantic Canada has a larger share of the workforce that has not completed high school than the rest of Canada (15 percent more).

The regional workforce is more oriented toward community college and trades education than is the country overall. As of 2022, 42 percent had a post-secondary certificate or diploma (well above the national share) but only 21 percent held a bachelor's degree (well below the national share) and 11 percent had a postgraduate degree (also well below the national share).

TABLE 5-1: EDUCATION ATTAINMENT LEVEL, WORKFORCE AGED 25+, ATLANTIC CANADA (2022)

	% of total	Compared to Canada*
Did not complete high school	7%	+15%
High school graduate only	17%	+6%
Post-secondary certificate or diploma	42%	+13%
University-bachelor's degree	21%	-17%
University-above bachelor's degree	11%	-19%

*DIFFERENCE IN THE SHARE OF THE WORKFORCE BY EDUCATION LEVEL IN ATLANTIC CANADA COMPARED TO THE COUNTRY OVERALL

Source: Statistics Canada Table 14-10-0118-01

WHERE PEOPLE WORK: INDUSTRIES

Atlantic Canada's economy has changed a lot in the past thirty years. Economies can be broken into two main categories: goods-producing industries and services industries. Over the past thirty years, employment in the region's services industries has risen 3.6 times faster than employment in goods-producing industries.

THE CONTINUING IMPORTANCE OF FISH AND WOOD

As a driver of export revenue, the region's goods-producing industries remain very important to the health of the economy. The fishing sector has seen a 37 percent drop in total employment over the past thirty years, even as output and export levels have increased. In 2022, the fishing workforce was eighteen thousand across the four provinces (excluding value-added processing and other activities). The fishing sector had a workforce 13.5 times larger than the rest of the country, which makes sense given our proximity to the Atlantic Ocean. The relative importance of the sector has only risen over the past three decades.

The forestry sector workforce (excluding value-added manufacturing) has seen similar trends as the fishing sector. Productivity gains mean there are fewer workers now (total employment is down 37 percent between 1992 and 2022), but output and export values have remained relatively strong—although there has been more disruption in the sector in Nova Scotia than in New Brunswick. As of 2022, there were only eight thousand workers employed directly in the forestry and logging sector across the region. However, with downstream value-added manufacturing (wood and paper products) and other indirect and induced employment, the region's forests supported more than thirty thousand workers during the year and were the third most important export sector by value behind fishing and energy. There were 2.6 times as many people employed in the logging sector in 2022 than in the country overall (as a share of total employment).

The region's mining sector has seen considerable employment growth (up 41 percent over the twenty-year period between 2002 and 2022) and it continues to have a higher share of employment than the country overall, mainly as a result of mining in Labrador and Newfoundland and Labrador's offshore oil and gas sector. There are now twenty thousand people directly employed in the sector and many thousands more jobs are supported by industry elsewhere in the economy.

FARMING

Total agricultural employment has declined across the region, but the sector's relative employment impact has risen. As of 2022, there were an estimated seventeen thousand people in Atlantic Canada's direct agricultural workforce, down 28 percent over the past three decades. But employment has also been declining nationally, even faster than in this region. As a result, the relative share of agricultural employment has risen and there is now a higher concentration of workers in agriculture here than in the rest of the country. The agriculture sector in the region holds considerable potential for growth both to meet local demand and to serve export markets.

MANUFACTURING EMPLOYMENT

The number of manufacturing jobs across Canada has declined in recent decades as certain types of lower-value manufacturing have shifted out of the country and other industries have become more productive. This trend has played out in Atlantic Canada as well. Manufacturing employment dropped from 112,000 in 1992 to 88,000 in 2022, a decline of 21 percent. However, relative to the national manufacturing workforce, the region's relative share has increased slightly over that time frame. Still, manufacturing employment is less important to the Atlantic Canadian economy than to the country overall.

Durable goods employment has held up; the sector employed thirty-five thousand people in 1992 and thirty-six thousand in 2022. This includes the rubber-products sector in Nova Scotia (Michelin), wood products across the region, and other durable goods. The non-durable goods sector has seen a sharp decline in total employment from seventy-eight thousand in 1992 to only fifty-two thousand in 2022. This sector includes food and seafood production, paper manufacturing, and other goods that are consumed in a short time frame. The region is still more reliant on non-durable goods employment than the rest of the country. This doesn't tell the whole picture, as much of that employment decline has been as a result of gains in labour productivity. In a later chapter, we discusses the importance of productivity growth to support the regional economy in the years ahead.

PUBLIC SERVICES

The services-producing sector in Atlantic Canada added 218,000 jobs over the past thirty years, a growth rate of 29 percent. This growth rate was slower than the country's overall, as services employment increased 60 percent over the same time frame. Population growth elsewhere in Canada is the main reason why services sector employment was slower here, as services employment is highly correlated to population growth.

Table 5-2 shows both the percentage change and the absolute growth in employment over the thirty-year period. In this case, percentage change in the workforce by sector doesn't accurately portray the impact of health-care sector employment. Health-care employment rose by 70 percent between 1992 and 2022, a slower growth rate than both professional, scientific, and technical services (+171 percent), and business, building, and other support services (+85 percent). However, in absolute terms, the health-care sector added eighty-two thousand jobs over the thirty-year period, more than the next three top sectors combined. In fact, health care was responsible for 38 percent of services-sector employment growth over the thirty-year period. The public sector, including public administration, health care, and education, was responsible for 52 percent of services-sector employment growth between 1992 and 2022.

The professional services sector across the region has been increasing its employment numbers over many decades. This sector includes legal services, accounting, engineering, architecture, and other professional services, including information technology services, which have been an important contributor to the growth story. The business, building, and other support services sector includes business services, office administrative services, and other related employment. The region, particularly New Brunswick, has added a lot of jobs in this sector over the thirty years, although the total workforce peaked way back in 2006 at nearly seventy thousand. As of 2022, total employment in this sector across Atlantic Canada has dropped back to forty-four thousand. It is still an important export industry, as companies here provide services across the country and beyond (such as hotel reservations, IT support, banking, and insurance services).

The accommodations and food services sector, a proxy for tourism employment, has seen increasing employment numbers over the three decades, although the rise has not been nearly as fast the rest of Canada's. Further, the pandemic hurt employment in this sector more than most, and as of 2022 it had not recovered its losses. In 2018, accommodation and food-services employment across the region peaked at 89,500. As of 2022, there were only 72,900 employed in the sector. Some of this is related to the pandemic, but there has been substantial pressure on the workforce as not enough people are showing interest in that type of employment, forcing hotels and restaurants to look for productivity gains.

TABLE 5-2: CHANGE IN ATLANTIC CANADA'S WORKFORCE BY VARIOUS SERVICES SECTOR

	1992	2022	# change	% change
Services-producing sector (total)	760,000	977,000	+218,000	+29%
Health care and social assistance	117,000	198,000	+82,000	+70%
Professional, scientific and technical services	29,000	78,000	+49,000	+171%
Business, building, and other support services	24,000	44,000	+20,000	+85%
Educational services	77,000	95,000	+19,000	+24%
Public administration	86,000	99,000	+13,000	+15%
Accommodation and food services	61,000	73,000	+12,000	+19%
Wholesale and retail trade	179,000	191,000	+12,000	+6%
Finance and insurance	33,000	41,000	+8,000	+24%
Information, culture, and recreation	35,000	40,000	+5,000	+16%
Transportation and warehousing	52,000	55,000	+4,000	+7%

Source: Statistics Canada Table 14-10-0023-01

Compared to the country overall, the importance of the transportation and warehousing sector has been waning, in large part, because of the challenges finding workers. Employment in the truck transportation sector, for example, has been increasing in the Toronto region while declining in Atlantic Canada. Truckers doing the route between the Toronto region and Atlantic Canada can be based either in this region or in Toronto. Increasingly it has been easier to find these workers there.

As discussed above, the business, building, and other support services sector has become relatively more important here as an employer, but its relative impact peaked way back in 2004 when the sector had a 30 percent larger workforce than the country overall. Now, the share of employment in this sector has dropped back to the national level.

The region is becoming far more reliant on health-care employment as compared to the country overall, and there are now 40 percent more people employed in public administration relative to the national workforce. Chapter 8 discusses the region's growing reliance on the public sector.

PROVINCIAL DIFFERENCES IN WORKFORCE GROWTH

Fishing is the one industry that is common across Atlantic Canada. Beyond that, each province has relied on different industries to create new jobs over the past three decades. Newfoundland and Labrador's economy and workforce have shifted toward the mining and oil and gas sectors since the discovery and exploitation of offshore oil and gas began in the late 1990s. As shown in table 5-3, employment in this sector is up by more than 200 percent. The oil and gas sector also helped drive the growth in professional services employment, which doubled in size across the province between 1992 and 2022. As elsewhere, health-care employment has been rising fast, adding more jobs than any other industry in the province over the past thirty years.

TABLE 5-3: FASTEST GROWING EMPLOYMENT SECTORS 1992–2022, NEWFOUNDLAND AND LABRADOR

	Workforce (2022)	% workforce change (1992–2022)
Mining, quarrying, and oil and gas extraction	13,200	+222%
Professional, scientific, and technical services	12,100	+109%
Health care and social assistance	46,000	+72%
Business, building, and other support services	6,800	+42%
Construction	23,300	+27%
Information, culture, and recreation	7,800	+22%

Source: Derived using Statistics Canada Table 14-10-0023-01

Nova Scotia's economy and workforce have shifted more toward services than the other three Atlantic provinces, led by the growth in professional services and business services employment. The provincial economy has become far more reliant on these services than the rest of the country. The health-care sector added more than thirty five thousand jobs between 1992 and 2022, making it the largest job creator in the province. The accommodations and food services sector has been another driver of job creation, pointing to the province's important tourism industry. The location of Nova Scotia Power's parent company, Emera, in Halifax has been the main reason why employment in the utilities sector has risen 29 percent over the thirty-year period—faster than in any other province.

TABLE 5-4: FASTEST GROWING EMPLOYMENT SECTORS 1992–2022, NOVA SCOTIA

	Workforce (2022)	% workforce change (1992–2022)
Professional, scientific, and technical services	38,500	+201%
Business, building, and other support services	20,500	+109%
Health care and social assistance	81,300	+77%
Construction	44,900	+67%
Accommodation and food services	30,000	+33%
Utilities	4,500	+29%
Finance and insurance	19,300	+25%

Source: Derived using Statistics Canada Table 14-10-0023-01

Employment in the professional, scientific, and technical services sector in New Brunswick increased by 158 percent over the 1992 to 2022 time frame, but the growth rate lagged behind Nova Scotia and Prince Edward Island's growth rates. Professional services still represent a much smaller share of the workforce compared to the country overall. The business, building, and other support services sector remains an important employer with 14,500 in the workforce as of 2022. However, no other province in Canada saw such turbulence in this sector's employment. Between 1990 and 2006, the sector added 17,500 jobs (a 350 percent growth rate), but as of 2022 employment had dropped by 41 percent.

New Brunswick's health-care employment rose by 57 percent over the thirty-year period and educational services also registered strong employment gains.

TABLE 5-5: FASTEST GROWING EMPLOYMENT SECTORS 1992–2022, NEW BRUNSWICK

	Workforce (2022)	% workforce change (1992–2022)
Professional, scientific, and technical services	22,700	+158%
Business, building, and other support services	14,500	+79%
Health care and social assistance	58,700	+57%
Finance and insurance	15,300	+47%
Educational services	32,900	+44%
Construction	32,800	+41%

Source: Derived using Statistics Canada Table 14-10-0023-01

Prince Edward Island saw the fastest growth among the Atlantic provinces in the workforce between 1992 and 2022. At 40 percent cumulative growth, the increase was only slightly lower than the country's overall (45 percent). On a sector basis, the Island benefitted from strong growth in professional, scientific, and technical services; business, building, and other support services; and health-care and social assistance workforces. The province's manufacturing sector expanded total employment by 68 percent. As of 2022, the Island now has a larger share of workers in manufacturing compared to the country overall.

The Island has the largest public administration employment in the country. There are more than twice as many public administration workers in the Island workforce than in the country overall, as a share of total employment.

TABLE 5-6: FASTEST GROWING EMPLOYMENT SECTORS 1992–2022, PRINCE EDWARD ISLAND

	Workforce (2022)	% workforce change (1992–2022)
Professional, scientific, and technical services	4,900	+227%
Business, building, and other support services	2,500	+108%
Health care and social assistance	12,300	+95%
Public administration	10,700	+78%
Manufacturing	9,400	+68%
Educational services	6,200	+51%
Construction	7,700	+48%

Source: Statistics Canada Table 14-10-0023-01

EXPORT-FOCUSSED VERSUS LOCALLY FOCUSSED INDUSTRIES

The Atlantic Canadian economy relied on growing export revenue through the 1980s and into the early 2000s. This export revenue supported a strong economic growth rate and boosted personal income and tax revenue for governments. A relative decline in the value of exports since has been a main reason why the region's economy has lagged behind. The importance of ensuring Atlantic Canada has the workers needed for export industries to support their growth in the coming years is discussed in a later chapter. The region's economic growth and prosperity relies on having an available talent pool.

LOOKING TO THE FUTURE

Atlantic Canada's workforce has been shifting in recent years toward service industries such as health care, professional services, and business services. However, the region is still heavily reliant on natural resource industries such as oil and gas, fishing, forestry, and agriculture. In the years ahead, the region will need a broad mix of workers to meet the needs of industry.

In a recent *Insights* podcast, Jim Irving, co-CEO of J. D. Irving, Ltd, told us about the company's international recruitment efforts. They have recruited truckers out of central Europe, including Ukraine and Poland. Loggers are being recruited from Brazil and tree planters from Mexico. Irving suggested that immigration would be key to filling workforce demand in his firm and the rest of the economy in the years ahead.

CHAPTER 6
AN AGING WORKFORCE

IN CHAPTER 5, WE DISCUSSED HOW THE WORKFORCE HAS CHANGED IN RECENT years. Now, we turn to the specific challenges of the aging workforce and how we can ensure we have enough workers to meet workforce demand in the coming years.

FROM A SURPLUS TO A DEFICIT OF TALENT

The workforce story in Atlantic Canada has dramatically shifted over the past several decades. The region went from a surplus of workers in the 1980s and 1990s to a significant deficit by the early 2010s. To illustrate this trend, between 1996 and 2004 the regional workforce expanded by 120,000 workers. By contrast, during the 2012 to 2017 period, the number of people participating in Atlantic Canada's workforce declined by 27,000.

In the 1980s and 1990s, thousands of young people were joining the regional workforce every year and relatively few were retiring; this resulted in a significant expansion of the regional workforce. But this expansion also coincided with a large number of people leaving the region to advance their careers elsewhere in Canada.

Figure 6-1 shows net interprovincial migration by year between 1972 and 2024 for the four Atlantic provinces combined. For thirty-six of the forty years between 1977 and 2016, annual interprovincial migration was negative. The only time more people moved to the region than moved out was when there was a recession or a significant downturn in Alberta—then, people tended to move back to the region. As shown in figure 6-1, net interprovincial migration has turned positive since 2017, boding well for the future economic potential of the region.

FIGURE 6-1: NET INTERPROVINCIAL MIGRATION BY YEAR, FOUR ATLANTIC PROVINCES COMBINED

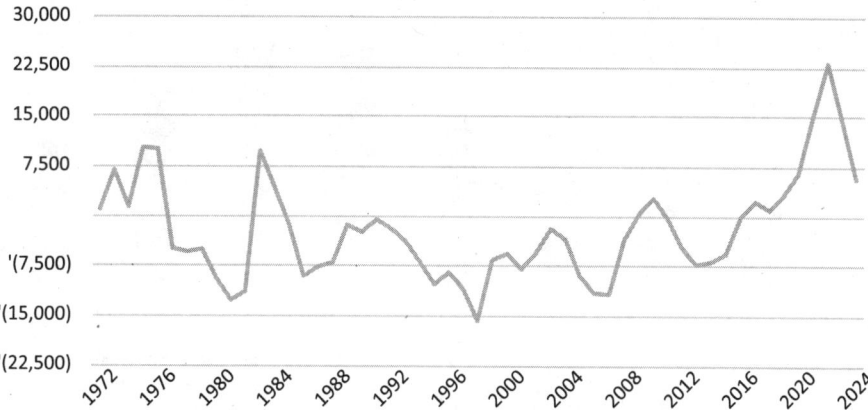

NOTE: THIS CHART SHOWS THE COMBINED NET INTERPROVINCIAL MIGRATION FOR EACH OF THE FOUR ATLANTIC PROVINCES. SOME OF THE MIGRATION WAS WITHIN THE REGION AND IS NOT PROPERLY CAPTURED IN THIS CHART, WHICH IS FOR ILLUSTRATIVE PURPOSES TO SHOW THE LONG-TERM TRENDS. THE DATA COVERS THE PERIOD OF JULY 1 TO JUNE 30 EACH YEAR.

Source: Statistics Canada Table 17-10-0008-01

IMMIGRATION AND INTERPROVINCIAL MIGRATION

The retention of immigrants is covered in more detail below. The long-term retention rate has been less than 50 percent, and the concern among some is that the boost in immigration to the region will turbocharge outward interprovincial migration. When immigrants move from one province to another, they are included in the net interprovincial migration statistics. Along with a surge in new immigrants moving to Atlantic Canada in the past few years, net interprovincial migration has remained positive. This is an indication that retention rates among immigrants are improving.

A SURGE IN JOB VACANCIES

Total job vacancies in Atlantic Canada more than doubled between 2017 and 2022, accelerating in the post-pandemic era. In the first quarter (Q1) of 2020, just before the onset of the pandemic, there were twenty-five thousand vacant jobs across Atlantic Canada. By spring 2023, there were over forty thousand. Within the region, Prince Edward Island saw the largest increase, with job vacancies almost tripling between spring 2016 and spring 2021. Due in large part to the increase in immigrants, international students and interprovincial migrants, job vacancies in the region have come down from the peak in 2022. However, across the four provinces combined there were still 46 percent more vacancies in October 2024 than in October 2017.

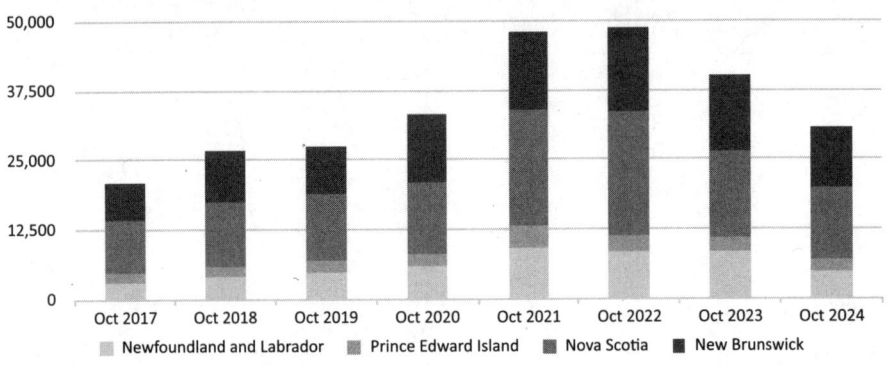

FIGURE 6-2: JOB VACANCIES BY PROVINCE, OCTOBER OF EACH YEAR, ATLANTIC CANADA

Source: Statistics Canada Table 14-10-0371-01

THE CHALLENGE OF THE AGING WORKFORCE

The top challenge facing the regional workforce—and the challenge with the most potential to curb economic growth—is the wave of retirements that is well under way in Atlantic Canada. In just the past twenty years, the number of people aged fifty-five and older in the region who worked for wages (as opposed to those who had self-employment income) has increased nearly 180 percent. Almost all of these people will be retiring from the workforce over the next ten to fifteen years. Figure 6-3 contrasts the increase in older workers with the number aged fifteen to twenty-four across Atlantic Canada from the mid-1970s until 2022. From the 1970s until the early 1990s, there were around 250 people aged sixteen to twenty-four participating in the workforce for every 100 aged fifty-five and older. By 2021, there were only 54 young people participating for every 100 aged fifty-five and up. It is no coincidence the decline in the region's GDP growth started roughly when the number of older workers exceeded that of younger workers.

The implications of this demographic tsunami go well beyond workforce considerations. In 1990, there were only twenty people collecting public pensions such as the Canada Pension Plan (CPP) and Old Age Security (OAS) in Atlantic Canada for every one hundred individuals earning employment income. By 2022, that had jumped to forty-eight retirees on government pensions for every one hundred in the workforce. On current trends there could be as many retirees as workers across Atlantic Canada within twenty years. This has considerable implications for health care and other public services, as well as the high likelihood of increased taxes.

The good news is that many of the people moving to the region in the past few years have been relatively young. They are helping to fill gaps in the workforce and turn back the tide. In fact, in 2022 there were forty-eight people reporting CPP income for every one hundred that report employment income, down from fifty in 2020.

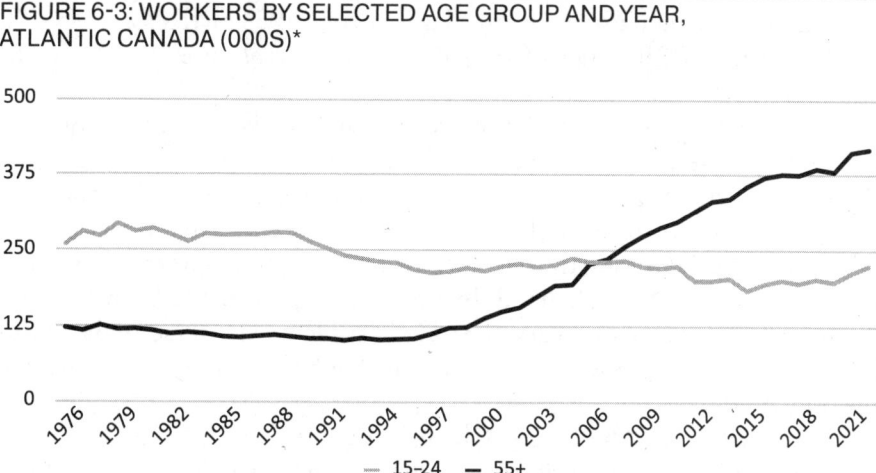

FIGURE 6-3: WORKERS BY SELECTED AGE GROUP AND YEAR, ATLANTIC CANADA (000S)*

*THE NUMBER OF PEOPLE REPORTING EMPLOYMENT INCOME ON THEIR ANNUAL CRA TAX RETURNS

Source: Statistics Canada Table 11-10-0239-01

PROVINCIAL VIEW

There have been considerable differences in the trajectories of each Atlantic province's population and economy. Newfoundland and Labrador has the largest gap between older and younger people in the workforce. In 2022, there were only forty-eight people aged sixteen to twenty-four in the workforce for every one hundred aged fifty-five and up. By contrast, Prince Edward Island has seen an improving situation in recent years. In 2015, there were fifty-seven people aged fifteen to twenty-four in the workforce for every one hundred aged fifty-five and up, and by 2022 the ratio had improved to sixty-eight per one hundred. Nova Scotia and New Brunswick have seen modest improvements in the past couple of years.

THE STRUCTURAL TALENT PIPELINE SHORTAGE

In chapter 2 we introduced the unprecedented demographic challenge facing Atlantic Canada and, in this chapter, have shown how the wave of retirees currently under way is impacting the workforce. Now we turn to the challenge of the talent pipeline. How are governments and the education system responding to this generational challenge?

Historically, Atlantic Canada has relied almost exclusively on natural population growth to support labour market needs. Natural population growth is the difference between births and deaths. Population moving into the region from elsewhere in Canada and from around the world has been relatively limited. As discussed earlier in this book, the natural growth rate in Atlantic Canada has gone from a large surplus (253 births for every 100 deaths in 1972) to a substantial annual deficit (74 births for every 100 deaths in 2022).

How has the post-secondary education system responded to this unprecedented increase in workforce demand across the region? Figure 6-4 shows the ratio of annual graduates from the region's post-secondary education institutions relative to the population aged fifty-five and older. Ideally, as the demand for workers rises, the entities that turn out the talent should expand enrollment to meet that demand. In reality, the opposite has been the case. After increasing for many years, the ratio of students in post-secondary education to the workforce aged fifty-five and up has been steadily declining since the mid-1990s.[4]

In absolute terms there were only slightly more post-secondary graduates from Atlantic Canadian institutions of higher learning in 2022 than in 2014. Over the same period, the number of graduates has increased by a robust 20 percent across the country. The main reason the post-secondary education talent pipeline is not keeping up with demand is that the pool of young people to draw from has been declining every year. In fact, as a share of the population, there are more people under the age of twenty-five enrolled in post-secondary education than ever before across the region.

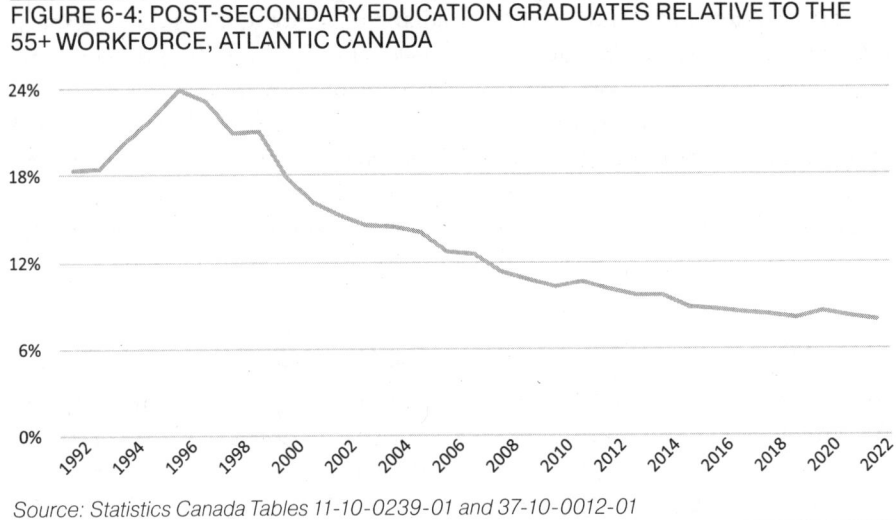

FIGURE 6-4: POST-SECONDARY EDUCATION GRADUATES RELATIVE TO THE 55+ WORKFORCE, ATLANTIC CANADA

Source: Statistics Canada Tables 11-10-0239-01 and 37-10-0012-01

Without international students, the problem would be even more pronounced. The number of domestic students (those born in Canada) graduating from universities and colleges across Atlantic Canada peaked back in 2011 and has been declining ever since. This had to do with an aging population leading to fewer children being born after the baby boom generation.

THE LACK OF INTEREST IN TRADES

The talent pipeline is particularly acute in certain segments of the workforce. Despite considerable effort on the part of the government, the number of people enrolled in Red Seal trade apprenticeships was no higher in 2021 than it was in 2003, a year when very few trades workers were retiring from the workforce. Over that time frame the number of apprentices to become Red Seal carpenters dropped by 11 percent. The number apprenticing to be welders is down 32 percent, and the number who are training to be Red Seal industrial mechanics is down 16 percent.

The main reason the post-secondary education talent pipeline is not keeping up with demand is that the pool of young people to draw from has been declining every year. In fact, as a share of the population there are more people under the age of twenty-five enrolled in post-secondary education than ever before across the region. Until recently, the population aged eighteen to twenty-four living in Atlantic Canada was declining every year. Between 1984 and 2017, the population of this age group declined by 38 percent.

GREEN SHOOTS

One of the main themes of this book is that we are seeing positive trends in a wide variety of economic and demographic indicators in the past few years. Young people living in the region is one good example. After more than thirty years of decline, the number of people aged eighteen to twenty-four living in Atlantic Canada has increased slightly between 2017 and 2022 as a result of a boost in immigration and young people moving here from other parts of Canada.

THE CHRONIC LACK OF IMMIGRATION

Another labour market challenge facing this region, at least until recently, has been a chronic lack of immigration. For decades, attracting talent from around the world has been key to the growth of places like southern Ontario, Greater Vancouver, and other regions in the country. As workforce demand increased, immigration expanded.

Across Canada, in 2013 there were 14.5 million people participating in the national workforce who were born in Canada. A decade later, in 2023, the number is only slightly higher at 14.7 million. Over the same period, the number of immigrants, temporary workers, and international students in the national workforce rose by 46 percent, or 2.1 million. In other words, immigrants accounted for almost all net growth in the national workforce.

There was little focus in Atlantic Canada on attracting immigrants to meet workforce demand until just the past few years. The introduction of the Atlantic Immigration Pilot Program in 2016, as well as other initiatives designed to make it easier for employers to attract immigrant workers, led to a significant rise in immigrants participating in the Atlantic Canadian workforce. Between 2016 and 2023, the number of immigrants, international students, and other temporary foreign workers participating in the region's workforce rose by more than double, an increase of eighty-six thousand. It is hard to understate the importance of this new workforce. The number of people born in Canada and working in Atlantic Canada has been declining for more than a decade. Without immigrants and other temporary foreign workers, there would have been severe shortages of workers in most industries across the region.

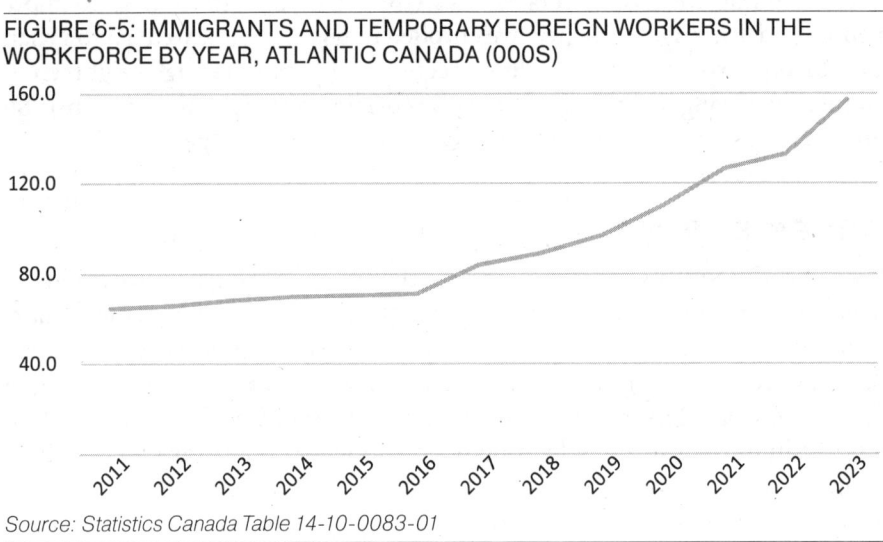

FIGURE 6-5: IMMIGRANTS AND TEMPORARY FOREIGN WORKERS IN THE WORKFORCE BY YEAR, ATLANTIC CANADA (000S)

Source: Statistics Canada Table 14-10-0083-01

International students are also starting to help fill the chronic gap in the workforce. The number enrolled in regional universities and colleges more than tripled between 2010 and 2022. In 2022, 6,550 university and college graduates from Atlantic Canada's post-secondary education system had not been born in Canada. Many of those graduates stayed in the region and took roles in the workforce. Further, a large share worked while in school.[5] This has been an important pool of workers for service and retail industries across the region. Still, the growth in international students in the region has not kept pace with the rest of the country. In 2004, 10 percent of all international students in Canada's post-secondary education system were studying in Atlantic Canada's schools. By 2022, the share had dropped to only 5 percent. The impact of the federal government's decision in January 2024 to reduce the number of international students will significantly slow the pace of growing the workforce in Canada.

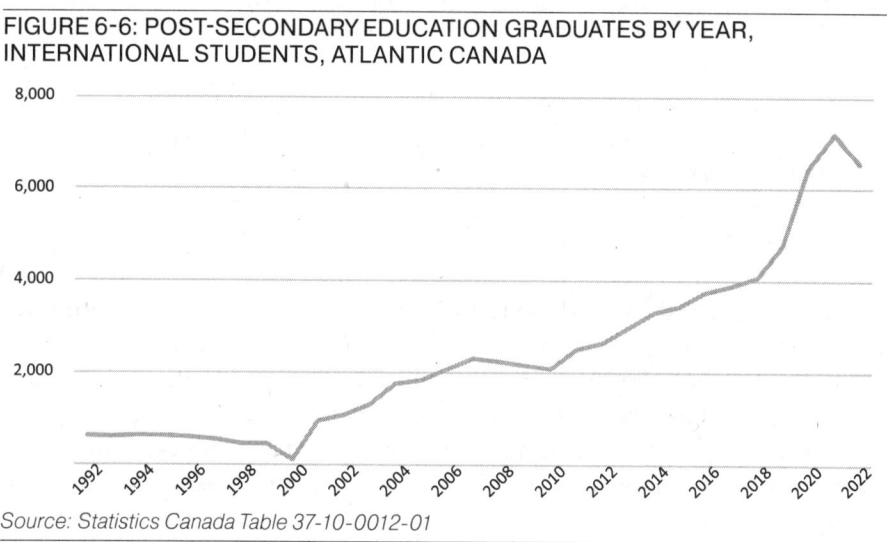

FIGURE 6-6: POST-SECONDARY EDUCATION GRADUATES BY YEAR, INTERNATIONAL STUDENTS, ATLANTIC CANADA

Source: Statistics Canada Table 37-10-0012-01

WILL WE RETAIN THEM?

It will be critically important for the region to retain a large share of newcomers moving to the region. It is not realistic to expect all immigrants, or even the vast majority, to stay in Atlantic Canada because the region is relatively small, and labour mobility has been a prominent feature of the Canadian economy for decades. People moving to advance their careers is important to a flexible national labour market. However, it is important to retain a large share of newcomers. Some have suggested 75 to 80 percent long-term retention should be the goal.

The data from Statistics Canada shows the region has work to do. Among those who landed in Nova Scotia in 2017, 62 percent were still in the province in 2022. In New Brunswick and Newfoundland and Labrador the shares were 52 percent and 46 percent, respectively. Prince Edward Island had the lowest retention rate in the country at 26 percent.

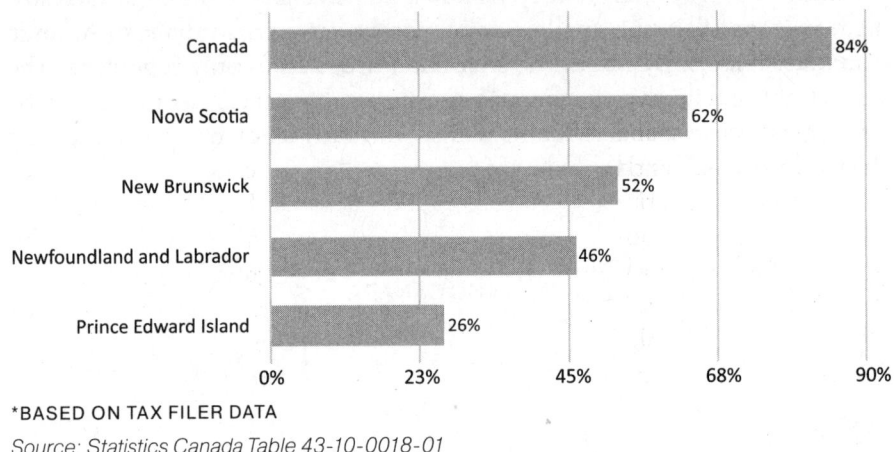

FIGURE 6-7: SHARE OF IMMIGRANTS WHO LANDED IN 2017 STILL IN PROVINCE OF LANDING AS OF 2022, ATLANTIC CANADA*

*BASED ON TAX FILER DATA
Source: Statistics Canada Table 43-10-0018-01

While it is still too early to tell, it looks like immigrant retention rates have been improving in recent years. More immigrants are finding employment directly aligned with their skills, which is the top indicator of long-term retention. Communities across the region are investing more in immigrant settlement support services and integration support and this is having a positive impact, but there is more work to be done. Family class immigration (those coming to join family and relatives already living in the community) has the highest retention rates of any immigration stream, and yet this region attracts fewer through this stream than most other provinces.

THE EI CHALLENGE

One of the challenges facing Atlantic Canada has been its significant reliance on seasonal industries and the seasonal workforce. This is a problem dating back decades. After the end of the Second World War, Canada was asked to settle 1.5 million European refugees. New Brunswick's premier at the time was not interested in attracting a share of these refugees, citing the province's high unemployment rate and his concern that returning local residents would not be able to find work.[6] These immigrants to Canada went on to help power a postwar economic boom across the country.

The Employment Insurance (EI) program was initially established as a typical unemployment insurance scheme, similar to those put in place around the industrialized world. Employees and employers pay an annual premium into the program and, if a person loses their job through no fault of their own, they receive income support while seeking other employment. However, in the 1970s, in certain parts of rural Canada, the program emerged as a de facto seasonal-industries income-support program. People working in industries such as fishing, fish processing, forestry, and agriculture would work for a portion of the year and then collect EI for the rest of the year, making no effort to seek other formal employment.[7] There have been attempts over the years to reform the program, but for the most part the use of the EI system as a seasonal income support program remains strong in many parts of Atlantic Canada and Quebec.

Figure 6-8 shows the implied Employment Insurance usage rate by province relative to the national rate. In 2022, 12.4 percent of employment income earners across the country also reported Employment Insurance income during the year.[8] How the provincial EI rates compare to the national rate is shown in the figure, with the national level set at 1.00. Newfoundland and Labrador workers collect EI 2.7 times more than the national workforce. Prince Edward Island workers are 2.2 times more likely to collect EI, and New Brunswickers use the program twice as much as the country overall. Nova Scotia workers are 45 percent more likely to collect EI during the year than those at the national level. In total, across Atlantic Canada there were 330,000 people who earned EI income at some point during 2022—24 percent of the entire population that earned employment income.

Of course, not all people who receive EI each year are seasonal workers. Some are unemployed for more traditional reasons, and some are using the program for parental leave. But the differential between the provincial and national EI rates is mostly accounted for by the differences in seasonal EI usage.

FIGURE 6-8: IMPLIED EI USAGE BY PROVINCE COMPARED THE NATIONAL RATE (CANADA = 1.00), 2022

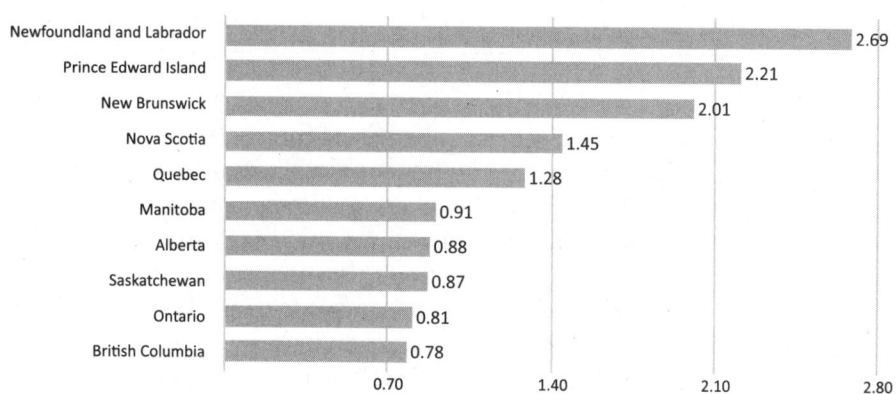

NOTE: THE RATIO OF EI INCOME-EARNERS TO EMPLOYMENT INCOME-EARNERS ACROSS CANADA IS USED AS THE BASE (1.00), AND THE PROVINCES ARE COMPARED TO THE NATIONAL EI USAGE RATE.

Source: Statistics Canada Table 11-10-0007-01

This challenge is mostly related to rural areas and smaller communities. To show just how important the EI program has become in rural regions of Atlantic Canada, figure 6-9 shows the implied EI usage rate outside the urban centres in the region. Urban centres include the census Metropolitan Areas (CMAs) and the smaller census Agglomeration (CA) areas.

In non–CMA-CA Newfoundland and Labrador, nearly half of all employment income earners also reported receiving EI income in 2022. On Prince Edward Island the share was 40 percent and in New Brunswick, 35 percent. Contrast this with western Canada, where the EI usage rate outside the urban centres is less than half the rate in Atlantic Canada.

FIGURE 6-9: IMPLIED EI USAGE OUTSIDE URBAN CENTRES, BY PROVINCE, 2022

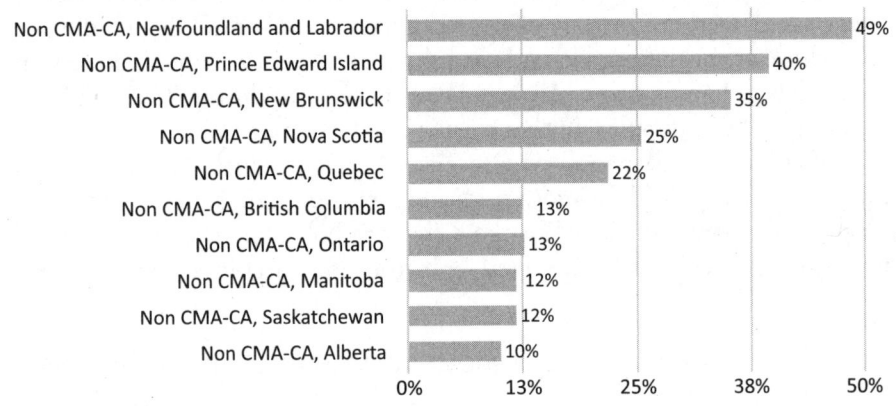

Source: Statistics Canada Table 11-10-0007-01

There are many potential implications arising from very high EI usage in a community. Companies that need year-round workers may be hesitant to invest in areas where a large share of workers are not accustomed to working year-round. The biggest implication, however, has been the distortion of the labour market picture in these regions. People who are seasonally unemployed are counted in Statistics Canada's formal unemployment rate for regions and communities. As a result, communities can have a nominal unemployment rate of 15 to 20 percent or more but still be in a situation where many businesses cannot find workers. For example, the unemployment rate in the Campbellton–Miramichi region in April 2023 was 12.1 percent, even as the region faced a record-high level of job vacancies. In the South Coast–Burin Peninsula and Notre Dame–Central Bonavista Bay region of Newfoundland and Labrador, the unemployment rate was over 19 percent, even though the job vacancy rate has nearly tripled over the past three years.

If the unemployment rate was defined as the number of people actively seeking employment and willing to work the jobs on offer, the rate in much of Atlantic Canada would be approaching zero.

Chapter 7 provides more insight into possible ways to address the EI conundrum.

THE RURAL WORKFORCE CHALLENGE

Atlantic Canada has a much larger population and workforce living in rural areas than the country has overall, and the number who are about to hit retirement is much higher than in urban centres. Over 30 percent of the workforce outside the urban centres in Atlantic Canada is over fifty-five. Figure 6-10 shows the share of all communities by province in Atlantic Canada with at least one-third of the workforce fifty-five or older.[9] In Newfoundland and Labrador, the workforce is fifty-five and older in over half of all communities. In the Maritime provinces, the share is 33 percent.

FIGURE 6-10: PERCENTAGE OF COMMUNITIES WITH AT LEAST ONE-THIRD OF THE WORKFORCE 55 AND UP, 2021

Province	Percentage
Newfoundland and Labrador	56%
Prince Edward Island	35%
Nova Scotia	34%
New Brunswick	32%

Source: Statistics Canada 2021 Census

This is a particular challenge because it is harder to encourage population migration into smaller communities and rural areas. The availability of housing is limited, the immigrant settlement services capacity is limited, and it is harder to find such supports as child care. There is almost no recent history of immigration into the region outside the largest cities. In many communities, over 95 percent of all residents are at least third-generation Canadian.

One of the positive dynamics, however, is that most of this rural population is located within a 60-kilometre drive of an urban centre (census metropolitan area or census agglomeration),[10] allowing people to access urban services within a reasonable commute.

GREEN SHOOTS

Despite these challenges, there are signs that things could be improving across much of the region. The four provinces are divided into forty-seven counties (census divisions); between 2021 and 2023, all but six saw population growth. Municipal governments across the region are looking at ways to boost housing construction and immigrant settlement services.

CHAPTER 7

THE EMPLOYMENT INSURANCE CONUNDRUM

ATLANTIC CANADA'S WORKFORCE IS FAR MORE RELIANT ON THE EMPLOYMENT Insurance (EI) program than the rest of the country's, and this is creating some distortion in the labour market across the region, particularly in rural areas.

DAVID CAMPBELL: In 2020, I wrote a report on this subject for the Public Policy Forum (PPF)[11] that included a detailed analysis of the usage of the EI program in the region, high-use industries and jurisdictions, and other characteristics. The report, called *Making EI Work: For Consistent Economic Growth and the Atlantic Seasonal Workforce*, also outlined six potential reforms that could help ensure the program is not a continued barrier to economic development in certain areas in Atlantic Canada.

This chapter expands on the themes and recommendations in that report.

SEASONAL EI USAGE

Throughout this section of this book, EI income and recipients will be described in aggregate. Not all EI recipients are seasonal workers. Some have lost their job and needed to find a new one during the year. The federal maternity/paternity leave program is administered under the EI program. The federal government does not publish data at the regional or community level on the share of EI recipients who collect EI income year after year. Therefore, the data herein is based on all the people who reported EI income at some point during the year.

The Canada Employment Insurance Commission (CEIC) does report by province on the share of regular EI claims that are seasonal claims. As shown in figure 7-1, including those receiving fishing benefits, in 2018/2019 the share of seasonal claims ranged from 49 percent in Nova Scotia to 73 percent in Prince Edward Island.

FIGURE 7-1: SEASONAL REGULAR CLAIMS AS A SHARE OF TOTAL REGULAR CLAIMS 2018–2019
INCLUDES THOSE RECEIVING FISHING BENEFITS

Source: Canada Employment Insurance Commission (CEIC)

AN IMPORTANT SOURCE OF RURAL INCOME

In 2019, Atlantic Canadians received $3.2 billion in payments from the Employment Insurance program—an amount equivalent to 3.5 percent of total income from all sources. Statistics Canada has published data on 2020 and 2021, but those years are influenced by the COVID-19 pandemic. While the total amount of EI payments has been rising, the share relative to total income has slowly declined over the past twenty years. In 2001, EI payments provided 4.6 percent of total income across the region.

The number of workers who rely on EI income each year across Atlantic Canada is much higher when compared to Canada overall. In 2019, across Canada only 12 percent of workers reported both employment income and Employment Insurance income on their tax forms. In Nova Scotia, the share was 18 percent and in New Brunswick, it was 24 percent. Twenty-seven percent of all employment-income earners in Prince Edward Island reported EI income in 2019 and 32 percent of all employment-income earners in Newfoundland and Labrador.

Outside of the region's urban centres, the share of workers relying on EI income increased substantially to 25 percent in non-urban centre Nova Scotia, 35 percent in non-urban centre New Brunswick, and 48 percent in Newfoundland and Labrador.

FIGURE 7-2: EI INCOME RECIPIENTS RELATIVE TO TOTAL EMPLOYMENT INCOME EARNERS, 2019

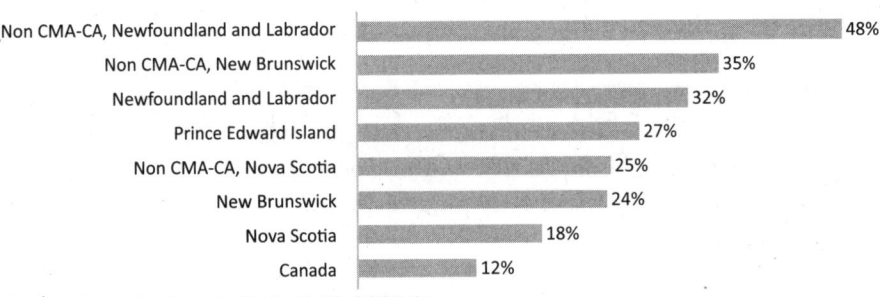

Source: Statistics Canada Table 11-10-0007-01

There are eighteen counties/census divisions across Atlantic Canada where EI income represents an amount equivalent to at least 10 percent of employment income. In some parts of the region, the ratio rises to 20 percent or more.

It is important to recognize the importance of this source of income to much of the region when considering any changes to the program in the years ahead.

TABLE 7-1: EI INCOME RELATIVE TO EMPLOYMENT INCOME, SELECTED CENSUS DIVISIONS, 2019

County/Census Division:	Total EI income ($Million)	EI income relative to total employment income
Division No. 9, NL	$507.0	23%
Division No. 8, NL	$1,069.0	20%
Victoria County, NS	$251.6	18%
Division No. 3, NL	$459.8	17%
Division No. 7, NL	$1,091.6	15%
Division No. 4, NL	$584.9	15%
Kings County, PEI	$586.7	14%
Gloucester County, NB	$2,570.3	14%
Guysborough County, NS	$245.0	13%
Division No. 2, NL	$665.5	12%
Kent County, NB	$1,045.5	12%
Division No. 11, NL	$64.8	11%
Northumberland County, NB	$1,443.6	11%
Inverness County, NS	$591.5	11%
Shelburne County, NS	$481.1	10%
Richmond County, NS	$312.7	10%
Prince County, PEI	$1,527.1	10%
Restigouche County, NB	$951.1	10%

Source: Statistics Canada 2021 Census

SEASONAL EI AND THE NEXT GENERATION

In the early 1990s, an assistant deputy minister in the New Brunswick Department of Advanced Education and Labour stated in a meeting that as long as the EI rules allowed it, tens of thousands of New Brunswickers would never work year-round no matter what the provincial government did to incentivize them. The good news, he said, was that young New Brunswickers would not accept that "lifestyle," and he expected a steep decline in seasonal EI use in the years ahead.

Nearly thirty years after that meeting, data from the 2021 Census suggests that he was wrong. While the absolute number of young people collecting EI income at some point during the year has declined around the region as a share of the total workforce, young people in many areas still rely on EI as a source of income each year.

Figure 7-3 shows the share of persons aged fifteen to thirty-four who reported both employment income and EI income on their tax returns in 2020. Outside of the urban centres (CMAs/CAs), across Atlantic Canada 37 percent of all employment-income earners also reported EI income on their tax returns. Outside the urban centres in Newfoundland and Labrador, 45 percent of all persons aged fifteen to thirty-four with employment income also reported EI income during the year.

While the data in 2020 was influenced by the pandemic, the effect was modest—for example, only 6 percent more young people living in Newfoundland and Labrador collected EI income in 2020 compared to 2019. In fact, the effect was much higher nationally; 36 percent more people reported EI income in 2020 compared to 2019.

FIGURE 7-3: SHARE OF 15- TO 34-YEAR-OLDS REPORTING BOTH EMPLOYMENT INCOME AND EI INCOME, 2020

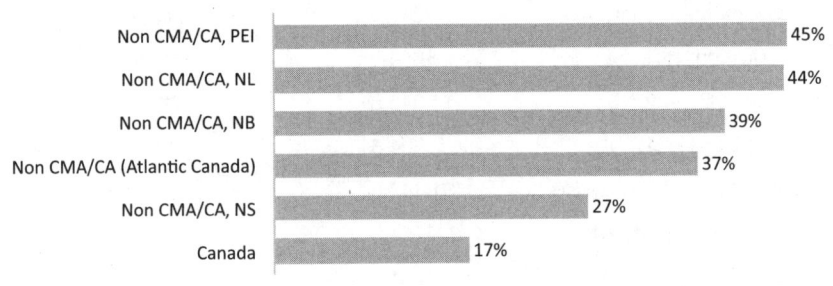

Source: Statistics Canada 2021 Census

NOT JUST THE FISHING SECTOR

One of the arguments about why the region has a higher EI usage rate is that Atlantic Canada has more people in fishing and forestry occupations. The fact is EI usage in Atlantic Canada is higher in all sectors of the economy. It is also important to point out that EI usage is primarily an issue outside the main urban centres in each province. Table 7-2 shows the EI usage rate in the main urban centres in Atlantic Canada (Halifax, Charlottetown, St. John's, Moncton, Saint John, and Fredericton) and the rest of the region compared to the national EI usage rate (with the national usage rate set at 1.00).

In the main urban centres, the EI usage rate is only slightly higher than in the country overall. The usage of EI in the construction sector is considerably higher, along with several other sectors, but the big variances are in smaller urban centres and rural areas. Outside the main urban centres, the EI usage rate in the construction sector was 53 percent in 2020 (i.e., over half of all workers that year collected EI). Thirty-six percent of all workers in the administrative support services sector, and 23 percent of all workers in the professional services sector also collected EI during the year. The share of workers collecting EI in most sectors outside the main urban centres was well above the share across the country. Even in the public administration sector, the EI usage rate was 2.3 times higher than the country's overall.

TABLE 7-2: EMPLOYMENT INSURANCE USAGE RATES IN ATLANTIC CANADA RELATIVE TO THE CANADIAN LEVEL
PERCENTAGE OF EMPLOYMENT INCOME EARNERS ALSO REPORTING EMPLOYMENT INSURANCE INCOME IN 2020

	Main urban centres	CAN = 1.00	Rest of ATL CAN	CAN = 1.00
All industries	16%	1.09	33%	2.18
11 Agriculture, forestry, fishing, and hunting	41%	2.01	67%	3.23
21 Mining, quarrying, oil and gas extraction	22%	1.33	39%	2.33
22 Utilities	7%	0.80	21%	2.23
23 Construction	33%	1.29	53%	2.09
31–33 Manufacturing	17%	0.99	42%	2.36
41 Wholesale trade	14%	1.16	23%	1.91
44–45 Retail trade	14%	1.11	22%	1.70
48–49 Transportation and warehousing	17%	1.18	30%	2.07
51 Information and cultural industries	12%	1.02	16%	1.37
52 Finance and insurance	9%	1.26	12%	1.78
53 Real estate and rental and leasing	14%	1.36	24%	2.38
54 Professional, scientific, and technical services	12%	1.19	23%	2.40
56 Administrative and support**	21%	1.14	36%	1.93
61 Educational services	16%	1.10	28%	1.95
62 Health care and social assistance	14%	1.08	24%	1.92
71 Arts, entertainment, and recreation	23%	0.98	40%	1.68
72 Accommodation and food services	27%	1.08	40%	1.58
81 Other services (except public administration)	18%	1.14	26%	1.67
91 Public administration	8%	0.98	20%	2.34

*INCLUDES THE REGIONS OF HALIFAX, CHARLOTTETOWN, ST. JOHN'S, MONCTON, SAINT JOHN, AND FREDERICTON
**INCLUDES WASTE MANAGEMENT
Source: Statistics Canada 2021 Census

IMPLICATIONS OF RELIANCE ON EI

The biggest challenge posed by the EI usage numbers is the distortion of local labour markets around the region. This distortion has both statistical and practical implications. First, Statistics Canada includes seasonal workers in its calculation of unemployed workers. As a result, the unemployment rate in much of the region is distorted because some areas have a large share of seasonal workers. Although these seasonal workers are able to work while on their seasonal EI claims, the vast majority do not. As an example of this effect, the number of job vacancies across Newfoundland and Labrador nearly doubled between the first quarter of 2019 and the first quarter of 2023 even as the unemployment rate remained high, at 12.3 percent. In the Campbellton–Miramichi region of New Brunswick, the number of job vacancies tripled over the same time frame, even as the official unemployment "rate" remained at 12.1 percent.

In a well-functioning labour market, a sharp spike in job vacancies (and the related increase in average wages on offer) would normally lead to a sharp decline in unemployment. But in a labour market environment where 30–50 percent or more of workers collect EI each year, the relationship between formal unemployment and available jobs becomes distorted.

In addition to distorting published labour market information, there can be many practical distortions arising from the current approach to the seasonal workforce. One important example is that federal government officials have been more reluctant to allow companies to bring in temporary foreign workers because of the perceived high rate of unemployment. Thankfully this is changing somewhat, but there is still a lingering perception that temporary workers and immigrants should not be attracted into areas with high unemployment.

Another distortion is that many people who collect EI income each year only work enough hours or weeks to qualify and then leave their employment. This creates instability for employers who are looking for year-round workers and creates a disincentive for companies to invest in a number of communities across the region.

But the biggest concern is that there seems to be a long-term correlation between dependency on EI and weak economic growth. Between 2006 and 2016, across the country census divisions with the highest EI usage rates also had the steepest declines in the size of the workforce. Correlation is not causation, but it is not hard to draw a link between EI dependency and weak economic growth over the long term.

SOLUTIONS

The Public Policy Forum report included six potential policy changes that are summarized in table 7-3.

TABLE 7-3: PUBLIC POLICY FORUM'S SUGGESTED POLICY CHANGES

Policy change:	Considerations:
Tighten rules to significantly reduce the use of EI for seasonal income support.	Government could restrict how often workers could access EI (e.g., no more than two consecutive years), restrict to certain industries (e.g., fisheries but not construction), or use some other formula meant to decrease the number of people who voluntarily use the program each year when their skills could be put to use in other jobs in the community. Past efforts to tweak the program have met with significant pushback. The political case for substantial reforms is not strong. Municipal governments benefit from the hundreds of millions of dollars pouring into local communities each year, boosting household spending and property tax revenues. Provincial governments do not pay for a program that brings over $3 billion into the region with a large share going to rural communities, and the federal government doesn't pay out of general tax revenues as the EI program is funded through employee and employer premiums. However, employers in these communities are increasingly insistent that something be done. The number of job vacancies in many communities around Atlantic Canada has doubled or even tripled in recent years, and with 30–40 percent of all workers over the age of fifty-five, the workforce shortage is set to increase significantly in the coming years.
Grandfather everyone over a certain age and change EI eligibility rules for new workers only.	This idea has been proposed in the past but, as described above, a large number of young people also access the program on an annual basis. Still, with a strong plan, appropriate phase-in periods, and other safeguards, this could be one way to significantly increase the number of people available for year-round work in rural Atlantic Canada. An important caveat here is that this isn't just an Atlantic-Canada issue. There would likely be pushback from younger workers across the country that use the program each year.
Create a new program specifically for seasonal workers.	Another option would be to stop using the current EI program for those who are collecting EI every year. In this case, the EI program would be exclusively to provide income support while people who have lost their jobs seek new employment. (This is the current definition of the program.) Seasonal workers would have their own program. Funding it would be challenging, as current EI premiums would only be a fraction of EI claims paid out. The federal government would either have to continue funding it with EI premiums or find some other way. The general public would likely push back against funding an income-support program such as this. In the past when there was a perceived need (i.e., high unemployment made it hard to find work), the program might have made more sense. Today, it is hard for the general public to understand why hundreds of thousands of workers can receive income from the government and not work while hundreds of thousands of jobs go vacant across the country.

Policy change:	Considerations:
Expand the use of temporary foreign workers (TFWs) to address seasonal surges in labour demand.	This idea would involve encouraging employers to use temporary foreign workers rather than local people for truly short-term seasonal jobs. If a company needs fifty workers to harvest crops, process fish, or make Christmas wreaths, they would bring in workers from outside Canada to work those jobs. These workers would not receive EI payments and would not be much of a burden on health care, education, or other public services. This is already happening in certain industries and regions across Atlantic Canada. It would become a political challenge if the TFWs were displacing resident seasonal workers.
Provide incentives for and/or strengthen off-season work requirements.	There are already rules in place to encourage seasonal EI workers to take on other jobs while their claims are active. There is little uptake. Government could just strengthen the rules and enforcement related to working while on an open EI claim. Again, this has been tried before and was not particularly successful. One of the biggest challenges is enforcement. There are no real incentives for bureaucrats to enforce these rules. In certain US states, unemployment insurance case workers are incentivized when unemployed workers they work with find employment. There are no such incentives in the Canadian system.
Classify long-term seasonal workers differently.	The easiest policy change would be to stop the statistical fiction that seasonal workers are available for work. They would be removed from the unemployment data entirely. They would not be "looking for work" while waiting for their seasonal job to start. This would create some challenges with reporting and with eligibility. Right now, areas with higher nominal unemployment rates require fewer hours/weeks of work to be eligible for EI payments. If the unemployment rate in these communities reflected the reality on the ground, seasonal workers would be required to work considerably more during the year to be eligible.

Source: *Making EI Work: For Consistent Economic Growth and the Atlantic Seasonal Workforce.* Public Policy Forum. September 2020.

TIME TO TAKE A SERIOUS LOOK

For decades, seasonal EI has been a way of life for tens of thousands of Atlantic Canadians. For many families it has been an intergenerational source of income. Some of the region's top politicians have been toppled after introducing relatively minor tweaks to the EI program.

However, as the region faces unprecedented labour shortages and a growing number of retirees, it is time to take a serious look at the program. As the region looks to the future and the need to fill hundreds of thousands of jobs in both urban and rural areas, policy-makers should be looking to develop an EI system that is fit for that purpose.

CHAPTER 8
OVERRELIANCE ON GOVERNMENT

ONE OF CANADA'S MOST IMPORTANT ATTRIBUTES IS THAT IT IS A COUNTRY WITH relatively limited economic disparity between regions. The richest province, Alberta, has a real GDP per capita that is 65 percent higher than that of the poorest province, Nova Scotia.[12] In the United States, the richest state, New York, has a real GDP per capita 122 percent higher than the poorest state, Mississippi.[13] In many countries the disparity is even greater. The richest state in Brazil, São Paulo, has a GDP per capita 3.7 times higher than the poorest state, Maranhão.[14]

The lack of disparity also applies to households across the country. Atlantic Canada has significantly reduced the household income deficit with the rest of the country over the past sixty years. In 1960, household income per capita in the region was approximately 30 percent below the Canadian level. By 2021, the deficit had narrowed to less than 10 percent. In other words, while household income per capita was increasing across the country, it increased faster in Atlantic Canada over the six decades. While the growth of private-sector industries in the region is part of the story, the reduction in the income gap has been significantly influenced by the rise in government transfer payments to regional governments and to individuals and households. This chapter takes a look at the role of government support and its implications for the future.

RELIANCE ON GOVERNMENT FOR INCOME

Not that long ago, the village of Belledune in northeastern New Brunswick was known as a centre of industrial activity, but after a period of deindustrialization, the village has become more and more reliant on governments as sources of household income. In 2019, 32 percent of all income reported by residents in Belledune was coming from government sources.[15] Nearly one out of every three dollars in total income comes from the government. The average adult in the village receives 2.6 times as much money from the government each year as the average Canadian. This income is a mix of public pension income, Employment Insurance, and other government sources. While the amount of household income from government sources increased by 22 percent between the 1996 and 2021 Censuses, the amount coming from employment income has dropped by 21 percent.

While the reliance on government income is more pronounced in many rural areas, it also applies to all of Atlantic Canada. In 2021, government transfers to individuals (Employment Insurance, Old Age Security, Workers' Compensation, and social assistance, for example) amounted to 21 percent of total personal income reported to the Canada Revenue Agency. The share of total income coming from government transfers in Atlantic Canada is 34 percent higher than in the country overall.

Table 8-1 breaks down personal income by source in Atlantic Canada and compares the share of total income to the country overall. For example, Atlantic Canadians overall rely on employment income for just under 64 percent of total income. As a share of total income, this represents 7 percent less than the country overall. Atlantic Canadians, on average, receive more than twice as much EI income as Canadians in the rest of the country, 43 percent more Old Age Security (with net federal supplements), and 39 percent more Canada Pension Plan payments. Atlantic Canadians receive much more income from HST credits and workers' compensation than the rest of the country, although the total amounts are relatively small.

Again, the rural-urban divide in Atlantic Canada is significant, particularly in terms of EI, where many rural communities rely on three to four times as much income from this source, and OAS and CPP, as the retired population is much higher in most of rural Atlantic Canada.

TABLE 8-1: BREAKDOWN OF TOTAL PERSONAL INCOME BY SOURCE, ATLANTIC CANADA (2021)

	% of total	Compared to Canada*
Total employment income	63.9%	-7%
Wages, salaries, and commissions	60.5%	-6%
Net self-employment income	3.4%	-8%
Dividend and interest income	3.5%	-38%
Total government transfers	20.7%	+34%
Employment Insurance (EI) benefits	5.3%	+108%
Old Age Security (OAS) and net federal supplements	5.3%	+43%
Canada Pension Plan (CPP) benefits	5.3%	+39%
Federal Child Benefits	1.6%	+8%
Social Assistance benefits	0.6%	-22%
Other government transfers	1.2%	-15%
Private pensions	9.3%	+25%
Registered Retirement Savings Plan (RRSP)	0.3%	-5%
Other income	2.3%	-15%

*RELATIVE TO THE NATIONAL BREAKDOWN OF INCOME BY SOURCE

Source: Statistics Canada Table 11-10-0007-01

The reliance on government goes beyond the direct income transfers. Government jobs are more predominant in Atlantic Canada. Health care is now the most important sector employing more residents than any other industry. From the town of Bonavista in Newfoundland to Victoria County in Nova Scotia, rural communities across the region have become highly reliant on government as a source of direct income and, in many cases, the largest number of and highest-paying jobs in the community.

Some have suggested society has a moral and even constitutional obligation to support these communities even as they grow older and have less private-sector economic activity. Others have suggested we cluster older residents in cities and larger towns where they can better access support services. The region has considerable natural resources, forests, fish, minerals, agricultural land, and tourism potential. Many areas have other attributes such as ports and other transportation infrastructure. Rural areas are well positioned to benefit from the clean energy transition. Many of these opportunities are not being developed because of a lack of entrepreneurs, workers, and other supports.

In fact, as of the writing of this book, there is a serious effort under way to build a cluster of new industries in the village of Belledune, including wind and nuclear energy, green hydrogen, green steel, and possibly others. There are presently multiple green energy projects proposed in Nova Scotia and in rural Newfoundland and Labrador.

GOVERNMENT RELIANCE ON FEDERAL TRANSFERS

In Canada, provincial governments have the responsibility to deliver most public services, but the federal government raises around the same level of tax revenue from households and businesses each year as the total raised by all provincial and territorial governments. In 2022, the federal government brought in $360 billion in taxes, while the provincial and territorial governments raised $357 billion.[16] To help push national priorities, the federal government transfers a significant amount of the taxes it raises each year to provincial governments to help them deliver services and invest in infrastructure.

The federal government provides annual transfers to provincial governments in three main areas: the Canada Health Transfer, Canada Social Transfer, and, for provinces that qualify, Equalization. The federal government provides additional funds to provincial and municipal governments under various infrastructure and other programs, but these are the three main annual transfer programs.

The concept of "equalization" goes all the way back to Confederation, when it was agreed that not every province had the same capacity to fund public services but that all Canadians should have access to reasonably equivalent public services. The current federal Equalization program has been around since the 1950s, and the Constitution of 1982 specified that all Canadians should have "reasonably comparable levels of public services at reasonably comparable levels of taxation." In 2023–2024, federal Equalization payments amounted to $24 billion out of the total $89 billion in federal transfers to the provinces under the three programs.

FIGURE 8-1: FEDERAL GOVERNMENT TRANSFERS TO PROVINCIAL GOVERNMENTS, PER CAPITA, 2023–2024

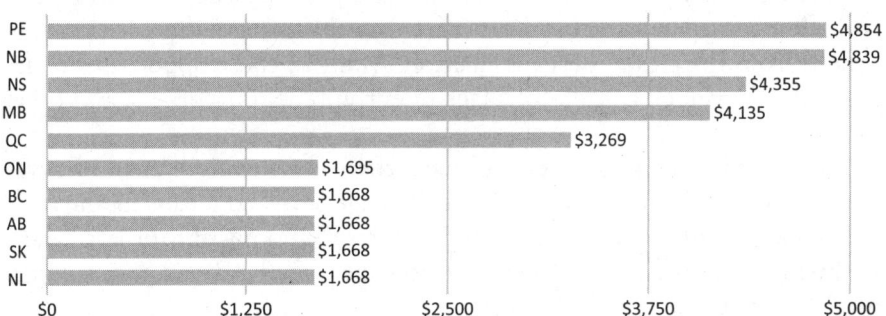

NOTE: INCLUDES THE CANADA HEALTH TRANSFER, CANADA SOCIAL TRANSFER, AND EQUALIZATION

Source: Department of Finance Canada

To put this into greater perspective, figure 8-2 shows the federal transfers from these three programs relative to total provincial government program spending in 2023–2024. Program spending does not include capital expenditures, servicing of debt, or other non-program spending. Relative to program spending, New Brunswick is the most reliant on federal transfers, with an amount equivalent to 34 percent of program spending that year. In Prince Edward Island and Nova Scotia, federal transfers amount to 31 percent and 29 percent of total program spending.

Between 2014–2015 and 2023–2024, the amount of federal transfers relative to program spending declined in two of the four Atlantic provinces. In Prince Edward Island, federal transfers relative to program spending dropped from 33 percent to 31 percent, and in Nova Scotia from 33 percent to 29 percent.

FIGURE 8-2: FEDERAL GOVERNMENT TRANSFERS RELATIVE TO PROVINCIAL GOVERNMENT PROGRAM SPENDING, PER CAPITA, 2023–2024

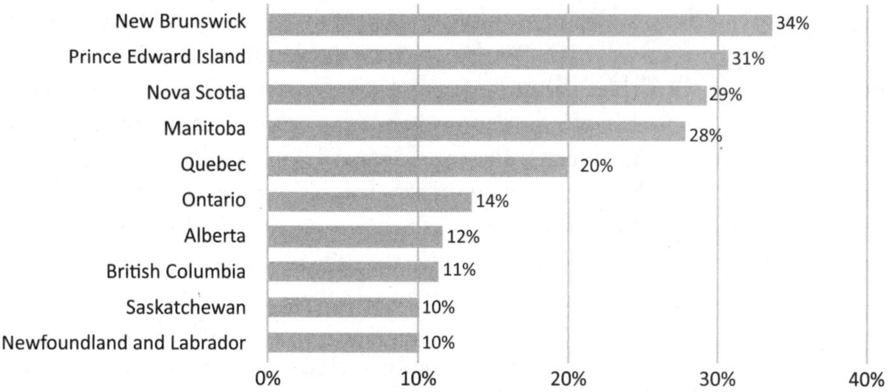

Province	%
New Brunswick	34%
Prince Edward Island	31%
Nova Scotia	29%
Manitoba	28%
Quebec	20%
Ontario	14%
Alberta	12%
British Columbia	11%
Saskatchewan	10%
Newfoundland and Labrador	10%

Source: Derived using RBC Economics and Department of Finance Canada figures

RELIANCE ON GOVERNMENT OVERALL

The public sector accounts for a larger share of economic activity in Atlantic Canada than in the country overall. In 2023, as measured by GDP, the public sector accounted for 31 percent of total GDP in Nova Scotia, 30 percent in Prince Edward Island, and 29 percent in New Brunswick. The share in Newfoundland and Labrador is not as large because of the impact of the offshore oil and gas sector (25 percent). This compares to Saskatchewan (19 percent) and Alberta (16 percent).

Compared to the ten-province average, the public sector in Nova Scotia accounts for 50 percent more GDP, in Prince Edward Island, 44 percent more, and in New Brunswick, 39 percent more.

FIGURE 8-3: PUBLIC-SECTOR GDP AS A SHARE OF TOTAL GDP, BY PROVINCE, 2023

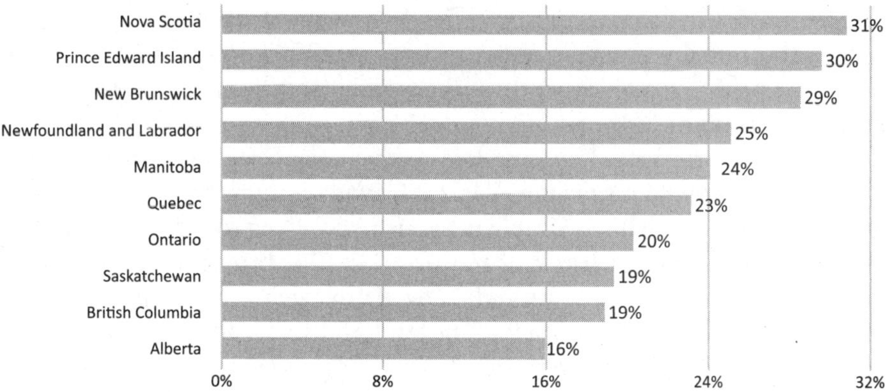

Province	%
Nova Scotia	31%
Prince Edward Island	30%
New Brunswick	29%
Newfoundland and Labrador	25%
Manitoba	24%
Quebec	23%
Ontario	20%
Saskatchewan	19%
British Columbia	19%
Alberta	16%

Source: Statistics Canada Table 36-10-0402-01

PUBLIC VERSUS PRIVATE SECTOR

The public sector as a share of the total economy is an important measure, but this is mostly a denominator problem—the public sector is relatively larger because the private sector has not been growing as fast in recent years. The private sector in the three Maritime provinces generates far less GDP per capita than in other provinces. Compared to the per capita average private-sector GDP across the ten provinces, Prince Edward Island's economy generates 36 percent less private-sector GDP, Nova Scotia 34 percent less, and New Brunswick 31 percent less. To put this another way, if the Maritime provinces had a private-sector economy similar to the average of the rest of the provinces, the public-sector GDP would be similar to the average of the provinces.

Over the twenty-six-year period from 1997 to 2023, private-sector GDP increased faster than the public sector in Atlantic Canada. In inflation-adjusted dollars, private-sector GDP across the region increased by 60 percent, while the public-sector GDP grew by 44 percent. New Brunswick was the only province among the four to see public- and private-sector GDP increase at about the same rate over that period.

However, there were considerable differences by time frame, as shown in table 8-2. Between 1997 and 2005, cumulative private-sector GDP growth was a strong 32 percent in New Brunswick, 32 percent in Nova Scotia, 25 percent in Prince Edward Island, and 67 percent in Newfoundland and Labrador. Between 2005 and 2014, cumulative private-sector GDP growth dropped substantially across the region to -1 percent in New Brunswick, 4 percent in Nova Scotia, 12 percent in Prince Edward Island, and 11 percent in Newfoundland and Labrador. As a result, in New Brunswick and Nova Scotia the public-sector share of the economy increased between 2005 and 2014. Public-sector GDP growth slowed as well in Prince Edward Island and Newfoundland and Labrador during that period.

In three of the four provinces, real private-sector GDP growth rebounded modestly in the 2014–2023 period, as did public-sector GDP. Newfoundland and Labrador's real private-sector GDP declined by 9 percent.

The bottom line is simple: between 1997 and 2005, economic growth was led by the private sector. Since then, the region has relied more on the public sector for economic growth.

The myth propagated in some areas is that provincial government spending on programs and services in Atlantic Canada is much higher than in the rest of the country. This is simply not true. According to RBC Economics, Nova Scotia ranks ninth out of ten provinces for provincial government program spending per capita and New Brunswick ranks eighth. While Prince Edward Island and Newfoundland and Labrador spend more per capita, the variation is not very significant. Program spending per capita in Newfoundland and Labrador, for example, is only 7 percent higher than in Alberta.

TABLE 8-2: CUMULATIVE REAL GDP GROWTH BY TIME FRAME, PUBLIC AND PRIVATE SECTORS

	1997–2005	2005–2014	2014–2023
New Brunswick			
Private-sector GDP growth	32%	-1%	13%
Public-sector GDP growth	16%	13%	12%
Nova Scotia			
Private-sector GDP growth	32%	4%	19%
Public-sector GDP growth	11%	11%	16%
Prince Edward Island			
Private-sector GDP growth	25%	12%	31%
Public-sector GDP growth	24%	8%	25%
Newfoundland and Labrador			
Private-sector GDP growth	67%	11%	-9%
Public-sector GDP growth	13%	9%	11%

Source: Statistics Canada Table 36-10-0402-01

FOCUS ON PRIVATE-SECTOR GROWTH

The three Maritime provinces are more reliant on the public sector than the other provinces in Canada, but this is mainly because the private-sector economy is much smaller. If the region had a larger private sector, the public sector share would be similar to the rest of the country. Newfoundland and Labrador is a good example of this, as its oil and gas sector has pushed GDP per capita to among the highest in the country.[17] Public spending on services is not particularly high in the region, specifically in New Brunswick and Nova Scotia.

The three provincial governments in the Maritimes are also far more reliant on federal transfer payments to meet budget needs, but again this needs to be put in context. Tax rates in the region tend to be higher than in most of the rest of Canada. This includes personal income tax rates, the sales tax rate, property tax rates, and even corporate income tax rates. The average Nova Scotian pays as much tax as the average Albertan, even though household income is considerably lower in Nova Scotia than in Alberta.[18] The impact of tax rates and the tax environment overall on economic development and population growth is discussed further in chapter 22.

There is a risk associated with being overly reliant on the federal government. The economist Richard Saillant told us in a podcast covering fiscal federalism that "for every dollar Albertans put into the Canadian federation they get a little over fifty cents back and, in Atlantic Canada, we get about two bucks." He went on to say the "centre of gravity in Canada is moving west progressively and therefore issues about redistribution are becoming somewhat more salient."

There are actually several risks. The first, as highlighted by Saillant, is that the formula used to calculate equalization changes over time, limiting the amount of funding received by provincial government in the region. Another risk is general fiscal belt-tightening. The federal government continues to run significant annual deficits and eventually may end up cutting transfer payments to provinces or reducing federal employment in the region. This happened before in the mid-1990s.

As we look to the future, Atlantic Canada should focus on growing its private-sector economy, particularly higher-value and productive sectors. This will help generate a sustainable level of taxes to fund public services without increasing tax rates or increasing the share of provincial spending that comes from federal transfers.

CHAPTER 9

THE PRIVATE-SECTOR INVESTMENT GAP

BUSINESS INVESTMENT IS CRUCIAL TO THE GROWTH OF ECONOMIES. WHEN businesses invest in a community, they are making a bet on the future. They are betting they can achieve a good return on that investment over a period of years.

The New Brunswick Innovation Foundation (NBIF) has done an excellent job of attracting private-sector investment to support technology-based start-up companies in New Brunswick. According to a report published in 2024, NBIF has invested $24 million in the forty-two companies currently in its portfolio.[19] This early-stage, higher-risk investment has helped bring in $443 million in other venture capital and $65 million in angel investment. Adding in other public sources of funding, these forty-two companies have attracted $730 million of investment that is being used to build new companies that are developing markets across Canada and the world.

Private-sector investment is vital to a growing economy. The NBIF primarily invests in information technology and other technology-based companies that do not tend to require large investments into plants and equipment, but they do require capital to support early product and market development and then to rapidly scale.

Statistics Canada tracks private sector investment relative to GDP year-by-year on an inflation-adjusted basis. With the exception of Newfoundland and Labrador, the rest of Atlantic Canada has a significant business investment gap with the country overall.

Excluding investment in residential structures, business investment relative to GDP in Prince Edward Island ranked last in the country between 2013 and 2023. New Brunswick ranked ninth worst among the ten provinces and Nova Scotia ranked eighth.

The obvious question raised by this data relates to Prince Edward Island. It has been among the top performers in recent years for GDP growth and population growth in Canada, and yet has a relatively low level of business investment. This relates to the structure of the economy. Some industries are more capital-intensive than others. The reason Newfoundland and Labrador has such a high relative level of capital investment is due mainly to its offshore oil and gas and its mineral mining industries. Prince Edward Island has few capital-intensive industries and therefore does not attract a high level of investment.

To illustrate the weak trend in business investment at an industry level, New Brunswick is an instructive example. Between 1998 and 2007, the level of investment in non-residential structures, machinery, and equipment in the province increased at an inflation-adjusted rate of 6 percent per year. Between 2008 and 2023, the rate of change in business investment has been negative, averaging -1 percent per year.

Some industries are investing more than others. The paper manufacturing sector has seen two and a half times the level of capital investment in the rest of the country.[20] The wood products manufacturing sector has attracted 51 percent more investment. The IT sector has attracted a higher share of investment than the rest of the country, at least in part due to the work of the NBIF discussed above. Companies in these sectors are betting this investment will pay off with a good return on investment over the next twenty to thirty years.

Other industries are not investing as much in New Brunswick. The food manufacturing sector has seen significantly less investment than the rest of the country. The transportation and warehousing sector have attracted much less investment, as has the utilities sector.

There has been almost no investment in the mining sector in New Brunswick in recent years. In 1997, mining accounted for 6 percent of provincial GDP. By 2023, the industry's share had dropped to only 0.5 percent. In fact, mining is an excellent example of an industry that has not achieved its potential, particularly in New Brunswick and Nova Scotia. Newfoundland and Labrador has done a much better job of creating an environment and fostering investment in mining. In the two Maritime provinces, the real GDP contribution from mining, quarrying, and oil and gas extraction has dropped by 80 percent between 2001 and 2023. If the sector's GDP contribution had continued to grow after 2001, the two provinces' economic performance could have been significantly improved over the interim period.

In chapter 30 we will explore ten ways to strengthen the environment for business investment in the region.

CHAPTER 10

THE CHALLENGE OF ACCESSING CAPITAL

ONE OF THE PERENNIAL CHALLENGES FACING ENTREPRENEURS AND START-ups in Atlantic Canada has been accessing capital. The good news is that there is more and more interest among people seeking investment opportunities in Atlantic Canada and, with many green energy projects under development and growing potential for offshore wind energy, the region is gaining increasing attention as a good place to invest. Both the proposed hydrogen projects in development and the offshore wind opportunity will require billions of dollars of capital to realize their potential.

But obstacles remain, especially for women and entrepreneurs from marginalized populations. The formation of Sandpiper Ventures, aimed specifically at female entrepreneurs, has been a positive development in this regard. Sandpiper Ventures is one of the few venture capital funds targeting women in Canada and the only one in Atlantic Canada focussed on early-stage investments with women-led businesses.

Sandpiper initially raised $20 million for its first investment fund, of which more than 70 percent of private investments came from other women. But as Sandpiper's co-founder and managing director Rhiannon Davies underscored in an *Insights* episode with us, the motivation behind establishing a venture capital fund targeting women was to fill a gap in the market:

> We were founded in 2020, and we focus on companies that not only have women in leadership positions, but a woman needs to be in the C-suite for more than a year and she needs to have equity ownership. We're doing this because we know, and statistics have proven, that having diversity in your team and your C-suite and your board leads to better ideation and essentially better company development. So that was the motivation. We saw that only 3 percent of venture capital dollars were going to women-led companies. We recognize that's an incredible gap. We've made progress in other areas such as board leadership and company leadership, but in this area of innovation and early-stage start-ups, very little women's innovation was being commercialized.
>
> ...I see huge opportunities to invest in and support an incredibly rich

pipeline of women-led technologies in Canada, and particularly in Atlantic Canada, and these opportunities are growing. Our biggest challenge is to ensure that we continue to raise funds to ensure that we can continue to support and invest in these opportunities and provide them, not only with capital, but with the right level of operator support to enable them to grow their businesses in Canada—and particularly as export opportunities. So, access to capital is our most pressing challenge for the fund and for the companies that we work with.

RENEWED INVESTMENT INTEREST IN ATLANTIC CANADA

Atlantic Canada has caught the attention of the investment community. In September 2024, the Association for Corporate Growth (ACG) held its annual Atlantic Network conference for investors in Halifax. The ACG's third annual conference in 2024 attracted two hundred investors from across the region, from the rest of Canada, and from the northeast US. The ACG's first conference in the region in September 2022 drew about forty participants. Mike Fenton, the President of ACG Toronto and the individual behind the Atlantic conference, described the motivation for launching a conference in Halifax during a 2024 *Insights* podcast:

> What we've seen in bringing ACG to the Atlantic region is there was a gap, a niche that needed to be filled because there isn't really anything like our conference in the region. So we had companies like Seafort and HanMac and a few of the big advisory firms like Deloitte and Grant Thornton, whose senior members would come to Toronto to our national conference, to our events, to meet clients who expressed an interest in having such a conference in the region. I talked about the progression of how we've expanded to Ottawa, then Montréal, then the Atlantic region in the last five years. It just seemed to be the right time. …I've heard it mentioned on your podcast that the Atlantic region is now fast-growing from a business perspective.

The ACG was founded in 1954 and is promoted as the premier merger and acquisitions (M&A) deal-making organization globally driving middle-market growth. It has fifty-two chapters worldwide with more than fifteen thousand members. ACG Toronto, in partnership with ACG Quebec, is the sponsor of the conferences in Halifax. The 2024 conference focussed on issues like succession planning, the use of private equity for investment purposes, partnerships with Indigenous communities, sources of growth capital, and the best growth and investment opportunities in Atlantic Canada. The growth in attendance of this conference is evidence of changing attitudes about the investment opportunities and environment in Atlantic Canada and a clear positive signal for the future of the region.

Canada is in the midst of a generational transfer of business assets that is being driven by the exit from the workplace and business ownership by the baby boom generation. In a recent *Insights* episode, CFIB CEO Dan Kelly said, "We've done tons of work in this area, and it is a big worry for us as an organization that serves small businesses…but it should be a big worry for public policy-makers more broadly. If you can believe it, 76 percent of small [and medium] business owners plan to exit their business within the next decade. This represents $2 trillion worth of business assets that could change hands over the course of that decade."

The question is, how will this transfer of business assets be financed? Few of these businesses would meet the investment criteria employed by the ACG. This will require an enormous amount of capital to facilitate. At the same time, few business owners are prepared for this transition. When asked how prepared business owners were for this transition, Kelly said, "Sadly, not so prepared, as only 9 percent of them (according to CFIB's own research) have a formal succession plan in place. That's deeply worrisome."

Don Mills: I have had personal experience in this regard, having purchased and sold a number of companies over the course of my career, including the sale of my former company, Corporate Research Associates Inc., in 2018 to my senior management team. This had been in the planning process for nearly a decade. I had always intended to sell the company to those who helped build it with me as my preferred exit option, but a senior management buyout is perhaps one of the most challenging types of business transactions. There were a number of challenges to overcome in the sale of the company, including preparing the new owners for ownership of the company and preparing the company for the transition in leadership. One of the biggest challenges was related to financing such a transaction. In my case, I personally financed the transaction myself over a period of time in order to ensure the viability of the company during the transaction period. In the end, the transition to the new owners went extremely well, despite the impact of the pandemic during the timing of the repayment period. The company (now Narrative Research) continues to be owned and operated by Nova Scotians and remains the only national market research firm headquartered in Atlantic Canada.

With so many companies about to change hands, owners should consider how those transitions should be financed and, if there is an opportunity for a management buyout, their willingness to finance a portion of the transaction.

THE CASE FOR A REGIONAL EQUITY TAX CREDIT

It may surprise many, but early-stage start-up companies in Atlantic Canada are eight times less likely to have access to angel capital (individuals who invest personally) than in the rest of Canada, averaging less than $4 per capita versus $31 per capita nationally, according to the recently released study by the National Angel Capital Organization of Canada. Having four smaller provinces only exacerbates the challenge start-ups face in accessing capital.

Angel capital is often the source (sometimes the only source) of early-stage funding for emerging new businesses and is considered high-risk capital. Equally importantly, angel investors frequently provide mentorships and access to their networks to start-up businesses, which can dramatically increase their chances of success. Sandpiper Ventures is an example of a source of early-stage funding in the region.

A group of business leaders and entrepreneurs has been working behind the scenes for the past few years on an idea they believe will help accelerate investment and growth across the region. The group, which does not have a formal name, advocates for the establishment of an "Atlantic investment bubble" or an "Atlantic growth investment rebate" or some equivalent incentive to increase investment in Atlantic Canadian companies. This initiative would allow Atlantic Canadians to invest in companies outside their home province but within the region, and receive a tax credit for such investments. Currently, each of the four Atlantic provinces have their own individual equity tax credits, each with different tax credit limits and different sectors eligible for those tax credits. This group argues that lack of access to angel or venture capital (managed pooled investments) is limiting economic growth in the region.

CURRENT SITUATION

The purpose of equity tax credits or investment rebates is to encourage private-sector investment in sectors where the availability of capital to start or grow a business is otherwise limited. Often the sectors eligible vary depending on the circumstance within each province. Nova Scotia has an Innovation Equity Tax Credit for approved corporations in the oceans technology and life sciences sectors, with a tax credit of 35 percent (45 percent for investments in the ocean tech and life sciences sectors) for individuals with investments up to $250,000 annually. The credit for a corporation that invests in an eligible company is 15 percent for investments up to $500,000 per year. Corporations must first apply for a Certificate of Registration before being able to accept investment from eligible investors.

New Brunswick has a broader program (Small Business Investor Tax Credit) aimed at the small business sector in general. Individual investors receive non-refundable personal income tax credits of 50 percent, up to a maximum of $125,000 per year, based on an investment of $250,000. The tax credit for corporations is 15 percent for investments of $500,000.

In Newfoundland and Labrador, investors can take advantage of the province's Direct Equity Tax Credit program. Newfoundland targets its tax credit for eligible small businesses with fewer than fifty full-time equivalent positions and assets of less than $20 million. There is a fundraising cap of $3 million per eligible business. There is a maximum tax credit of $50,000 available for any given year. Newfoundland recently introduced a separate Resort Property Investment Tax Credit.

In Prince Edward Island, the Equity Investors Incentive is the least generous, providing a 20 percent tax credit for eligible investments. To be eligible, companies must have fewer than fifty employees and assets of less than $10 million. Companies are limited to $200,000 in total in terms of equity raised.

NEW INTERPROVINCIAL EQUITY TAX PROPOSAL

The proposed new regional equity tax or investment rebate would not replace the current equity tax programs that exist in each of the four Atlantic provinces. Rather, the proposal is for a separate equity tax that would apply to investments made in one of the Atlantic provinces by individuals or corporations that are based in another of the Atlantic provinces. The belief is that this equity tax credit or rebate would dramatically increase the pool of funds available for companies requiring such capital to grow their businesses. The proposal would see each provincial government continue to manage the regional tax credit along with their own provincial tax credit program. The federal government would play a role by backstopping those interprovincial tax credits by reimbursing each province for any out-of-province tax credits paid, so no single province would be disadvantaged. It is suggested that the program be a four-year pilot to validate the concept and that the evaluation of the return on the investment be separately undertaken by ACOA. The group is suggesting the establishment of a collaborative working group that includes both public and private representation from each of the four Atlantic provinces to work out the details. It had been hoped that there would be an agreement to proceed with this work by April 1, 2023, but it has not yet been activated.

SOURCES OF PRIVATE CAPITAL

There is increasing demand for risk capital across Atlantic Canada both from the start-up sector and those businesses seeking capital to expand their business. Early pre–seed-stage capital has the highest risk for investors and often comes from friends and family.

In terms of regional sources of private capital, the region has a small but active group of angel investors—individuals who invest their own money in businesses with perceived opportunities for growth. A growing number of investment and venture funds are based within Atlantic Canada. Venture capital is different from angel capital in that it is generally a strategically managed pool of capital, often from a variety of sources. In addition to Sandpiper, which targets women-led companies, there are venture funds backed by high-net worth families in Atlantic Canada, including Seafort Capital backed by the Sobey and McCain families, CFFI, John Risley's private venture fund, HanMac Capital, Colin MacDonald's private venture fund, Killick Venture Fund, focussed primarily in Atlantic Canada and run by Mark Dobbin, and Founders East, a venture fund run by Mickey MacDonald, Jim Spatz, and Rob Steele. Most of these high–net worth individuals are focussed on regional opportunities, although not exclusively.

A recent *Insights* podcast with Rob Normandeau, the managing partner and president of Seafort Capital, highlighted two important trends in Atlantic Canada. One is related to the growing investment opportunities in the region and the other is related to the unprecedented transfer of business ownership that is currently under way as large numbers of baby boom business owners begin their transitions from their companies. Normandeau outlined his rationale for starting Seafort:

> I had the idea of setting up a private firm. One of the things I noticed was that there was a huge demographic shift going on in Canada with an aging entrepreneurial class or a lot of businesses—small or medium-sized—that I knew were going to be available for sale in the coming years, and that trend has continued. What I really needed was capital partners to come in and support me because I didn't have the means on my own to make all these investments. And it wasn't just a regional opportunity. It was a national opportunity.

In spring 2023, Normandeau presented to the ACG investment event in Halifax, where he talked about the investment opportunities in the region and the focus of his company's investment strategy. It was the second such conference held in Halifax and attracted more than 175 interested investors from inside and outside the region. In fall 2023, he presented a very interesting and thought-provoking presentation entitled "Grow or Sell" at the Regional Enterprise Network conference in New Glasgow where he provided a path for business owners to either scale their businesses or prepare their companies for sale.

Seafort Capital is a private investment company that Normandeau and his partners founded in 2012. The company is positioned to provide financial and strategic support to help Canadian businesses grow. Initial funding for the company came from the Sobey and McCain families; they are represented on the company's board of directors and Max St-Pierre is the chair. The company, headquartered in Halifax, looks for opportunities across Canada.

Seafort focusses on the business services and industrial sectors but is not limited to those sectors. Companies need to have minimum earnings before interest, taxes, depreciation, and amortization (EBITDA) of $2 million, and up to about $15 million EBITDA to be of interest to Seafort. The company seeks a majority interest in the companies it partners with.

Seafort just recently announced that its second fund of $200 million for investment has been raised.

THE INVESTMENT ENVIRONMENT

In addition to funding the start-up community, the transition to a green environment will require enormous capital investments in the region. This is particularly the case for utilities in the three Maritime provinces seeking renewable sources of power, and for the various green hydrogen projects under development. For example, the first phase of World Energy GH2's project near Corner Brook, NL, is expected to cost $6 billion alone. A similar amount will be needed for EverWind's hydrogen facility at the Strait of Canso. Financing for these projects will come from financial institutions and export programs from the countries manufacturing the equipment (electrolyzers for green hydrogen production and wind turbines, for example), much in the way Export Development Canada provides our manufacturers with assistance for sale of their equipment to global markets.

Beyond these mega-projects, the need for capital for our burgeoning start-up community continues to increase. Then there is the transition of generational business ownership that needs to be funded. It is safe to say the demand for capital in our region has never been greater. This is good news, because Atlantic Canada as a whole has trailed the rest of the country in capital investment for decades. There is also the offshore wind opportunity, which, according to Peter Nicholson, the author of the *Catching the Wind* report for the Public Policy Forum, could turn the region into an energy superpower but would cost tens of billions to bring to market. As Nicholson stated in an *Insights* podcast, "Offshore wind could have the same impact on Atlantic Canada as hydro has had on Quebec and oil has had on Alberta."

All four provincial governments have a stated goal of attracting investments to their individual provinces as a way of accelerating growth in high-performing businesses and increasing the number of private-sector investors. The Atlantic investment bubble proposal only serves to enhance the possibility of success in achieving this goal and furthering the economic prosperity for the region.

CHAPTER 11

THE WEAK ENTREPRENEURIAL ENVIRONMENT

BEFORE CONFEDERATION, THE MARITIME PROVINCES WERE CONSIDERED TO be highly entrepreneurial, especially in terms of export trade with other markets. Over time, the region has been become much less entrepreneurial and this decline in entrepreneurism has had a detrimental impact on economic prosperity in the region. There are encouraging signs of improvement in that regard which we will cover later in the book.

THE PRIVATE SECTOR

At the time of the 2021 Census, 16.2 million people were employed in Canada. The private sector (including large publicly traded companies) represented nearly 76 percent of total employment in the country at the time of that census.

The census of 2021 also indicates that there are 1.2 million employer businesses in Canada, of which nearly 98 percent are small businesses (companies with fewer than 100 employees), with three-quarters having fewer than ten employees. Small business represents nearly 64 percent of all private-sector employment. There are also another 2.1 million self-employed individuals in Canada. Medium-sized businesses (companies with between 100 and 499 employees) represent nearly 2 percent of all private sector businesses (but over 21 percent of total private-sector employment), while large businesses represent only 0.2 percent of all businesses and 15 percent of all private-sector employment. Small businesses in Canada employ over 10 million people. Small and medium-sized businesses are most associated with entrepreneurs.

One interesting fact is that, again according to the most recent census, one in four new companies in Canada was started by immigrants. Until only recently this has been one of the key weaknesses in the creation of new businesses in Atlantic Canada. There have simply been too few immigrants for our region to benefit from the entrepreneurism of these newcomers Fortunately, this is no longer the case. Many immigrants have a relatively high tolerance for risk and bring new energy, ideas, and innovations to the communities where they live. This is evidenced by the number of incubators and accelerators in the region that report a significant number of start-ups led by newcomers to Canada, in some cases up to 30 percent or more. This coincides with data from StatsCan which indicates that immigrant entrepreneurs account for 33 percent of all businesses in Canada with paid staff. This represents more than a quarter of a million immigrant-owned and -operated businesses. As Dan Kelly, CEO of the Canadian Federation of Independent Business has told our podcast, "Economic immigration has always been the lifeblood of Canada's economic success and has played a key role in building our great nation."

Nearly 80 percent of all employer businesses are in the service-producing sector, while the remainder (21 percent) are in the goods-producing sector. It is important to note the significant role that small and medium enterprises (SMEs) contribute to exports in the country. According to the 2021 Census, SMEs contributed nearly 43 percent of the $575 billion in total goods exported that year.

SMEs are even more important to the economy in Atlantic Canada, where the number of large companies is proportionately smaller. Dan Kelly told us, "Smaller provinces typically have fewer large enterprises. Atlantic Canada, generally speaking, has fewer large enterprises and more small and medium-sized companies. Of course, there's a whole bunch of strengths that come along with that for the region. One of the strengths, of course, of small businesses is when you are hit with an economic downturn, these businesses tend to be more resilient than larger companies and slower to reduce employment."

EMPLOYMENT BY SECTOR IN CANADA

It has long been the reality that Atlantic Canada is more dependent on public-sector jobs than anywhere else in Canada. According to Statistics Canada, in 2024, across the country more than one in five workers (22 percent) was employed by some level of government. Within the region, the percentage of those working for the public sector is much higher and growing. More than one in four Atlantic Canadians (28 percent) works for the public sector.

This has a direct and negative impact on the region's economic performance, and contributes to the higher levels of taxation across the region because, while these tax-funded jobs are well-paid and contribute to the regional economy through spending, they do not contribute much to the prosperity of the region in terms of wealth creation through the production of goods and services for sale. At the same time, these jobs negatively impact the competition for talent for private-sector employers who increasingly find it difficult to compete with the salary, benefits, and pensions provided by public-sector employers. In simple terms, Atlantic Canada is playing a person short in terms of growing its economy relative to other parts of Canada.

Unfortunately, that trend appears to be increasing, not only in Atlantic Canada but across the country. It seems the era of big government has arrived.

Newfoundland and Labrador currently has the highest percentage of public sector workers in the country: 29.6 percent in 2024, up from 28.8 percent in 2019. Prince Edward Island is the next highest at 29.3 percent, up from 26.4 percent in 2019. New Brunswick's percentage of public-sector workers is next at 27.5 percent, up from 23.6 percent in 2019. Relatively speaking, Nova Scotia is closest to the Canadian average in the region, but still high at 26.6 percent. Nonetheless, the growth in the percentage of public-sector workers has been more modest in Nova Scotia than elsewhere within the region. Regardless, the trends are not favourable across the region.

Between 2019 and 2024, overall job growth was highest in Prince Edward Island (a robust 18 percent), but much of that job growth was mainly the result of the growth in public-sector jobs (up 32 percent) while growth in private sector and self-employed jobs increased less than 14 percent. This is unsustainable in the long term. The story is concerning in New Brunswick where overall job growth between 2019 and 2024 was nearly 11 percent) but growth in the public sector was 29 percent, while private sector jobs grew by only 5 percent.

Nova Scotia also saw a big difference between public sector and private sector job growth between 2019 and 2024, with public sector employment up 23 percent and private sector employment up only 9 percent. In Newfoundland and Labrador, overall job growth during that same period was a more modest 6 percent, with the growth in public-sector jobs leading the way by 9 percent, while private-sector jobs and those self-employed grew by only 5 percent.

Clearly, there is a need to rebalance jobs between the public and private sectors to ensure healthy and sustainable economic growth.

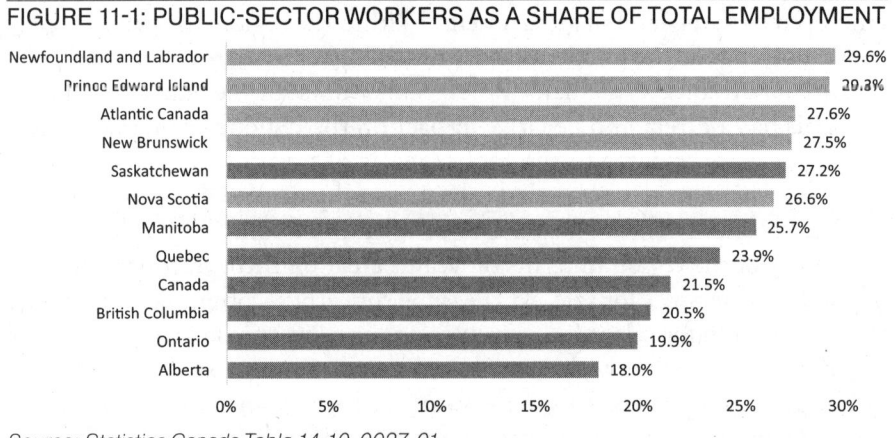

FIGURE 11-1: PUBLIC-SECTOR WORKERS AS A SHARE OF TOTAL EMPLOYMENT

Region	Percentage
Newfoundland and Labrador	29.6%
Prince Edward Island	29.3%
Atlantic Canada	27.6%
New Brunswick	27.5%
Saskatchewan	27.2%
Nova Scotia	26.6%
Manitoba	25.7%
Quebec	23.9%
Canada	21.5%
British Columbia	20.5%
Ontario	19.9%
Alberta	18.0%

Source: Statistics Canada Table 14-10-0027-01

ENTREPRENEURISM IN ATLANTIC CANADA

Perhaps surprisingly, Prince Edward Island has more businesses per capita (46.2) than any other province. This is followed by Alberta (45). Nova Scotia has the fewest such businesses (35.7), followed by Newfoundland and Labrador (36.3). New Brunswick is also below the national average, at 37.1 businesses per thousand.[21]

The history of entrepreneurism in Atlantic Canada is mixed. The region is famous for a handful of successful entrepreneurial families, including the Sobeys, the McCains, the Irvings, the Braggs, the Jodreys, and the Crosbys. Some have suggested that the dominance of these family dynasties has served to dampen the environment for other entrepreneurs in the region. This may or may not be true; it is hard to prove. But other factors have impacted the entrepreneurial environment in the region, not the least of which is the high dependence on, and influence of, government in the regional economy. The most important advantages of being an entrepreneur are the independence and self-determination that go along with running your own business, so those who choose the entrepreneurial route clearly give up the security of a permanent job for their own personal fulfillment.

THE COMPETITION FOR TALENT

There was a time when there was an equilibrium in the competition for talent between the public and private sectors. In the past, the private sector generally had the advantage of more competitive base compensation, while the public sector had the advantage of better benefits and pensions. The increasing competitiveness of base compensation in the public sector has disrupted the competitive market, which now generally favours public-sector employers. With little or no disadvantage on base compensation, it has become increasingly difficult for private-sector employers to compete for talent with the public sector. As a private-sector employer, it is frustrating to compete against your own tax dollars. I (*Don Mills*) had firsthand experience with this problem during my time at Corporate Research Associates, often losing employees to the public sector because my company could not compete with the benefits and pensions provided by governments that were funded by my own taxes.

GROWING SUPPORT FOR ENTREPRENEURISM

The weak entrepreneurial environment has long been recognized in Atlantic Canada. There have been many efforts to address this weakness, at both the provincial and federal levels. The Atlantic Canada Opportunities Agency (ACOA) is one of seven regional economic development agencies in Canada; it was formed in 1985 to coordinate the federal government's economic development initiatives in Atlantic Canada, with its focus on programming to help develop more entrepreneurs within the region. Other federal agencies include the Business Development Bank of Canada (BDC), which is mandated to help create and develop Canadian businesses through the provision of advisory services and financing with a focus on small and medium-sized businesses.

These federal agencies are supported by similar provincial and municipal agencies. We estimate that the total amount spent on economic development activities within Atlantic Canada by the three levels of government exceeds $1 billion per year, with half of that amount from ACOA alone. One could argue that there are too many agencies, often with overlapping mandates, to be effective, and the lack of metrics for most of these agencies makes it difficult to effectively measure their true impact on the economies of the four Atlantic provinces. One thing is clear, however. Atlantic Canada has chronically underperformed the rest of the country for decades, despite the significant investment in economic development in the region.

In Nova Scotia, Invest Nova Scotia has the economic development mandate for the province; in New Brunswick, it is Opportunities NB (ONB); in PEI, it is Innovation PEI; while in Newfoundland and Labrador, it is the Department of Business and Economic Development.

In addition to these provincial agencies, there are also sub-regional agencies. In Nova Scotia, seven different regional enterprise networks (RENS) support business growth outside Halifax. The Halifax Partnership has responsibility for economic development activities within the capital region.

In New Brunswick, the Regional Development Corporation has the responsibility for five economic regions within the province. There are a variety of municipal agencies in New Brunswick as well, including Envision in Saint John, the Southeast Regional Service Commission (SERSC) in Moncton, and Ignite in the capital region. In Prince Edward Island, there are several other economic development agencies, including the Central Development Corporation, the Prince Edward Island Co-operative Council (PEICC), the Summerside Regional Development Corporation (SRDC), and CBDC–West Prince Ventures Limited.

It seems that economic development in Atlantic Canada has become its own employment sector. The region has too many agencies with not enough focus on outcomes and return on investment.

ACCELERATORS AND INCUBATORS

In recent years, there has been a growing trend of a new kind of agency, one focussed squarely on start-ups. These agencies include Propel, Ignite, COVE, Genesis, the PEI BioAlliance, the Verschuren Centre, Volta, Invest Nova

Scotia (formerly Innovacorp), and the Creative Destruction Lab and the ideaHUB at Dalhousie University. These organizations are focussed on providing accelerator and incubator services to the start-up community. Through our *Insights* podcast, we have had the opportunity to interview many of the people involved in these accelerators and incubators and have been impressed not only with their focus but also the success of those efforts.

THE ROLE OF EDUCATION

The debate about entrepreneurs is usually about whether people are born to be entrepreneurs based on their personalities or whether people can be developed into entrepreneurs. Increasing efforts have been made across Atlantic Canada to train entrepreneurs, particularly within the post-secondary sector.

Saint Mary's University in Halifax has a dedicated entrepreneurial program through its Sobey School of Business; the university also offers a Master of Technology Entrepreneurship & Innovation degree. In 2016, Dalhousie University in Halifax opened its ideaHUB to specifically focus on those with an interest in entrepreneurism in the field of engineering. Dalhousie also has the Norman Newman Centre for Entrepreneurship. In addition, Dalhousie's Faculty of Management formed a partnership with Creative Destruction Lab (CDL) to create CDL-Atlantic, the east coast division of a national innovation accelerator that pairs early-stage start-ups with established business leaders.

The University of New Brunswick has a Master of Technology Management and Entrepreneurship program as well as an intensive three-month accelerator program called the Summer Institute.

At Acadia University, the Acadia Entrepreneurship Centre (AEC) has been recognized for its support of entrepreneurs by Startup Canada and boasts Alex McLean, the CEO of East Coast Lifestyle, as one its alumni.

In Newfoundland and Labrador, Memorial University has its own Centre for Entrepreneurship, as well as a sixteen-week entrepreneurship training program for graduate students.

The public education system should be an integral part of developing entrepreneurs. Unfortunately, in our opinion, it is not. Apart from Junior Achievement programs, there is little evidence we can find that students are exposed to the world of business through the curriculum. There are life-skill business courses that could be added like basic accounting or finance courses and introductory sales or marketing courses that would provide at least some exposure to the private sector while at the same time providing students with life skills that would be of value in any line of work. Unless a student's parents are entrepreneurs (which has a high correlation with the development of new entrepreneurs), there is little opportunity to be exposed to the potential of owning and operating a business.

In recent years, there have been efforts to open the Nova Scotia curriculum to include more business-related topics; a report in 2014 by Myra Freeman, the former lieutenant-governor of Nova Scotia, called for greater emphasis on math skills and literacy. Unfortunately, many recommendations from this report were never fully implemented, although funding to Junior Achievement in the province was increased to provide more hands-on entrepreneurial skills training, including financial literacy, for high school–aged students—something that should probably be a core subject for all students.

THE BOTTOM LINE

The bottom line is that the proportion of private-sector jobs must be brought in line with the rest of the country to achieve the rate of economic growth seen at the national level on a sustainable basis. An under-represented private sector makes that possibility unachievable, as the last fifty years of economic performance has shown. There should also be greater focus on exposing students to the world of business as part of the secondary education curriculum.

One of the most important advantages of being an entrepreneur is the independence and self-determination that goes along with running your own business. Those who choose the entrepreneurial route give up the security of a permanent job for their own personal fulfillment. It is not for everyone, but having more entrepreneurs within the region would lead to greater prosperity.

PART TWO

THE TURNAROUND: IS ATLANTIC CANADA POISED FOR GROWTH?

CHAPTER 12
IMMIGRATION AS AN ECONOMIC DRIVER

LITTLE OR NO GROWTH IN THE POPULATION HAS LED TO DECADES OF WEAK economic growth. Until very recently, the population in Canada had been growing at a steady and predictable rate of about 1 percent a year. The federal government's aggressive immigration strategy has led to a growth rate of twice that or more. That has recently been reduced in recognition that that level of population growth was unsustainable, especially from a housing availability and affordability perspective.

That 1 percent population growth over decades has translated into economic growth for most of the country. The same has not been true, however, for Atlantic Canada. The rate of economic growth in Atlantic Canada has trailed the rest of the country for much of the last half-century or more.

Until recently, 71 percent of population growth in Canada has been attributed to immigration. That is largely because the birth rate has fallen below the replacement rate for the population (2.2 births per female). The birth rate across Canada and within Atlantic Canada has been well below the replacement rate for decades. Until quite recently, Atlantic Canada had more deaths than births. It is expected for the foreseeable future that the percentage of population growth in Canada attributed to immigration will continue to increase, despite the recent reduction in the number of immigrants being allowed in the country.

FOOD, CLOTHING, SHELTER, AND OTHER LIFE NECESSITIES

When a new family moves into a community, the priority is usually finding suitable housing followed by finding a job. That family adds to consumption and economic activity in that community. They pay property taxes (either indirectly through rent or directly through home ownership), consumption taxes, and income taxes. The family needs food and clothing, transportation, insurance. Family members need dental and medical care. They become involved in social and cultural activities and might join a church or volunteer in their community. The children need to go to school. The family becomes an economic unit, whose members contribute to the local economy through their expenditures.

ECONOMIC IMMIGRATION

Economic immigrants help fill labour-force gaps caused by an aging workforce and low birth rates. But until only very recently, Atlantic Canada has not received its fair share of the immigrant stream coming to Canada. Newcomers can not only boost economic activity, they can promote new ideas and innovation and improve the productivity of other workers by exemplifying a hard work ethic.

THE ATLANTIC IMMIGRATION PILOT PROGRAM

Perhaps the most important initiative that changed the prospects for Atlantic Canada in terms of attracting immigrants to the region was the Atlantic Immigration Pilot Program that was introduced in 2017 by the federal government. The objective was to attract seven thousand newcomers and their families to the region by 2021. Based on the success of the pilot, the program, now called the Atlantic Immigration Program, became permanent in January 2022. This program provides a pathway to permanent residency for skilled foreign workers and international graduates.

The program is driven by marketplace demand; designated employers provide job offers to qualified immigrants, and applicants must have an individualized settlement plan in place for themselves and their family. The program targets not only experienced and skilled workers but also international graduates who have attended a recognized post-secondary institution in one of the four Atlantic provinces. All those accepted must have a certain level of language proficiency in either French or English.

GROWING NUMBER OF IMMIGRANTS

Between July 1, 2023, and June 30, 2024, over thirty-eight thousand immigrants settled in Atlantic Canada. This represents 1.4 percent growth in the population from immigration alone. This is the highest number of immigrants ever to come to Atlantic Canada and eleven times the number recorded twenty years ago.

TABLE 12-1: IMMIGRANTS ARRIVING IN ATLANTIC CANADA BY YEAR*

	1974	1984	1994	2004	2014	2024
Newfoundland and Labrador	1,128	311	704	536	1,025	5,353
Prince Edward Island	377	103	139	268	1,400	4,149
Nova Scotia	3,064	939	3,084	1,707	2,779	13,736
New Brunswick	2,279	558	589	761	2,300	14,988
Atlantic Canada	6,848	1,911	4,516	3,272	7,504	38,226

*BETWEEN JULY 1 AND JUNE 30 EACH YEAR
Source: Statistics Canada Table 17-10-0008-01

About fifty years ago, the region attracted modest numbers of immigrants, with the numbers fluctuating from year to year. In fact, the number of immigrants was higher in the 1970s than thirty years later in the early 2000s. Until recently, Nova Scotia outperformed the rest of the region in terms of immigrant attraction. This may at least be attributed to the higher number of post-secondary institutions in the province. In the last decade, Prince Edward Island has outperformed the rest of the region in immigrant attraction. Part of the reason for the Island's success has been its growing bioscience cluster. On the other hand, Newfoundland and Labrador has been underperforming the rest of the region in attracting immigrants. One of the reasons for this underperformance has been a much slower response by the provincial government in terms of developing and executing an immigration strategy relative to the other three provinces in the region. The good news is that Newfoundland and Labrador is finally gaining traction in attracting newcomers from other countries.

ATLANTIC CANADA'S SHARE OF IMMIGRANTS

Until only recently, the number of immigrants coming to Atlantic Canada has been well below that for other regions of the country, both in absolute terms and on a per capita basis. Atlantic Canada currently represents a little over 6 percent of the Canadian population. According to the 2021 Census, the region received 3.5 percent of all immigrants coming to the country that year, or roughly only about half its share. As documented elsewhere, the share of immigrants settling in Atlantic Canada has been increasing since 2021.

This helps explain why Atlantic Canada lags so far behind the rest of the country in terms of the percentage of its population that is from other countries, as well as the relative lack of diversity in our regional population. As of the 2021 Census, nearly a quarter of people living in Canada had been born in another country. Meanwhile, Atlantic Canada was in the single digits, although, as discussed earlier, this is improving. The challenge is most apparent in Newfoundland and Labrador, where only 3 percent of the population at the time of the census was made up of immigrants—the lowest percentage in the country, including the North. As the following graph illustrates, the distribution of immigrants across Canada has been very uneven. This historic lack of diversity means many Atlantic Canadians have little experience with people from other cultures. Although Atlantic Canadians are known to be friendly, some have been less than welcoming at times to people they consider "come from aways," but this is changing. We should expect some considerable time will be needed to adjust to the increasing diversity in our Atlantic populations.

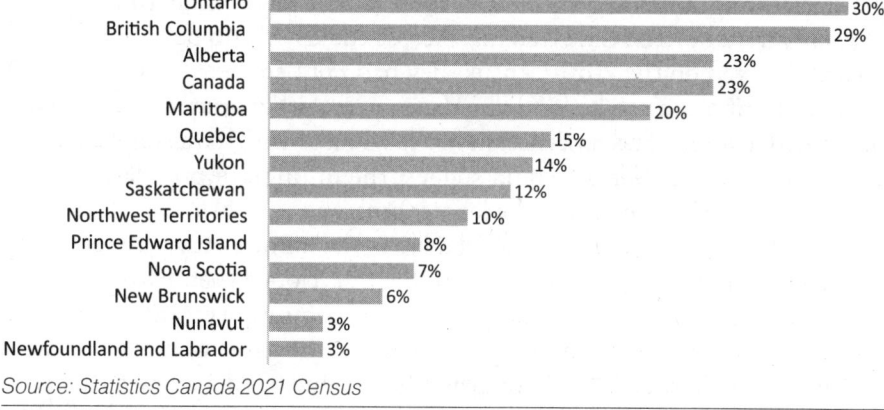

FIGURE 12-1: IMMIGRANTS AS A SHARE OF THE TOTAL POPULATION, 2021

Region	%
Ontario	30%
British Columbia	29%
Alberta	23%
Canada	23%
Manitoba	20%
Quebec	15%
Yukon	14%
Saskatchewan	12%
Northwest Territories	10%
Prince Edward Island	8%
Nova Scotia	7%
New Brunswick	6%
Nunavut	3%
Newfoundland and Labrador	3%

Source: Statistics Canada 2021 Census

Not surprisingly, the news is better for the region's major urban areas. Halifax leads the region in the percentage of immigrants that make up the population, but this is still less than half of the rate in the country overall. Halifax benefits from its post-secondary sector as an attraction to the city. Charlottetown is close behind Halifax in the region with its bioscience cluster, an important attraction for newcomers from elsewhere.

TABLE 12-2: PERCENTAGE OF IMMIGRANTS IN THE POPULATION, 2021

City	%
Halifax, NS	11.2%
Fredericton, NB	8.9%
Moncton, NB	8.7%
Saint John, NB	6.6%
St. John's, NL	4.6%
Charlottetown, PEI	10.8%

Source: Statistics Canada 2021 Census

INTEGRATING IMMIGRANT POPULATIONS

Historically, the majority of immigrants coming to Canada ended up settling in three major urban centres: Toronto, Montréal, and Vancouver. According to the 2021 Census, nearly half the population now living in Toronto was born in another country.

Immigrants tend to want to congregate with other people who share their nationality, which is an advantage for larger urban communities in attracting newcomers from other countries. It is one of the reasons Montréal, Toronto, and Vancouver have historically attracted the largest number of immigrants.

In the Toronto CMA, some neighbourhoods are made up of nearly 100 percent immigrants, and there are others where fewer than 10 percent of residents were born outside Canada. Across the CMA, 46 percent of all residents reported on the 2021 Census they had not been born in Canada.[22] A similar distribution can be found in Vancouver. Although immigrants make up a smaller share of the population in the Moncton CMA, a simple analysis of population distribution would suggest the immigrant population is not clustering as much there as in the largest centres.

Those cities have achieved critical mass in the immigrant groups attracted to their communities, and those groups have developed their own social and cultural infrastructure, including churches, community centres, grocery stores, and restaurants. There is debate about the value of having clusters of immigrants in specific neighbourhoods. On one hand, having a cluster of immigrants from the same region can foster support networks and enable the sharing of religious and cultural events. On the other hand, it can be harder for newcomers to integrate into other aspects of Canadian society when there are large and concentrated ethnocultural communities.

Atlantic Canada is still in the process of creating critical mass in its immigrant communities. In Charlottetown, there is growing evidence of critical mass for some Asian communities. In Halifax, the Lebanese community has long held a dominant role in the development community. The improving rate of retention provides some indication that critical mass is slowly but surely being achieved for some immigrant groups.

Nonetheless, the larger urban areas within the region are attracting the vast majority of immigrants coming to Atlantic Canada and there is an urgent need to find ways to more evenly distribute this population, given widespread labour shortages everywhere, particularly in rural communities.

IMPACT OF GROWING POPULATION

There are a number of consequences that accompany a growing population, especially in a region that has had little population growth over a long period. Perhaps the most obvious is the impact on housing demand, especially longer term. As Duncan Williams, CEO of the Construction Association of Nova Scotia (CANS) indicated on an *Insights* podcast in 2023, the number of housing units under construction in Nova Scotia for that year was 5,500 units. He anticipated that the need would grow to between 12,000 and 15,000 units per year by 2030 to meet demand, based on current population trends. CANS has eight hundred members, and Williams underscored the importance of the construction sector to the Nova Scotia economy during our podcast. "As of today, we're about 6.5 to 7 percent of the GDP for Nova Scotia. It obviously fluctuates, but generally it's been growing and is continuing to grow over the last decade or so. In terms of employment, we're somewhere between thirty thousand and thirty-five thousand people actively participating in the industry today. That includes the industrial, commercial, and the residential sides." At its current percentage of GDP for Nova Scotia, as with the rest of the region, the sector is proportionately lower in terms of contribution to the economy than the country as a whole.

A similar story can be found elsewhere in the region. In New Brunswick, a recent study conducted by David Campbell for the New Brunswick Business Council predicted a tripling of the number of houses needed by 2030 to 8,000 units per year based on a moderate growth scenario.

In the meantime, cities like Halifax and Moncton have near-zero rental vacancies and rapidly rising rental costs and housing prices. The housing market is clearly out of equilibrium at the moment and rising interest rates have not helped the supply side, although declining rates at the time of writing should help stimulate housing construction. Equally challenging: many communities, large and small, lack the developers and the labour force to build homes for a growing population. This will slowly be resolved as new entrants emerge in the housing market to take advantage of demand. In the meantime, patience will be required to allow supply to catch up with demand, which it will eventually do, and to guard against blaming newcomers for the current housing challenges.

Until the recent surge in population growth, especially in the major centres in Atlantic Canada, enrollment in schools had been in a slow and steady decline as a result of decreasing birth rates. That trend has now been reversed as the result of significant population growth. Enrollments are on the rise, and the debate now is not about closing schools but about building more to accommodate increasing demand. This will mean more teachers and other staff.

A growing population puts additional pressure on our health-care system, as evidenced by the growing number of people across the region who don't have a family doctor. The health-care system in Canada and those responsible for managing health care have failed Canadians—first, by not foreseeing the shortage in medical personnel that was predicted decades ago as the result of the impending retirements of baby boomers and, second, by not accounting for increased demand as a result of a growing population. Some provinces have finally started to increase the supply of medical practitioners to deal with these issues. Again, there is a disequilibrium between the supply and demand for medical practitioners that will eventually be resolved. At the same time, new approaches to health-care delivery are being implemented, including the use of collaborative health clinics for primary care and the use of pharmacists to deliver some elements of primary care.

The good news is that, with a growing population, there is a growing number of taxpayers to help fund the increases needed to deliver education and health services.

THE CHALLENGE OF RETENTION

The five-year retention rate is the key metric used by Statistics Canada to measure retention. The most recent five-year retention numbers are for those who were granted permanent residency in 2017 and still filing their taxes in the province they were admitted to as of the 2022 tax filing year.

TABLE 12-3: FIVE-YEAR AND TEN-YEAR IMMIGRANT RETENTION RATES AS OF THE 2022 TAX FILING YEAR

	5-year retention*	10-year retention**
Newfoundland and Labrador	45.6%	37.5%
Prince Edward Island	25.7%	22.8%
Nova Scotia	62.1%	59.2%
New Brunswick	51.7%	37.1%

*ARRIVED IN 2017, STILL FILING TAXES IN PROVINCE AS OF THE 2022 TAX FILING YEAR
**ARRIVED IN 2012, STILL FILING TAXES IN THE PROVINCE AS OF THE 2022 TAX FILING YEAR
Source: Statistics Canada Table 43-10-0018-01

Based on a 2012 admission year, Nova Scotia's ten-year retention rate was a respectable 59.2 percent. Prince Edward Island's ten-year retention rate was only 22.8 percent.

Atlantic Canada has historically had trouble retaining immigrants in the region, but there is growing evidence that the Atlantic Immigration Program is significantly improving retention rates. The reason is simple: immigrants are being recruited to specific jobs in the region and those employees are working with settlement agencies to ensure a smooth transition for immigrant families.

Governments in the region have only recently come to understand both the need to attract immigrants to replace an aging workforce and the importance of developing strategies to retain those newcomers. Settlement agencies like Immigrant Services Association of Nova Scotia (ISANS), with a staff of three hundred, are making a difference. ISANS serves more than ten thousand immigrants per year with a variety of settlement services, plus language and employment training. Jennifer Watts, the former CEO of ISANS, spoke on our *Insights* podcast about the challenge of retaining immigrants:

> They came to settle here. They came for opportunity. They came to contribute, and they have incredible things to offer us beyond an attachment to the labour market. I think that's one of the things that's really important for all of us to grasp if we're going to be about supporting retention and having people stay here. Because there's a huge investment. We all make a huge investment

> when we bring someone here and settle them and go through training, and if people leave and go to other parts of Canada, it's a loss. It's not necessarily a loss to our whole Canadian identity but it's a loss to our region.
>
> So we really need to pay very close attention to the fact that this is not just about the labour market. It's about people developing a sense that "I belong here. I have a contribution to make, and I see my family settling here. We're welcome here. This is the place that I want to be." And there's a whole series of factors that can support that, but it's critically important for all of us to understand that, and to be ready and open to change ourselves, our workplaces, and in our communities and our schools.

There are other settlement agencies in the region doing similar work, including the Immigrant and Refugee Services Association (IRSAPEI) in Prince Edward Island. There is even a regional association for settlement agencies called the Atlantic Region Association of Immigrant Serving Agencies, which serves thirty-five member organizations across the region through the sharing of information and the development of policies and programs regarding the immigrant community.

THE IMPORTANCE OF DIVERSITY

It is important for governments to monitor public attitudes toward diversity and immigration to limit misunderstandings between Canadian-born and foreign-born residents. Some people may blame immigration for the problems around housing supply and access when these issues are primarily the result of poor public policy over a long period of time—for example, the lack of affordable housing built by governments over the past twenty years.

There is already wide recognition that population growth and immigration have had a positive impact on the economy of Atlantic Canada. This attitude needs to be continually reinforced, not only by governments at all levels, but by the private sector. The reason new schools are being built rather than closed is because there are now more children who require schooling. This is largely driven by immigrant families who tend to have more children than their Canadian-born counterparts. Many of the service-related jobs in areas such as fast food are increasingly being filled by newcomers. Some immigrants are demonstrating that they are more entrepreneurial and risk-tolerant that their Canadian-born counterparts. They tend to have a strong work ethic as well. This is reflected in the high percentage of immigrants involved in start-ups across the region and is leading to a more entrepreneurial environment in the region. One of the most high-profile entrepreneurs is Tareq Hadhad, whose Peace by Chocolate company has a manufacturing facility in Antigonish, NS. In our *Insights* conversation with Hadhad in 2022, he proudly talked about giving back to his adopted country and creating jobs for other immigrants and other Canadians. The number of employees fluctuates seasonally, but ranges from forty-five to seventy-five people.

Immigrant success stories need to be told so Atlantic Canadians can better understand and appreciate the value that immigrants bring to their communities. Government and the private sector have a responsibility to keep the population informed about the contributions of immigrants to our economic growth and prosperity. Atlantic Canadians need to find ways to be more welcoming and help immigrants integrate into our communities. There is a difference between offering a friendly wave to a newcomer in your neighbourhood and inviting that person into your home for a meal.

CHANGING ATTITUDES TOWARD IMMIGRATION

Attitudes toward immigration have shifted in the past couple of years according to recent research released by Narrative Research. Their quarterly Atlantic Omnibus indicated in May of 2024 that the majority of the general public thought the pace of population growth was too fast. This contrasted with the May 2023 results where the majority felt the pace of population growth was either about right or even too slow.

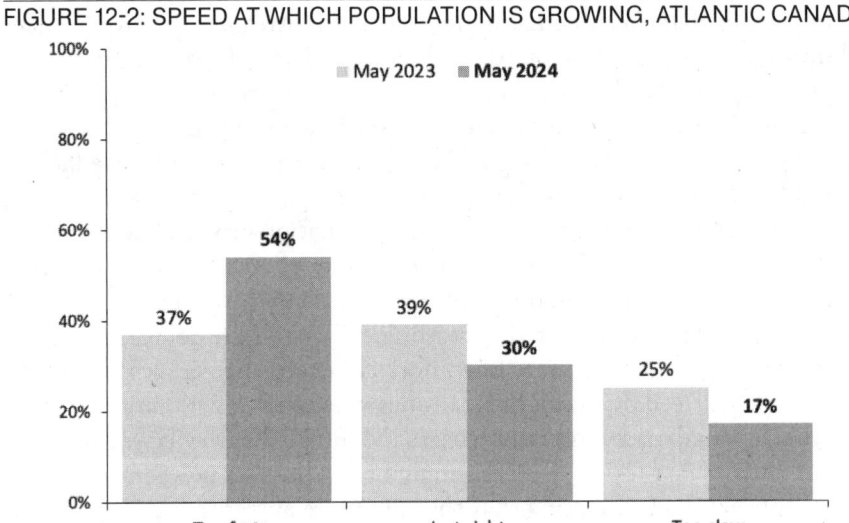

FIGURE 12-2: SPEED AT WHICH POPULATION IS GROWING, ATLANTIC CANADA

Source: Narrative Research

The pace of population growth was especially a concern in Prince Edward Island (88 percent) and Nova Scotia (67 percent). This sentiment was driven by concerns that there was insufficient housing to support the pace of growth.

FIGURE 12-3: WHY POPULATION IS GROWING TOO FAST

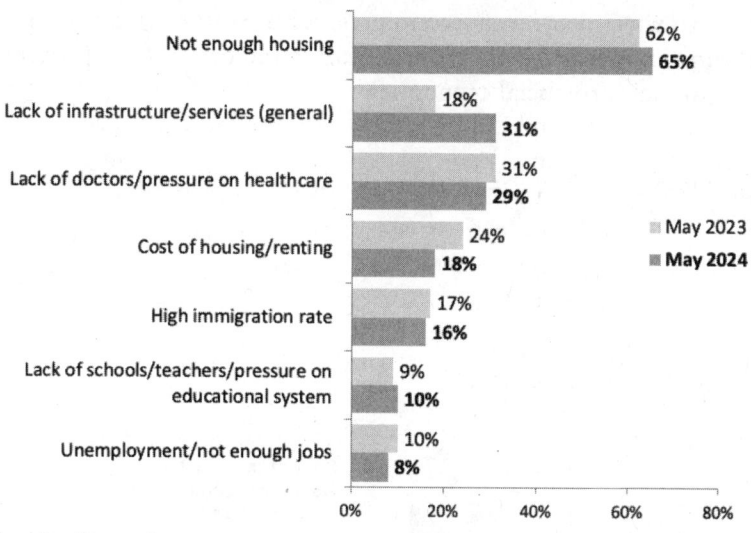

Source: Narrative Research

The good news is that the importance of population growth continues to be well understood by the general population across the region, except in Prince Edward Island, where population growth has been the highest over the last decade or so.

FIGURE 12-4: IMPORTANCE OF GROWING THE POPULATION, ATLANTIC CANADA

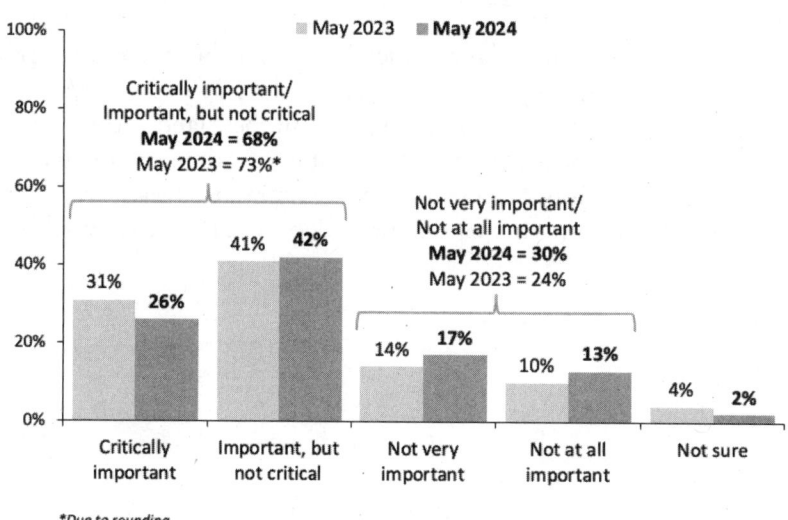

Source: Narrative Research

IMMIGRATION AS AN ECONOMIC DRIVER **115**

The general population continues to recognize the importance of immigration to their provinces' economies, with nearly eight in ten residents indicating immigration was either critically important or important but not critical to their provincial economies.

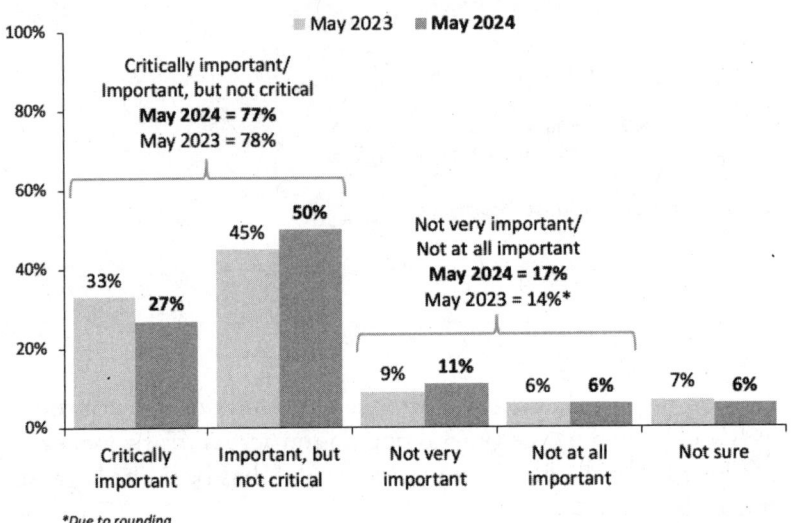

FIGURE 12-5: IMPORTANCE OF IMMIGRATION TO ECONOMY, ATLANTIC CANADA

*Due to rounding

Source: Narrative Research

Even in Prince Edward Island, which has been subjected to the greatest impact and pressure from population growth, the population continues to recognize the important role immigration plays in the Island's economy. Since 2023, there has been a weakening in the number of Atlantic Canadians who believe their province is best served by having more immigrants rather than fewer immigrants. Again, this sentiment is highest in Prince Edward Island.

FIGURE 12-6: THE PROVINCE IS BEST SERVED BY HAVING...,
ATLANTIC CANADA

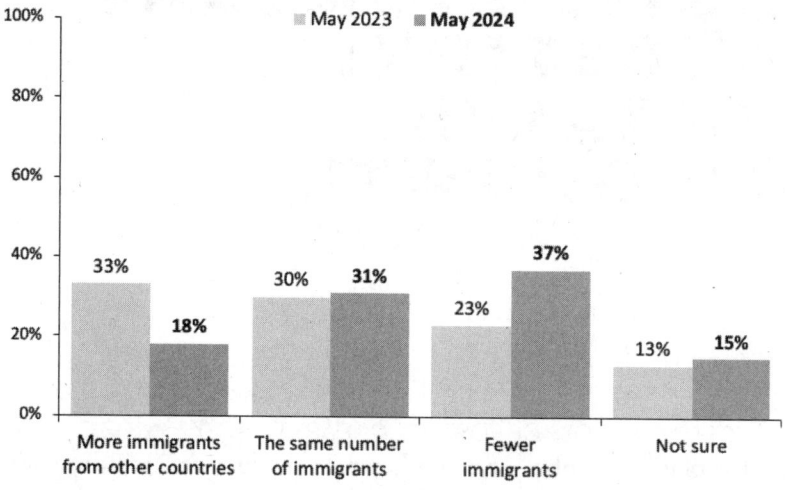

Source: Narrative Research

NOTE OF CAUTION

The decision by the federal government in 2024 to reduce the levels of immigration, foreign students, and temporary workers has reduced the pressure created by too-rapid growth in the population. At the same time, there is an opportunity to decide on a more orderly process to manage population growth in our region and to continue to promote the benefits of population growth overall and the benefits of welcoming newcomers from around the world to Atlantic Canada. It will be important to counter the shifting opinions toward immigration in our region before they turn negative, and against immigrants in particular. This work needs leadership from both the private and public sectors.

CHAPTER 13

POST-SECONDARY EDUCATION: A CATALYST FOR GROWTH

WHILE THE PRIMARY ROLE OF POST-SECONDARY INSTITUTIONS IS EDUCATION, this sector plays a number of other key roles in society, including advancing social justice and creating intellectual capital. Without question, post-secondary institutions in our region and country are key economic enablers from a number of perspectives. In Canada, post-secondary institutions spend nearly $40 billion per year—money that stays in the communities where these institutions are located.

There are fifteen universities in Atlantic Canada, along with community colleges in each province. The overall economic impact of post-secondary institutions through employment alone is significant. In Atlantic Canada, universities and community colleges employ nearly twenty thousand people in well-paying staff and faculty jobs. Total budgets for the post-secondary sector in the region, including community colleges, are well in excess of $3 billion per year, generating thousands of jobs for people and companies that supply these institutions with goods and services. Through the multiplier effect—indirect benefits associated with the expenditures from this sector—the economic impact is even higher.

RESEARCH AND DEVELOPMENT

According to the Association of Atlantic Universities (AAU), universities in the region attract more than $500 million in research funding annually, representing 63 percent of all R & D conducted in Atlantic Canada. At the same time, the private sector within the region invests proportionately less in R & D than elsewhere in Canada. Dalhousie University (ranked sixteenth in Canada in 2022 in research funding) attracts nearly half of the R & D funding to the post-secondary sector within the region.

It has been long recognized that the commercialization of post-secondary research efforts within Atlantic Canada (by both universities and community colleges) has generally been weak. To address this weakness, the AAU, with the support of ACOA and the national granting councils, created Springboard Atlantic, which works to encourage the transfer of knowledge and technology to the marketplace.

In addition, Dalhousie University has partnered with the Rotman School of Management at the University of Toronto to create CDL-Atlantic, modelled on the University of Toronto's successful Creative Destruction Lab, and is focussed on the development of blue-green technologies to support Dalhousie University's research activities. Dal has also created the Emera ideaHUB, which is an early-stage tech incubator associated most closely with the faculty of engineering that provides physical facilities for prototyping ideas. The ideaHUB opened in 2019 and has had eighty early-stage start-ups to date working within so-called oceantech, cleantech, agtech, and medtech sectors.

Other universities in the region are also ramping up efforts to commercialize their research. Memorial University in Newfoundland and Labrador is second after Dalhousie University in attracting research funding and has established a research innovation office to assist in the commercialization of research efforts. The Verschuren Centre works closely with Cape Breton University to help commercialize biotech opportunities. At the University of New Brunswick, the Research and Innovation Partnerships team works to commercialize research being conducted at the university through partnerships with ACOA and Springboard Atlantic. The University of Prince Edward Island has the Office of Commercialization, Innovation, and Industry to help commercialize its research opportunities.

CHANGING DYNAMICS OF POST-SECONDARY EDUCATION

In Atlantic Canada, total full-time and part-time enrollment in universities during the 2024–25 academic year was nearly 95,000. This number was down slightly from nearly 98,000 the previous year as a consequence of the cap on international students. Up until the imposition of the cap on foreign students, enrollments had been steadily increasing over the past decade. Even with the slight decrease, enrollments have increased by a healthy 9 percent since the 2018–19 academic year. Another 60,000 people are estimated to be enrolled in community colleges across Atlantic Canada.

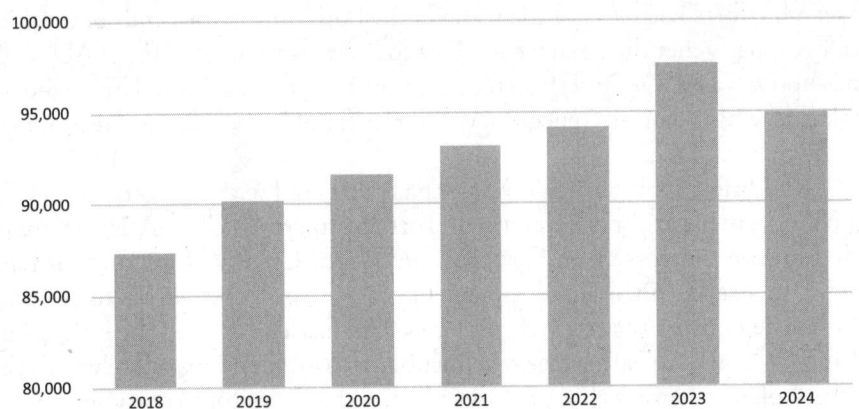

FIGURE 13-1: UNIVERSITY ENROLLMENT ACROSS ATLANTIC CANADA

NOTE: INCLUDES FULL- AND PART-TIME ENROLLMENT AT THE UNDERGRADUATE AND GRADUATE LEVELS

Source: Association of Atlantic Universities (AAU)

The composition of students attending post-secondary institutions across the country has been changing over the past decade, with an increasing percentage of international students. The number of foreign students in Canada tripled in the last decade to more than 640,000 prior to the pandemic (50 percent of whom study in Ontario).

According to the AAU, there were 26,220 international students studying at universities in the region in the 2023–24 academic year. The number of international students in Atlantic Canada increased by 68 percent between 2017 and 2024—and even more when community colleges are included. It is worth nothing that Nova Scotia accounts for more than half (53.7 percent) of all the university enrollments in Atlantic Canada. It is one of the reasons post-secondary education is a more important contributor to Nova Scotia's GDP.

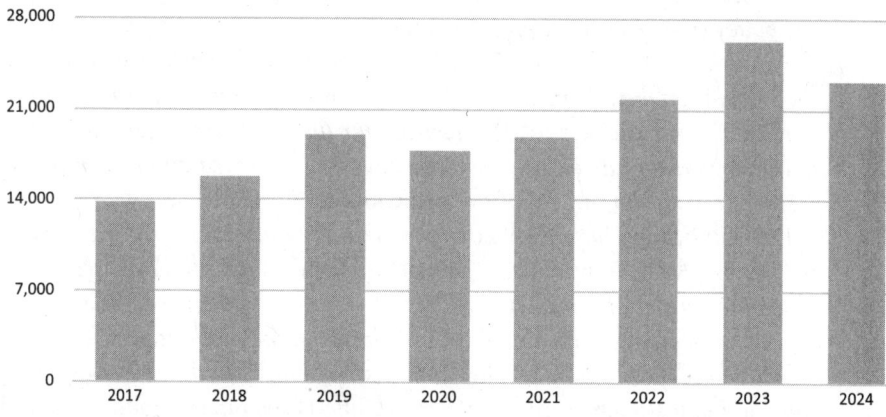

FIGURE 13-2: INTERNATIONAL STUDENT ENROLLMENT IN ATLANTIC CANADA UNIVERSITIES BY YEAR

Source: Association of Atlantic Universities (AAU)

The rapid increase in the number of international students studying in Canada is due to a variety of things. Chief among them is a rapidly growing middle class in developing countries and emerging markets like Asia, where citizens are seeking both education and immigration opportunities. The number of international students worldwide has grown from around 2 million in 2000 to more than 5 million. This increasing interest in international study has greatly benefitted Canadian institutions, which had previously relied on the domestic market for students. At the same time, the availability of eighteen- to twenty-four-year-old Canadian students has greatly diminished over the years as the children of the baby boomers have worked their way through the education system. This has forced post-secondary institutions to increasingly look to international students to provide them with financial sustainability.

It may surprise some that Canada has become the third most popular destination for foreign students in the world, trailing only the United States and Australia. Canada is sought after because of its reputation as a multicultural and largely tolerant society with high educational standards.

In 2024, the federal government imposed a cap on international students coming to Canada, resulting in three thousand fewer enrollments in the region for the 2023–24 academic year. Peter Halpin, the executive director of the AAU, told Insights:

> From the outset of the unanticipated Immigration, Refugees and Citizenship Canada (IRCC) policy announcement [in January 2024] placing an immediate cap on the numbers of international students entering Canada and its

> post-secondary education institutions, Atlantic universities expressed serious concerns. Even the minister [the Honourable Marc Miller] characterized the policy change as a "blunt instrument."
>
> Atlantic universities and the Atlantic region have a greater dependence on international students than the rest of Canada [about 30 percent of total enrollment versus closer to 20 percent]. Our universities also tend to have a lower conversion rate on students who have been accepted and have received visa approval than institutions across Canada.
>
> Early indicators [as of July 2024] are that the initial concerns are coming to fruition. A few universities are reporting significant declines in acceptance of Provincial Attestation Letters (PALS)—required under the IRCC policy—and subsequent institutional revenue losses in the millions of dollars.
>
> The IRCC policy is indeed a "blunt instrument." In addition to affecting international student enrollments, which affects the internationalization of our campuses and short- to long-term institutional financial sustainability, the IRCC policy undermines the federal government's Atlantic Immigration Policy (AIP). The retention of international students is one of the key streams of new citizens for Atlantic Canada [for which the 2024 retention rate was 56 percent].
>
> In short, the IRCC policy on international student recruitment is hurting our universities, the communities in which they are located, local and regional economies, and regional population growth strategy.

To help mitigate the negative effects of IRCC policy changes, Peter Halpin says the AAU has recently proposed a federal-provincial pilot project: the Atlantic Education Destination (AED). The goal of AED is to promote Atlantic Canada as a unique post-secondary education destination internationally. The AED would strategically manage the number of international students choosing to study in Atlantic Canada and ensure that participating institutions have appropriate housing, health care, and other services in place.

ECONOMIC VALUE OF INTERNATIONAL STUDENTS

International students at both the secondary and post-secondary levels have had a significant economic impact on Canada and on this region. The average foreign student spends in excess of $45,000 a year while studying in Canada. Tuition fees for international students are significantly higher than those for domestic students, accounting for about $20,000 per academic year. This means international students are paying full market rate to cover all their costs without being subsidized by Canadian taxpayers, as it should be. In Atlantic Canada, according to a 2023 Gardner Pinfold Study called *The Economic Impacts of Canada's International Student Cap in Atlantic Canada for 2024/25*, which was prepared for the AAU, international students spent more than a $1 billion in the region in the last academic year. Just look to the local luxury car market to see the importance of foreign students to business; some dealerships have brought on Mandarin-speaking sales personnel to cater to this international segment.

In addition to tuition, foreign students purchase goods and services while studying in Canada and pay taxes on their purchases. In the Atlantic region, Gardner Pinfold estimated international students induced more than $310 million in tax revenue for governments in Atlantic Canada.

International students also support the creation of jobs. Again, the 2023 Gardner Pinfold study estimated that over eighteen thousand jobs in the region are attributed to international students from direct, indirect, and induced effects.

International students also have a tourism-related impact because friends and relatives often come to visit while they are studying in Canada. While difficult to quantify, an Australian study found that for every ten long-term international students there were five visitors per year.

POPULATION GROWTH IMPACT OF UNIVERSITIES

In 2018, Corporate Research Associates conducted a comprehensive study of foreign students for the AAU. One of the key findings was that more than 60 percent of those queried expressed a desire to stay in Canada upon graduation. A report by the AAU entitled *The Class of 2020 Atlantic University Graduates, Two Years On* said that 56 percent of international students chose not just to stay in Canada but to stay in the region after graduation. More importantly, these international students wanted to stay in the communities where they had studied. In the case of Cape Breton University, the influx of international students has reversed decades of population decline in the Cape Breton Regional Municipality (CBRM).

Given the need to grow the population (and especially the workforce) across the region, post-secondary institutions represent an important source of future immigrants. The federal government has recognized this opportunity by creating a post-graduate work permit for those who wish to stay in Canada after graduation. This is an important change for foreign students, as it allows them an opportunity to gain work experience that helps them qualify for the Express Entry program. Canada's Comprehensive Ranking System (CRS) awards points according to the applicant's potential to succeed in Canada. High proficiency in either official language, along with educational credentials and skilled work experience are the key ways to qualify. Providing foreign students with the opportunity to gain up to three years post-graduation work experience is a clear advantage to this segment in gaining permanent residence status over other applicants. More importantly, international students who have lived and studied in Canada for a number of years have the further advantage of being more acclimatized to Canadian society and require much less time to integrate.

Employers and the general public play an important role in welcoming international students—especially those who wish to remain in Canada and become citizens. Ensuring diversity in employment hiring is key to opening up job opportunities for international students after they graduate. At the same time, post-secondary institutions could enhance their approach to international students by pre-screening those with an interest in remaining in Canada after graduation, and by providing a more intensive language-training stream for those individuals while they are attending their institutions. One of the key barriers often mentioned in conversation with employers in hiring immigrants was the lack of language proficiency. (*Don Mills*: This has been my own experience as well.) In addition, post-secondary institutions need to do a better job of providing co-op work term opportunities for foreign students so they can gain critical Canadian work experience prior to graduation. Schools could also provide assistance to students who are applying for post-graduate work permits. We all have a role in creating the conditions to retain these high-value immigrants.

CHAPTER 14

THE DOWNSIDE OF HIGH POPULATION GROWTH

HOUSING

HOUSING AVAILABILITY AND COST HAVE BEEN THEMES THROUGH THIS BOOK. IT is vitally important to have enough housing and a good mix of housing options at costs aligned with household income to encourage people to move to the region. Very few people, if any, expected the level of population growth the region has witnessed over the past few years. The residential construction sector was also caught off-guard, and one of the results has been a dramatic increase in the price of housing—both purchasing and renting. Table 14-1 shows the benchmark price for a single-family dwelling in June 2024 for the ten provinces in Canada compared to the price in June 2019. The price has increased across the country, but nowhere faster than in the Maritime provinces, coinciding with the rapid increase in population. New Brunswick has led the country with an 83 percent rise in the benchmark price in just a five-year time frame. Nova Scotia has seen similar price rises. It's worth noting that the benchmark price for a single-family dwelling in Atlantic Canada is still considerably lower than in most other provinces in Canada.

TABLE 14-1: SINGLE-FAMILY BENCHMARK HOUSE PRICE BY PROVINCE

	June 2019	June 2024	% change
British Columba	$869,300	$1,344,800	+55%
Ontario	$653,900	$973,400	+49%
Alberta	$431,500	$598,000	+39%
Quebec	$368,200	$550,200	+49%
Nova Scotia	$227,700	$413,900	+82%
Manitoba*	$292,700	$383,000	+31%
Saskatchewan	$293,200	$366,400	+25%
Prince Edward Island	$223,700	$358,900	+60%
New Brunswick	$169,000	$308,500	+83%
Newfoundland and Labrador	$233,400	$295,900	+27%

*DATA ONLY AVAILABLE FOR WINNIPEG

Source: Canadian Real Estate Association

The Canada Mortgage and Housing Corporation (CMHC) released a report in September 2023 that estimated the demand for housing across Canada through 2030. The agency estimated Nova Scotia could have a housing supply gap of seventy thousand units by 2030 under a high-population growth scenario and sixty thousand under a low-economic growth scenario.[23] Duncan Williams, CEO of the Construction Association of Nova Scotia (CANS), indicated in a 2022 *Insights* episode that the challenge was not only to build more housing units but to build a workforce to construct the units needed to meet the increasing demand:

> *Labor force, no question about it, is probably the single biggest constraint we have right now. We do know there is a significant shortfall. We know we need at least seven thousand to ten thousand [people]. I would argue it's closer to eleven or twelve thousand that we're going to need by 2030 just to keep up with demand and replace our workforce. Those are big challenges. We have to tap more into underrepresented communities earlier. It took us decades to get here. It's going to take us a bit of time and effort to get back to right-sizing and putting in place the systems that we had when we moved away from trade schools and Industrial Arts.*

The New Brunswick Business Council released a report on housing demand that found an implied housing deficit of more than ten thousand units in just the 2021–22 time frame.

One of the top challenges is the shortage of workers in the residential construction sector, particularly in the skilled trades. This is an issue across the country, but it is particularly acute in Atlantic Canada. Because the region had a long period of virtually no population growth, annual housing starts were relatively limited compared to places in Canada where the population was growing. When the regional population started to increase, the size of the residential construction sector workforce kept pace. As shown in figure 14-1, across Atlantic Canada in 2022 there were just under ten thousand workers in the residential construction sector in an average month during the year. This represented a workforce similar in size to that in the 2010–15 time frame, when the population across Atlantic Canada was hardly growing at all.

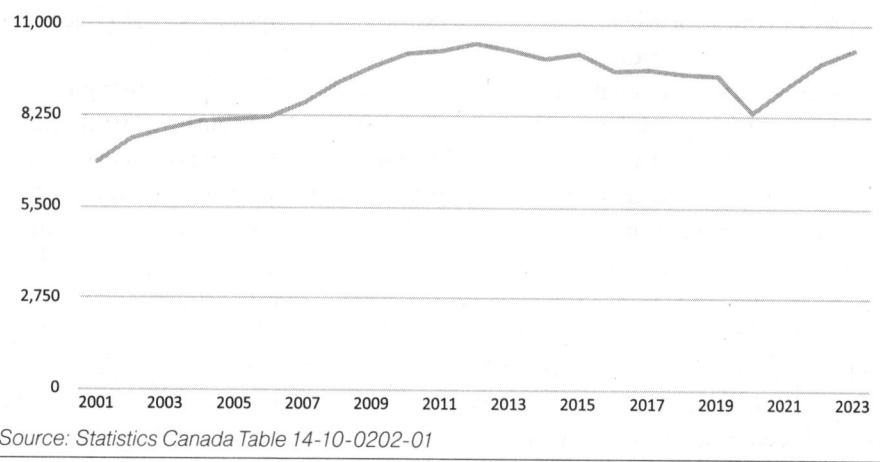

FIGURE 14-1: AVERAGE MONTHLY EMPLOYMENT IN THE RESIDENTIAL CONSTRUCTION SECTOR, ATLANTIC CANADA

Source: Statistics Canada Table 14-10-0202-01

Like most sectors, the construction industry is dealing with a rapidly aging workforce at a time when it needs to significantly increase the number of construction workers. In a 2023 *Insights* podcast, Duncan Williams of CANS captured the challenge when he said, "Nova Scotia will need to triple the number of housing units during a time that 40 percent of the workforce are forecasted to retire by 2030."

To put this into perspective, in the early 2000s the residential construction workforce in Atlantic Canada represented just under 9 percent of the total workforce across the country. By 2022, it was 30 percent smaller.

Provincial governments have responded. The number of people in skilled trades apprenticeship programs has increased significantly across the region. Further, there are now efforts under way to attract more skilled tradespersons from around the world. It is critically important that the region has enough housing to accommodate demand in the years ahead. This should include determining the rate of population growth that is in line with the economy's ability to keep pace in terms of housing availability.

HEALTH CARE

The challenges related to health care and population growth in the region are well documented. For many moving to the region, finding a family doctor has been very hard, if not impossible. In many parts of the region, the wait time to see a doctor in an emergency department has been rising. According to the Canadian Institute for Health Information (CIHI), between April 2022 and March 2023, the median emergency room wait time in Nova Scotia for patients who were eventually discharged was 4.7 hours, 20 percent longer than the average wait time across the country[24] and one of the longest wait times among the reporting provinces.

Wait times for surgeries, access to specialized physicians, and other services have been rising across the region.

One of the main roadblocks has been the difficulty in recruiting health-care provisions. A top example of this is the nursing workforce. The demand for registered nurses in the health-care sector and in support workers for the elderly population and other activities has never been greater; unfortunately, a large cohort of nurses is heading toward retirement. According to the Canadian Occupational Projection System (COPS) produced by Employment and Social Development Canada, there will be a significant shortage of registered nurses between 2023 and 2031 that will need to be made up for by increasing the number enrolled in post-secondary education or through immigration, although most immigrants require academic upgrading to meet Canadian requirements.

According to Statistics Canada's job vacancy and wage survey for the third quarter of 2023, the two Atlantic provinces for which data was published had a combined 1,485 vacant nursing positions (in just that quarter). This was 2.7 times as many as in the same quarter in 2018. Adjusted for population size, New Brunswick and Nova Scotia had well above-average nurse vacancy levels in that quarter compared to the country overall.

TABLE 14-2: NURSING WORKFORCE VACANCIES BY PROVINCE, Q3 2024

	Q3 2018	Q3 2024	% change	Vacancies per 100,000 population
Canada	10,230	23,905	134%	58
Newfoundland and Labrador	195	N/A	N/A	N/A
Prince Edward Island	N/A	N/A	N/A	N/A
Nova Scotia	330	800	142%	74
New Brunswick	215	685	219%	80
Quebec	2,550	8,640	239%	95
Ontario	3,935	7,555	92%	47
Manitoba	855	890	4%	60
Saskatchewan	190	N/A	N/A	N/A
Alberta	340	360	6%	7
British Columbia	1,585	3,705	134%	65

Source: Statistics Canada Table 14-10-0328-01

If the region's health-care system cannot accommodate population growth, it could undermine public support for the attraction of newcomers.

At the same time, there is a need for health-care reform in Canada. Nova Scotia is leading the way in this area. The appointment of Karen Oldfield as the Interim CEO of Nova Scotia Health has allowed the province to think outside the box in terms of health reform. The Houston government has not been shy about using the private sector to deliver publicly funded health care, whether that involves the expansion of the role of pharmacists in prescribing medications or allowing private eye clinics to perform cataract surgeries to reduce wait times, there is a clear willingness to involve more private-sector solutions.

The other important change is in access to primary care. Like most jurisdictions in Canada, there is a movement toward collaborative health-care practices to accommodate the changing needs of family practice doctors who seek a better work-life balance. There are fewer and fewer single-practice doctors. At the same time, the use of virtual health care has increased significantly. Now the public's expectations around primary care need to move from the expectation that everyone should have their own doctor to the expectation that everyone should have access to a doctor when needed, but not necessarily the same doctor. As Oldfield outlined the province's approach in our 2023 *Insights* podcast:

> We do have a number of collaborative clinics in the province of Nova Scotia. There's a hundred that are operated through Nova Scotia Health, and we are supporting to grow as a clinic another twenty or thirty. By "supporting to grow," I mean putting a nurse practitioner with them or some other form of clinician that's going to be geared to that clinic and to that community. The idea is you belong to the health home, not necessarily to this physician or this nurse practitioner, but if you need to see the dietitian or you need to see the physiotherapist, they're part of your health home and your medical record belongs to the health home. So, a physician may come or go, the physiotherapist may come or go, but your record is there and that's your home. That is the wave of the future. It's a big change. It's a different way of thinking about primary health.
>
> So that's one component. If I look at the last two years, we've created so many new pathways. We have a very robust pathway to pharmacies. Similarly, mobile clinics that are travelling across Nova Scotia to meet the needs of populations in their community. Thirdly, we have virtual care, and I'm really excited about the virtual care component of our health system. If I look at the numbers, last month there were 116,000 appointments completed outside of family physicians. So, I'm talking about mobile clinics, virtual, and pharmacies. That's a massive number and these are people who may otherwise be going to our emergency departments. The launch of the

> YourHealthNS mobile app, which you download, provides the ability to find health services close to you.

EDUCATION

After more than twenty years of population decline in most of the region, with the exception of Newfoundland and Labrador, the population under the age of fifteen is growing again. In PEI, the growth among the younger demographic started back in 2016. The number of persons under the age of fifteen is up 10 percent on the Island since then. Between 2019 and 2023, the population under the age of fifteen in the Halifax CMA increased by 9 percent. The Moncton CMA had the fastest growth among this age group among all CMAs across Canada. Fredericton, Saint John, Cape Breton, and Bathurst all benefitted from strong growth in the under-fifteen age group.

This has led to a significant expansion in K–12 (primary and secondary school) enrollment in these areas. Some communities, including the Moncton region, are reporting a record increase in the number of K–12 enrollments.

CRIME, HOMELESSNESS, AND OTHER CHALLENGES

The crime rate has been rising in Atlantic Canada in recent years. According to data collected by Statistics Canada, the rate of Criminal Code violations (excluding traffic) in Atlantic Canada has been rising faster between 2017 and 2023 than in other provinces. The crime rate is now above the national rate in all four Atlantic provinces. The violent crime rate is also higher in Newfoundland and Labrador, Nova Scotia, and New Brunswick than in the country overall.

This may or may not be related to population growth. There are many factors that drive up crime rates, but this is still a major concern that needs to be addressed moving forward.

There has been a rise in the past few years in the number of people who can't find housing and who have other social challenges that, again, seems to be correlated with the growth in population.

TABLE 14-3: CRIME RATE BY PROVINCE (2023) AND PERCENTAGE CHANGE 2017–2023

ALL CRIMINAL CODE VIOLATIONS (EXCLUDING TRAFFIC), RATE PER 100,000 POPULATION

	Rate per 100,000	% change 2017–2023
Canada	5,843	9%
Newfoundland and Labrador	7,175	31%
Prince Edward Island	6,147	47%
Nova Scotia	5,933	17%
New Brunswick	6,587	28%
Quebec	3,713	9%
Ontario	4,454	16%
Manitoba	10,599	17%
Saskatchewan	12,909	11%
Alberta	7,948	-8%
British Columbia	7,404	2%

Source: Statistics Canada Table 35-10-0177-01

THE RISK

The population in Canada is more mobile now than at any time in the country's history. When Statistics Canada undertook the 2021 Census, the organization reported that 7.7 million people had moved out of their community in the previous five years, or more than one out of every five people in the population (22 percent). If Atlantic Canada cannot manage its population growth and the associated costs of growth, this could prompt more outward migration or curtail the number of people moving into the region.

CHAPTER 15

REGIONAL INCUBATORS AND ACCELERATORS

THE ECOSYSTEM FOR START-UP COMPANIES IN ATLANTIC CANADA HAS NEVER been stronger. Through the *Insights* podcast, we have had the opportunity to interview the leaders of the major incubators and accelerators across the region. We have also had Peter Moreira, the CEO of *Entrevestor*—a site dedicated to providing news and data on start-ups in Atlantic Canada—on the podcast to discuss the number of start-ups across the region, and Rory Francis, the Executive Director of the PEI BioAlliance, a not-for-profit organization dedicated to building the bioscience industry in PEI, which has created a cluster of new businesses on the Island. In addition, we have spoken with Kendra MacDonald, the CEO of Canada's Ocean Supercluster, an industry-led, national ocean cluster that brings together organizations from coast-to-coast-to-coast across the fishery, aquaculture, bioresources, defence, transportation, and ocean technology sectors.

There is no doubt that the number of new start-up businesses within the region is on the rise and that much of that rise is due to the support being provided to these new companies by the various accelerators and incubators across Atlantic Canada. Most of the accelerators and incubators have only been in place for the past decade or so. Interestingly, a high level of collaboration already exists among the accelerator and incubator communities within the region. The opportunity to work together and learn together has important implications for Atlantic Canada—a rising tide lifts all boats, as they say. Success in one part of Atlantic Canada is good for all of Atlantic Canada.

THE START-UP ENVIRONMENT

According to a report from *Entrevestor* for 2023, the number of tech start-up companies has doubled to over eight hundred in the past seven years, while the number of employees working with these start-ups has tripled to 9,400 over the same time period. In its most recent report, *Entrevestor* noted that the growth in the number of start-ups was 4.4 percent year over year, but the pace of growth was slowing recently, likely because of the pandemic.

FIGURE 15-1: NUMBER OF START-UP COMPANIES TRACKED BY *ENTREVESTOR*, ATLANTIC CANADA–WIDE

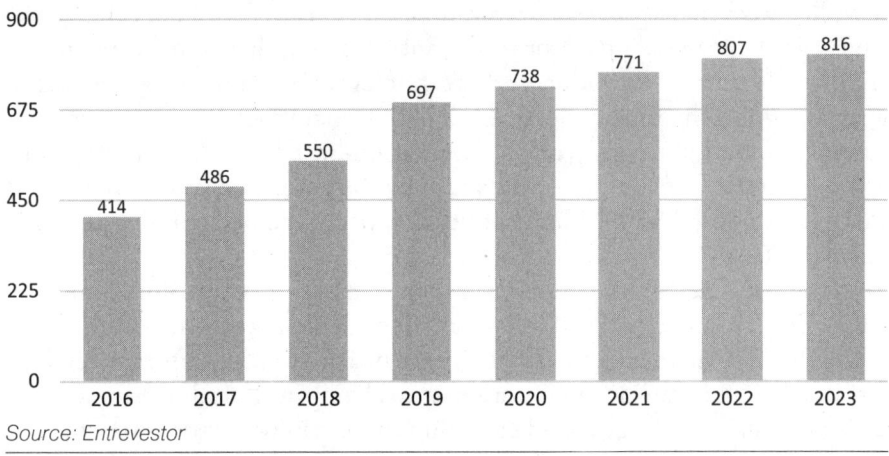

Source: Entrevestor

There have been some remarkable success stories over the past decade or so, including the sale of two Fredericton-based companies in the 2010 to 2011 time period. Radian6, which builds social media monitoring tools, was acquired by Salesforce for $326 million, and security intelligence company Q1 Labs was purchased by IBM for a reported $600 million. Meanwhile, St. John's-based fraud-detection and anti–money laundering software company Verafin was acquired by Nasdaq for US$2.75 billion in 2020 and continues to operate out of St. John's, recently surpassing one thousand employees.

PRINCE EDWARD ISLAND

There is little doubt that one of the most important drivers of economic growth in Prince Edward Island has been the PEI BioAlliance. The PEI BioAlliance is probably the region's most successful model of a purpose-built cluster. There are currently sixty-five companies in the cluster who collectively employ more than two thousand people with revenues approaching $600 million annually. This sector now represents nearly 5 percent of the Island's GDP and has a goal of reaching $1 billion in revenues with three thousand employees by 2030.

This is a private-sector–led not-for-profit organization charged with the responsibility of developing the strategy for and coordinating the growth of the bioscience cluster on the Island. The success of the PEI BioAlliance is in no small part due to the work of its executive director, Rory Francis. Since 2008, the number of bioscience-based companies has more than tripled, with most located in the capital city of Charlottetown. The focus of these companies has been on animal and fish health, industrial bioproducts, plant health, and human health. It has also led to the creation of the Canadian Alliance for Skills & Training in Life Sciences (CASTL) to ensure a continuing supply of skilled workers to grow the sector. It has led to the creation of Emergence, a bioscience business incubator for Atlantic Canada that is dedicated to the commercialization of products and technologies based on natural product chemistry, and the BioAccelerator, a 75,000 square foot facility designed to support biomanufacturing and fermentation-based business development across Atlantic Canada. Jointly financed by the governments of Canada and PEI, the proposed $50 million facility is expected to be operational by the fall of 2026.

One of the most important companies in the BioAlliance is BIOVECTRA, led by CEO Oliver Technow, who is also the current chair of the PEI BioAlliance. BIOVECTRA is a pharmaceutical contract development and manufacturing organization, specializing in clinical to commercial-scale production. Technow told us during an *Insights* podcast that the federal government's decision to repatriate drug manufacturing to Canada has led to his company being designated to manufacture mRNA vaccines used to fight COVID-19. Construction on the new manufacturing facility began in April 2022 and it is now operational. The new facility will be able to produce 160 million doses of the mRNA vaccine. BIOVECTRA also has facilities in Halifax and Windsor, NS, for R & D. It is interesting to note that BIOVECTRA has been in operation for more than fifty years and that its predecessor, Diagnostic Chemicals, was founded by Regis Duffy, who at the time was the Dean of Science at UPEI.

Another example is Elanco Animal Health, which was one of the first companies to join the PEI BioAlliance at its founding (it was then known as AquaHealth). The firm's Prince Edward Island–based operations produce aquaculture pharmaceuticals and was recently sold to Merck Animal Health for CAD$1.75 billion.

NEWFOUNDLAND AND LABRADOR

The Genesis Centre is an innovation hub for Newfoundland and Labrador. Its flagship incubator program, called Enterprise, has been in operation for more than twenty-five years and helps start-ups from concept to scaling the business. There are currently twenty companies in the program; half of the founders are immigrants and one-third are women. Based on a third-party independent assessment, the program has an 88 percent success rate, above the benchmark success rate of 67 percent for similar organizations.

The Genesis Centre, which opened in 1997, has helped raise more than $600 million in private capital for its clients, which in turn has created recurring annual revenues of $250 million and more than 2,500 jobs. The focus is on technology start-ups; it is perhaps best known for helping Verafin become the largest private-sector acquisition in Canadian history (US$2.75 billion). Importantly, Verafin continues to operate out of St. John's with a workforce of one thousand. According to Michelle Simms, the former long-time president and CEO of Genesis, the business model is one of the "most unique business models" for incubators in the country.

"We actually have a royalty agreement in place with all of our companies in the enterprise program stating that once the company reaches a million dollars in gross revenue, Genesis gets 2 percent of their gross revenues for five years or until they've paid Genesis $500,000 whichever comes first," Simms told *Insights*. "That is unique in the rest of the country and serves to support emerging start-ups following in the footsteps of companies like Verafin."

Another key organization driving innovation in Newfoundland and Labrador is techNL, a not-for-profit industry association representing the province's technology and innovation sector by working with industry and government partners to help shape policy. In 2022, it launched an Innovation Centre for remote operations in the province.

NEW BRUNSWICK

The New Brunswick Innovation Foundation (NBIF) is an independent private organization that focusses on venture capital financing and research funding. Its Startup Investment Fund provides up to $200,000 for eligible companies in New Brunswick in pre-seed equity investment, usually in the form of preferred shares, common shares, or convertible debentures. NBIF's Venture Capital Fund provides seed capital, ranging from $200,000 to $500,000 per round. NBIF has had a respectable return on its investments over time and currently has about twenty-six companies in its accelerator program, seventeen companies in its start-up investment fund, and more than thirty in its venture capital fund.

In an *Insights* episode, Jeff White, the CEO of NBIF, outlined their fund. "In the fund today, we have about twenty-five to thirty active companies that represent an investment value of around $35 million. What's more impressive about that group of companies: when you look at their total value, it is approaching $750 to $800 million worth of enterprise value for New Brunswick. That indicates how we just take a small sliver at a really important time in their journey when not a lot of other people will step in. You know, it's called the riskiest (time)."

Recently, there has been a realignment of NBIF responsibilities with Research NB, with CEO Damon Goodwin taking over full responsibility for funding research and promoting the work of New Brunswick researchers.

Another important accelerator in the region is New Brunswick–based Propel, which positions itself as "Atlantic Canada's e-accelerator for tech start-ups." It is focussed on tech start-ups across the region and is currently working with about one hundred companies across the region. Propel provides training and support programming virtually. It was founded by legendary innovator and entrepreneur Gerry Pond, along with business leaders Curtis Howe and Jeff White. Kathryn Lockhart is Propel's CEO.

NOVA SCOTIA

In Nova Scotia, there are several organizations supporting the start-up community, including Invest Nova Scotia, the Creative Destruction Lab at Dalhousie University, the Centre for Ocean Ventures & Entrepreneurship (COVE), the Verschuren Centre, the Emera ideaHUB, and Volta.

COVE is focussed on start-ups in the marine technology sector. Its waterfront facility provides access for marine product testing. The organization typically has sixty or more marine tech companies working on site. COVE works closely with Canada's Ocean Supercluster. Melanie Nadeau, COVE's CEO, outlined the objective of her organization in an *Insights* podcast with us:

> COVE was founded with a mission to propel and commercialize marine technology to create the world's next commercial and revolutionary tech advances. It's where start-ups and scale-ups find a home, where they can turn their ideas into reality with the support and resources they need to succeed. The infrastructure is designed to support and nurture budding entrepreneurs and established companies. But beyond the physical infrastructure, the spirit of innovation and collaboration truly sets the region apart. By fostering a culture of creativity and entrepreneurship, COVE has become a hub for innovative ideas and groundbreaking technologies driving the blue economy forward.

Volta, founded in 2013 as Volta Labs, is focussed on the tech sector across the region, providing tech start-ups with resources and mentorship during their early-stage development. Since its founding, Volta has supported nearly two hundred start-ups and has helped raise more than $400 million in venture capital for its clients, creating more than thirty-five hundred jobs. Matt Cooper is Volta's CEO.

Invest Nova Scotia, formerly Innovacorp, provides both equity and programming support for the start-up community. It provides early-stage venture capital, as former Innovacorp CEO, Malcolm Fraser, told us in our 2022 *Insights* podcast with him:

> Our mission is to find, fund, and foster early-stage companies that are trying to change the world. So we're looking for really interesting new technologies that are trying to commercialize at a global scale. That is really the focus. We have a $40 million venture fund where we make direct investments into

> *early-stage companies in Nova Scotia. We do some indirect investing as well into other funds.*

Innovacorp helped launch Meta Materials Inc. (META®) which was its first unicorn start-up (with a capital value of $1 billion). According to Fraser, Innovacorp invested $3 million into META and sold its shares for $101 million in 2021. It is highly unusual to have a thirty-five-times return on an investment, but that is both the risk and reward for venture funds. Unfortunately for Meta Materials, it has since been challenged to maintain its stock listing.

The Verschuren Centre, founded in 2011 and based in Sydney, NS, is an independent clean technology development and deployment facility. It offers support to companies in the sector by providing labs and manufacturing facilities and is focussed on biomanufacturing, bioagriculture, biomarine, energy, and decarbonization start-ups. The centre has only one of three bioreactors in the country and its capacity has been expanded more than ten times. Dr. Beth Mason, former CEO of the Verschuren Centre, told us:

> *The Verschuren Centre has built large-scale precision fermentation facilities to fill the capacity gap needed by scale-up companies across Canada. SME companies generating the materials, ingredients, and chemicals of tomorrow require access to this capacity to accelerate their path to market. By providing this shared-access business model, the VC provides efficient, cost-effective, and accelerated paths to deployment for companies in our shared ecosystem, with support from our Atlantic ecosystem partners, to ensure maximum success in deployment. Without access to these capital-intensive assets, companies would be unable to advance investment rounds and engage with large manufacturing partners targeted at a green supply chain.*

LOOKING FORWARD

One of the more interesting trends in start-ups within the region has been the diversification of entrepreneurs, as a recent cohort of the Genesis high-profile Enterprise program illustrates. This is a common trend among most of the accelerators and incubators in the region. The formation of the Sandpiper Venture Fund supports this diversification trend for women entrepreneurs. The increasing importance of First Nations in economic development is fostering opportunities for Indigenous communities, and organizations like the Black Business Initiative (BBI) have been instrumental in the development of Black entrepreneurs.

CHAPTER 16

RENEWED ENTREPRENEURSHIP AND ECONOMIC GROWTH

A SUCCESSFUL ATLANTIC CANADIAN ECONOMY IN THE YEARS AHEAD WILL BE one that has a good mix of national and international firms investing in the region as well as a thriving entrepreneurial culture. Entrepreneurs play a vital role in a successful economy as they strengthen competition between firms and are able to exploit new opportunities faster than larger, established firms. Because they are locally owned, decisions are made locally. This includes investment and growth-related decisions as well as supply-chain and charitable giving decisions.

We have interviewed dozens of entrepreneurs and the organizations that support them across Atlantic Canada since launching the *Insights* podcast in 2021 and have come away with a sense of optimism about the role they can play animating the regional economy in the coming years.

The data from Statistics Canada shows an increase in the number of Atlantic Canadians reporting self-employment income on their annual tax filings to the Canada Revenue Agency. While not all entrepreneurs are technically self-employed, the number working for themselves is a good proxy for what is going on with entrepreneurship in the region. After a number of years of decline, between 2010 and 2022 the number increased by nearly 14 percent, with much of that growth occurring in the past few years. Between 2019 and 2022, the number of self-employed persons across the four provinces increased by over ten thousand (figure 16-1). As of 2022, there were 157,000 self-employed persons in Atlantic Canada.

FIGURE 16-1: NUMBER OF TAX FILERS REPORTING SELF-EMPLOYMENT INCOME BY YEAR, ATLANTIC CANADA

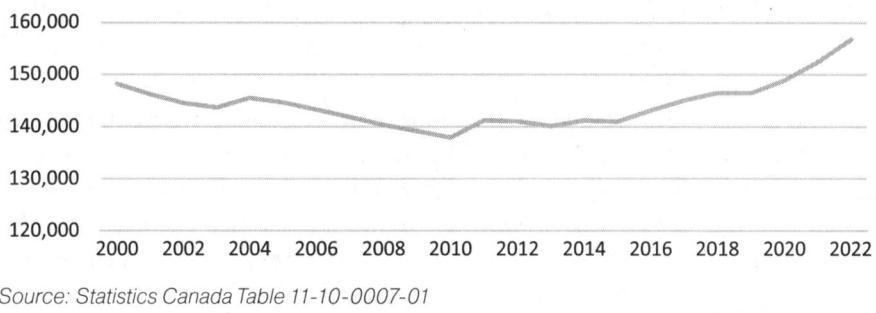

Source: Statistics Canada Table 11-10-0007-01

AGING ENTREPRENEURS

Atlantic Canada faces a challenge: a large number of people aged fifty-five and older who will be looking to retire in the next decade or so. Atlantic Canada needs a large influx of entrepreneurs just to take over from those about to exit their businesses. As shown in figure 16-2, over 40 percent of all persons identified as self-employed during the 2021 Census were over the age of fifty-five. Across the region, more than fifty-five thousand entrepreneurs will be retiring in the near future, and there is not a clear pathway to transitioning these businesses to new owners.

FIGURE 16-2: SHARE OF THE SELF-EMPLOYED WORKFORCE AGED 55 AND OLDER, 2021

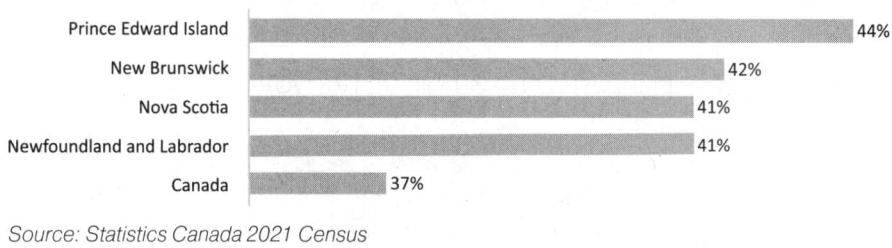

Source: Statistics Canada 2021 Census

Dan Kelly, CEO of the Canadian Federation of Independent Business, underscored the challenge the exit of the baby boomers from business poses in a 2024 *Insights* podcast:

> It is a big worry for us as an organization that serves small businesses, but it should be a big worry for public policy-makers more broadly. If you can believe it, 76 percent of small business owners plan to exit their business

within the next decade. That is such a huge number—$2 billion worth of business assets could change hands over the course of the next decade.... Sadly, only 9 percent of them have a formal succession plan in place. That's deeply worrisome.

The succession challenge exists in most industries but is particularly acute in the farming sector, where over 50 percent of farmers are set to retire in the near future. The Honourable Margaret Johnson, minister of Agriculture, Aquaculture, and Fisheries in New Brunswick discussed the extent of the challenge on *Insights*. She told us about her department's efforts to encourage young people to consider farming, such as going into middle and high schools to explain the career opportunities. The department also puts on fairs and other events to encourage people to consider farming. Increasingly, immigrant farmers are coming to New Brunswick to take over and expand farms.

It is clear that there are likely to be more sellers than buyers for all these businesses-in-transition over the next decade, and for many businesses looking to sell, there will be no buyers. This is an opportunity for governments to focus on attracting buyers from the immigrant community.

YOUTH ENTREPRENEURSHIP

Young people are less likely to be self-employed in Atlantic Canada than those in other parts of the country. This is a concern, particularly in light of the large share of entrepreneurs heading toward retirement. As shown in figure 16-3, Nova Scotia, New Brunswick, and Newfoundland and Labrador rank eighth, ninth, and tenth among the ten provinces for the share of persons aged twenty-five to thirty-four who claimed to be self-employed on the 2021 Census.

FIGURE 16-3: SELF-EMPLOYED AS A SHARE OF THE WORKFORCE AGED 25–34, BY PROVINCE, 2021

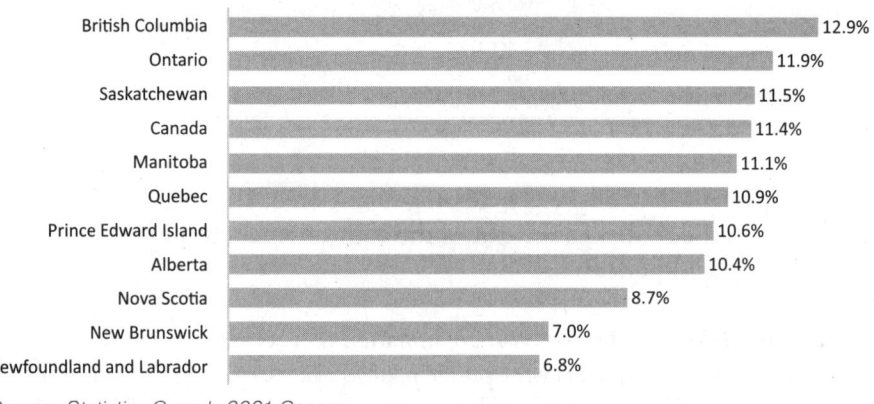

Province	%
British Columbia	12.9%
Ontario	11.9%
Saskatchewan	11.5%
Canada	11.4%
Manitoba	11.1%
Quebec	10.9%
Prince Edward Island	10.6%
Alberta	10.4%
Nova Scotia	8.7%
New Brunswick	7.0%
Newfoundland and Labrador	6.8%

Source: Statistics Canada 2021 Census

Among the twenty-five to thirty-four age group there are 40 percent fewer entrepreneurs in Newfoundland and Labrador than in the country overall. The variance in New Brunswick is about the same.

ENTREPRENEURSHIP BY INDUSTRY

There has been a shift in self-employment rates by industry in Atlantic Canada over the past twenty years or so. The share of employment in personal services industries such as hairstyling and pet grooming has declined across the region, likely due to the rise of firms that are consolidating business activity in those sectors. This consolidation is also happening in other industries such as veterinary services, dental services, and auto dealerships.

The transportation sector is also seeing a decline in self-employment numbers (this includes owner-operator truck drivers). In New Brunswick, the share of workers employed in the transportation and warehousing industry who worked for themselves declined from 18 percent in 1998 to 12 percent in 2022. In Nova Scotia, the decline was even more pronounced, dropping from 16 percent in 1998 to just over 9 percent in 2022. Newfoundland and Labrador saw a similar decline.

Following the national trend, there are now fewer self-employed people in agriculture. The data for Newfoundland and Labrador was not available, but in the three Maritime provinces, the number declined by 28 percent between 1998 and 2022.

The professional services sector in Atlantic Canada has also seen a decline in the relative share who are self-employed. This sector includes engineering firms, accountants, law firms, management consulting companies, and other professional services. While the total number of people employed in this sector across the region has risen strongly in the past twenty-five years, the share claiming to be self-employed dropped from 31 percent in 1998 to 23 percent in 2022. This is in part a national trend, but it is more pronounced in this region.

One final example is the construction sector. This is an industry with a traditionally high rate of self-employment as many plumbers, electricians, and other trades hang out a shingle and work for themselves. In recent years there has been less entrepreneurship in construction. The share of the construction sector workforce who identify as self-employed dropped from 27 percent of the total in 1998 to 20 percent in 2022.

THE RISE OF THE MICRO-ENTREPRENEUR

Another interesting trend has been the rise of the micro-entrepreneur. Atlantic Canada, like the rest of the country, is witnessing a rise in the number of small entrepreneurs reporting less than $30,000 in income to the Canada Revenue Agency (CRA) on an annual basis. These are referred to as non-employers by the CRA. There has been a 12 percent rise in non-employers in Prince Edward Island in just the four-year period between 2019 and 2023. In Nova Scotia and New Brunswick, the growth rate was 8 percent and 7 percent, respectively.

There are big variances based on industry. The number of micro-entrepreneurs in the fishing sector across Atlantic Canada has risen 15 percent over the four-year period between 2019 and 2023—a gain of over fifteen hundred non-employers. Not surprisingly, there has been a significant increase in the number of micro-businesses in the real estate sector responding to growing demand for real estate agents and other services. There were nearly forty-one hundred more non-employers in the real estate sector between 2019 and 2023, a 19 percent increase.

More self-employed people are setting up businesses in the health-care sector (up 23 percent) and the motion picture and sound recording industries (up 16 percent). The rise in delivery services across the country has led to a spike in self-employment. The couriers and messengers' sector has seen among the fastest growth in non-employers, with a 44 percent increase over 2019 to 2023 time frame.

ENTREPRENEURS WHO BREAK OUT

One of the constant debates is the definition of an entrepreneur. Most people equate business owners in general with entrepreneurship, but others reserve that term for people who have an idea they want to take to the world. For some, an entrepreneur is someone who wants to build a large company and not just someone operating a small business.

For the purposes here, we take the broader definition. We believe that an Atlantic Canada with a thriving entrepreneurial culture will lead to better local competition for goods and services; a few will step out of the pack and build globally competitive companies from this region. We have hundreds of examples of entrepreneurs from one end of the region to the other who have built a local company and then had the ambition to develop markets in the rest of Canada and around the world.

In our many podcast discussions with people involved with accelerators and incubators across the region, we've seen a change in the ambition of those in the start-up community that is important to emphasize. More and more, young entrepreneurs in the region are focussed on building products and services for national and international markets. As previously mentioned, it only takes a few winners, like Verafin with its thousand employees in St. John's, NL, to make a real difference in the region.

ENCOURAGING ENTREPRENEURSHIP

Not everyone is interested in or has the risk tolerance for entrepreneurship. But for those who do, Atlantic Canada provides a supportive environment. This includes access to capital and entrepreneur support services across the region. One important source of new entrepreneurs is the newcomer population. Immigrants in Atlantic Canada are 65 percent more likely to be self-employed than non-immigrants.[25]

We need to do more to expose young Atlantic Canadians to the possibilities of entrepreneurship as a career path. They need to be taught what it means to start a business, and about the process and the opportunities. Our educational system needs to do a better job of exposing young people to the possibility of becoming entrepreneurs. At the least, programs like Junior Achievement need to be better supported across our secondary school system in the region.

On the other end of the spectrum, we are seeing a rise in the number of entrepreneurs aged sixty and older, some of whom are starting small businesses to supplement their income and to stay active in the workforce.

As we look to the future, Atlantic Canada needs to be a place that is fostering more entrepreneurs across all sectors of the economy.

CHAPTER 17
BECOMING A MORE INNOVATIVE PLACE

ATLANTIC CANADA HAS ALWAYS RELIED HEAVILY ON NATURAL RESOURCES AS its primary source of economic development. In the Maritime provinces, fish, forests, and farming account for a large share of output, and Newfoundland and Labrador generates a larger share of its GDP from offshore oil and minerals development than any other province in Canada.

The region also has many other sectors that focus on export markets, including manufacturing industries such as rubber products (Michelin), and aerospace (Pratt & Whitney), and service industries such as information technology and business-support services. Because so much of what the region consumes is imported, a strong export economy will be key to the region's long-term prosperity.

Because of increasing global competition, rising operating cost pressures at home, and workforce-development challenges, many of the region's export-focussed sectors are under increased pressure. To maintain profitability and competitiveness, they will need to either find ways to drive down costs or to develop new, innovative products and services for which they are able to charge higher prices.

Many of the region's exporters are less productive than their competition in the rest of Canada and beyond. As shown in figure 17-1, across all business-sector industries combined, the three Maritime provinces have a much lower level of labour productivity than the country overall. ("Labour productivity" is the ratio between real value added and hours worked.) This is true for many of the region's important export sectors, including food manufacturing, wood products, chemicals, and fabricated metal products. Productivity is also a challenge in many export-focussed service industries including IT services, R & D services, and architectural, engineering, and related services.

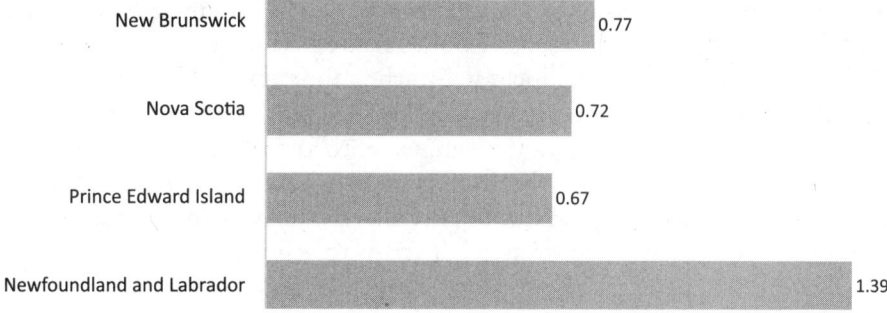

FIGURE 17-1: LABOUR PRODUCTIVITY IN 2023, BUSINESS-SECTOR INDUSTRIES (CANADA = 1.00)

NOTE: LABOUR PRODUCTIVITY IS THE RATIO BETWEEN REAL VALUE ADDED AND HOURS WORKED.

Source: Statistics Canada Table 36-10-0480-01

It should be noted that Newfoundland and Labrador's business sector is more productive than the country's overall, but this is mainly because of one industry. The offshore oil and gas industry generates $2,700 in value-added activity per worker hour, compared to only $76/hour across the economy. When productivity in the oil and gas sector (as well as in other mining) is removed, the province is actually less productive across most sectors of the economy. Of the more than three hundred industries for which Statistics Canada provides labour productivity data, Newfoundland and Labrador's productivity is below the national level.

It's also worth noting that the challenge of competitiveness increasingly applies not just to export sectors but also to industries that only operate in local markets. As an example, New Brunswick alone imported over $300 million worth of architectural, engineering, and related services from other provinces and countries in 2019, up 45 percent between 2010 and 2019. The province also imported over $370 million in information technology services, $145 million in office administrative services, and over $125 million in legal services. This is business that could be going to firms in the province. Firms doing business only in Atlantic Canada face increased competition from firms outside the region and will need to do more to increase competitiveness in the coming years to retain and grow their business.

HOW DOES THE REGION BECOME MORE INNOVATIVE?

According to the Conference Board (a non-partisan think tank whose areas of expertise include economic indicators, sustainability, corporate philanthropy, social responsibility, and sustainable capitalism), Atlantic Canada ranks near the bottom for its innovation capacity—not only in comparison to other provinces, but also to other countries. In its 2021 *Innovation Report Card*, the Board gave both New Brunswick and Prince Edward Island a D-minus; Nova Scotia and Newfoundland and Labrador both received a D. Among the twenty-six countries and provinces included in the report card, New Brunswick and Prince Edward Island ranked last and second-last. Nova Scotia and Newfoundland and Labrador ranked nineteenth and twentieth, respectively.

Table 17-1 shows how the four provinces scored on nine different innovation-related variables. New Brunswick received very low marks for the number of published scientific articles, access to venture capital, business R & D, number of patents, labour productivity, and automation vulnerability. Newfoundland and Labrador has been slowly moving up the rankings (to an A) due to substantial public investment in R & D and a rise in the number of start-up companies. Nova Scotia leads the country in public-sector R & D spending, but it is unclear if that spending is translating into broader innovation in the economy. Prince Edward Island also has a strong pipeline of new firms and good public-sector investment in R & D.

TABLE 17-1: 2021 INNOVATION REPORT CARD RESULTS BY VARIABLE

	NB	NL	NS	PEI
Overall	D-	D	D	D-
Public R & D	C	A	A+	B
Scientific articles	D	B	B	D
Entrepreneurial ambition	B	C	C	B
Venture capital	D	D	D	D-
Business R & D	D-	D-	D-	D-
Patents	D-	D-	D-	D-
Enterprise entry	C	A	C	A
Labour productivity	D-	C	D-	D-
Automation vulnerability	D	D	C	D

Source: Conference Board of Canada

The primary focus in the years ahead must be on driving a more innovative culture among the public and private sectors. The region has chronically invested far less in research than provinces such as Ontario, Quebec, and British Columbia. In 2022, industry, government, and institutions in Ontario invested nearly three times as much in R & D as their counterparts in New Brunswick, adjusted for population size. Even Alberta has per capita gross expenditure on research and development (GERD) 80 percent higher compared to New Brunswick. The good news in New Brunswick is that per capita R & D spending increased faster than the national average between 2017 and 2022. Prince Edward Island had the slowest growth among the ten provinces.

TABLE 17-2: GROSS EXPENDITURE ON RESEARCH AND DEVELOPMENT (GERD), $MILLION AND PER CAPITA (2022)

	2022 ($M)	Per capita	5 year % change*
Canada	$51,685	$1,327	34%
Newfoundland and Labrador	$467	$879	11%
Prince Edward Island	$102	$610	7%
Nova Scotia	$940	$917	30%
New Brunswick	$476	$588	38%
Quebec	$12,657	$1,459	28%
Ontario	$23,673	$1,563	39%
Manitoba	$1,000	$708	9%
Saskatchewan	$921	$782	35%
Alberta	$4,747	$1,052	35%
British Columbia	$6,657	$1,243	45%

*CHANGE TO THE PER CAPITA FIGURES.
Source: Statistics Canada Table 27-10-0273-01

PRIVATE-SECTOR INVESTMENT

The private sector in Atlantic Canada needs to invest more in research. According to Statistics Canada, businesses in Prince Edward Island only invested $44 million in total on in-house R & D expenditures in 2022. In Ontario, adjusted for population size, businesses invested three and a half times more than those in Prince Edward Island. New Brunswick and Nova Scotia are also at the bottom of the pile compared to other provinces.

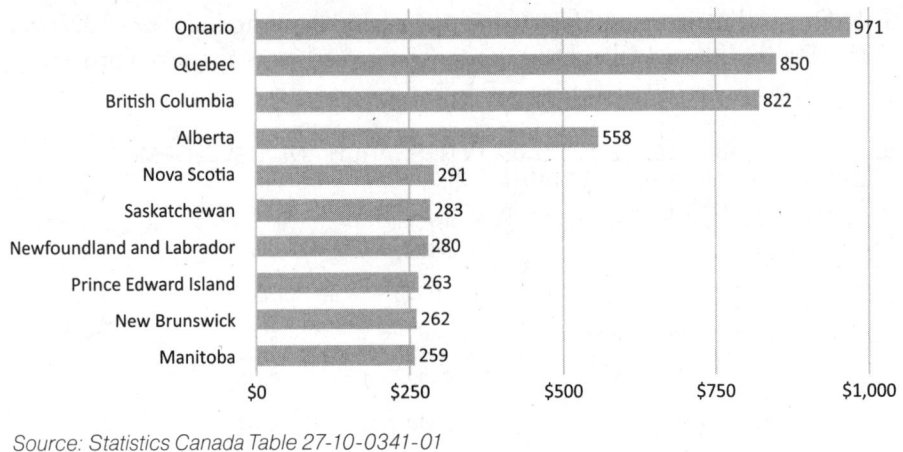

FIGURE 17-2: IN-HOUSE R & D EXPENDITURES PER CAPITA, BUSINESS ENTERPRISE SECTOR (2022)

Source: Statistics Canada Table 27-10-0341-01

RETURN ON RESEARCH INVESTMENT

Investing in research is not an end in itself. Nova Scotia leads the country in public-sector investment in R & D, but it is not clear that this investment is translating into more innovation across the economy. Governments, universities, and businesses should be focussed on driving innovation and competitiveness. The fact the Conference Board gave all four Atlantic provinces a D-minus for the number of patents is one indication that university, business, and institutional research spending is not translating into results.

This is not to suggest that early-stage research, or more speculative research, does not have a place on the research agenda. However, because the regional economy is falling behind in competitiveness, it is imperative that the research agenda be primarily focussed on investments that are meant to boost productivity and innovation.

LEVERAGING PRIVATE INVESTMENT

Atlantic Canada has relatively low levels of business enterprise investment in R & D. Another way to look at this is based on the gross domestic expenditures on R & D by funder data from Statistics Canada, as shown in table 17-3. Using this data, the Atlantic provinces rank comparatively low. Nova Scotia performs the best among the four provinces, but mainly because of high investment by the federal government and higher education sectors. New Brunswick ranks last in the country for R & D investment per capita and doesn't rank higher than eighth worst from any funding source.

Governments should use public investment to leverage private-sector spending on R & D. For example, Nova Scotia has relatively high levels of R & D investment from both the federal government and higher-education sectors. Why has that not translated into more business investment in R & D? Nova Scotia ranks eighth for provincial government investment in R & D. Would a larger provincial investment be able to leverage more private funding? Prince Edward Island generates less R & D spending across all sectors. Would a boost in provincial funding lead to more investment by other sectors?

TABLE 17-3: GROSS DOMESTIC EXPENDITURES ON R & D BY FUNDER, PER CAPITA (2022)

Funder	Newfoundland and Labrador	Prince Edward Island	Nova Scotia	New Brunswick	Canada-wide
Total, all sectors	$879	$610	$917	$588	$1,327
Federal government sector	$154	$114	$237	$99	$215
Provincial governments sector	$17	$24	$25	$23	$60
Business enterprise sector	$363	$209	$251	$214	$628
Higher education sector	$290	$197	$309	$180	$229
Private non-profit sector	$9	$24	$45	$27	$63
Foreign sector	$45	$42	$51	$43	$132
Provincial rank (out of 10)					
Total, all sectors	6	9	5	10	
Federal government sector	7	9	2	10	
Provincial governments sector	10	7	6	8	
Business enterprise sector	5	10	6	9	
Higher education sector	2	7	1	9	
Private non-profit sector	10	9	6	8	
Foreign sector	8	10	5	9	

Source: Statistics Canada Table 27-10-0273-01

THE NEED FOR MORE INNOVATION

A culture of innovation goes beyond just investing in R & D. An innovative jurisdiction will see hundreds of companies starting up to address specific market opportunities. These opportunities can be in targeted industries such as oceans, clean technology, and energy or in other sectors as well.

The Conference Board *Innovation Report Card* ranked the region fairly strongly in the area of entrepreneurial ambition (two Bs and two Cs) and enterprise entry (two As and two Cs). The Board uses the percentage of the population aged eighteen to sixty-four who report being early-stage entrepreneurs as the measure for entrepreneurial ambition. It uses the number of new firms as a share of all active firms as its measure for enterprise entry. The data site *Entrevestor* has tracked an increase in the number of start-up firms across the region in recent years.

ATTRACTING NATIONAL AND INTERNATIONAL INVESTMENT

According to the Canadian Venture Capital and Private Equity Association (CVCA), Canadian firms attracted $10 billion in venture capital in 2022. Atlantic Canadian firms attracted only about 2.3 percent of that venture capital. Relative to regional GDP, that represents less than half of the venture capital in the rest of the country. That underinvestment pattern has been largely the same for many years. The same trend exists with private equity. The CVCA reports that in 2022, Atlantic Canadian firms attracted less than 1 percent of the total private equity invested across the country.

As shown in table 17-4, adjusted for size, Atlantic Canada ranks last in the country for private equity and, with the exception of Nova Scotia, near the bottom for venture capital.

TABLE 17-4: VENTURE CAPITAL AND PRIVATE EQUITY INVESTMENT BY PROVINCE, 2022

	Private equity	Venture capital	Private equity	Venture capital	Private equity	Venture capital
	$million		per capita		provincial rank	
Newfoundland and Labrador	$2	$11	$4	$21	8	10
Prince Edward Island	$0	$4	$0	$25	10	9
Nova Scotia	$92	$149	$94	$152	7	5
New Brunswick	$2	$66	$3	$84	9	7
Quebec	$5,800	$1,500	$676	$175	1	3
Ontario	$2,200	$4,700	$149	$319	5	1
Manitoba	$146	$101	$106	$73	6	8
Saskatchewan	$240	$136	$204	$115	2	6
Alberta	$700	$729	$158	$165	4	4
British Columbia	$926	$1,600	$180	$310	3	2

Source: Canadian Venture Capital Association (CVCA)

INNOVATION AND A PROSPEROUS ATLANTIC CANADA

Despite the current turbulence in the global economy, there is no doubt innovation will be key to Atlantic Canada's prosperity in the years ahead. Continuing to rely on a model of low value-added commodity exports is not a good strategy. Driving productivity and innovation in traditional sectors and in new industries will help drive up incomes, create more wealth, and ensure the region is competitive in the years ahead.

CHAPTER 18
THE PROSPERITY DISPARITY

ATLANTIC CANADA, LIKE THE REST OF THE COUNTRY, IS BECOMING MORE urbanized with each passing year, although Atlantic Canada has been much slower to urbanize than the rest of the country due to much slower population growth over many decades. As a consequence, more than twice as many Atlantic Canadians than Canadians reside in rural communities. The overreliance on seasonal employment, especially from the resource sectors like forestry and fishing, has led to a higher proportion of the population living in less favourable economic conditions. As an example, the Halifax CMA is home to about 45 percent of Nova Scotia's population but represents nearly 58 percent of its GDP. Access to high-speed internet is allowing more people to make a living in rural communities across the country, but it is clear that the growth in the population in Atlantic Canada will be increasingly focussed on urban communities.

SIX DOMINANT URBAN COMMUNITIES

Within the region, Halifax, Charlottetown, St. John's, Fredericton, Moncton, and Saint John represent nearly 47 percent of the total population (based on the 2021 Census) and account for a disproportionate share of the total economy in the region. The five CMAs (Charlottetown is not a CMA) are home to only 42 percent of Atlantic Canada's population but contribute 53 percent of its GDP.

The six communities have enjoyed more economic prosperity and have had lower unemployment levels than the rest of Atlantic Canada, mostly in line with other cities in Canada. In Canada, 84 percent of Canadians live in census metropolitan areas (CMAs) or census agglomerations (CAs) that are formed by one or more adjacent municipalities centred around an urban core.

At the same time, all of these communities support the economies of smaller surrounding urban communities by providing nearby economic, educational, recreational, and entertainment opportunities, as well as retail and professional services, all within a reasonable driving distance.

The importance of urban centres like Halifax is not well enough understood. Halifax, as an example, draws thousands of people to the city every day from the Annapolis Valley, the South Shore, Colchester County, and the Eastern Shore, commuting up to an hour or more each day to the city for work. Halifax is an economic hub for more than half the population of Nova Scotia, allowing many living in more rural communities to benefit from the amenities and job opportunities provided by a nearby urban economy. To some extent, Halifax's importance as an economic driver is replicated by the other major urban centre in the region, supporting and benefitting those living in nearby rural communities. As previously referenced, more than 80 percent of Atlantic Canadians live within commuting distance of an urban community.

RURAL ECONOMIC DEVELOPMENT

Over the years, there has been a big effort by both governments and industry to help less prosperous communities with economic development through business attraction. Frankly, much of that effort has failed, although there have been notable exceptions like Michelin in Nova Scotia. Trying to attract or relocate business activity to more rural communities does not largely work. Unless there is a successful local entrepreneur such as John Bragg, the owner of Oxford Foods, willing to invest in their home community, it is very difficult to attract any type of investment beyond resource-based ventures like mining or forestry.

The importance of these rural business leaders is reflected in the innovative methods they use to attract talent to their rural businesses. In an *Insights* podcast, Bragg gave an example of housing assistance that he uses to attract and retain talent:

> *We're not so much in the mortgage business as we are an assistance program, where we contribute the down payment for a home, which amounts to say $20,000 as the down payment. It's hard for young people to collect the first $20,000 together; if they can get the down payment, then they can get a mortgage and they can move on. So, what we've done with sixty individuals is we've provided the down payment. And then we write that off over ten years; if they leave within three years, they have to pay it back. If they leave after four years, they get 40 percent credit, and so on. If they leave after seven years, they get a 70 percent credit, but this allows, especially young people, but also other people, to get the down payment.*

He went on to add that this program helped make the case for a new high school in the community during the term of Premier John Hamm. Bragg also provides a $3,000 bursary per year for anyone graduating from that high school who attends university, and a similar $2,000 bursary per year for those attending community college.

The best way to support rural economic development is by building the needed infrastructure to access—either physically or remotely via the internet—nearby economic opportunities.

I (*Don Mills*) have long argued for the creation of economic hubs to help support nearby rural communities. The best way to ensure the sustainability and economic viability of rural communities across the region is to ensure that nearby urban communities are the focus of economic development to generate full-time, year-round job opportunities for those living within reasonable commuting distances. Centralizing the delivery of public services, especially health care, is an example of an opportunity to utilize the critical mass associated with economic hubs to provide enhanced health-care services (like diagnostic equipment or specialized health-care practices like cancer treatment) in closer proximity to rural areas. To some extent, this is already happening through expanding larger regional primary care centres. There are thirty urban communities (communities with a population of five thousand or more) across Atlantic Canada that serve more than 80 percent of the population within a forty-five-minute commute. This creates the opportunity to enhance these regional primary care centres to deliver more comprehensive health-care services to those living in smaller nearby rural communities. Nova Scotia and New Brunswick are already moving in this direction by converting some rural hospitals to urgent care centres which are not open 24/7 but serve to divert less critical medical services from emergency rooms in larger communities.

THE CASE FOR IMPROVED INFRASTRUCTURE

Twinning the highway between Halifax and Moncton was one of the best economic development decisions at the time. The twinning of the highways created an economic corridor that not only improved the economic prosperity of the two cities but also facilitated transportation for tourism and provided quicker access to all of the communities between the two centres. The transportation of goods and services became more efficient, and road safety improved.

The twinning projects have continued over the years. In New Brunswick, the Frank McKenna government connected the three southern cities of Fredericton, Saint John, and Moncton in the 1990s. Later, the highway to the US border from Saint John was twinned. In Nova Scotia, twinning projects from Halifax to the Annapolis Valley, to the South Shore, and toward the Canso Causeway have recently been extended. There is still more work to be done to interconnect the economic corridors within each of the four Atlantic provinces.

The same case can be made for high-speed internet, which is now considered to be a right for citizens everywhere. The government of Canada's goal is to have high-speed connectivity available to 98 percent of the population by 2026 and 100 percent of the population by 2030. Currently 94 percent of all Canadians have internet access through a fixed broadband connection. With the advent of satellite internet services such as Starlink, the possibility of universal high-speed internet service is close to reality, providing almost everyone with the ability to work from home anywhere and to have the same access to the world. This is the democratization of geography, which essentially ensures an even playing field regardless of where people might choose to live.

Lee Bragg, the CEO of Eastlink, underscored the challenges of high-speed internet expansion on an *Insights* podcast. Bragg indicated that it cost about $50,000 a kilometre to construct the infrastructure required to deliver high-speed service to rural communities and that costs have to be subsidized by public funds because there are too few customers per kilometre to pay for those costs in very remote rural areas. Even the monthly costs of broadband services are subsidized to some extent by those living in urban areas in Atlantic Canada.

Access to educational facilities is another important aspect of ensuring a more even distribution of economic prosperity. Within Atlantic Canada, there are more than thirty communities that offer post-secondary educational opportunities, including either universities or community colleges or both, again serving more than 80 percent of the population within a forty-five-minute commute. Atlantic Canada has among the highest proportion of college graduates in Canada.

Increasing demand for skilled trades is opening up new opportunities for young people and helping with youth retention within the region. Atlantic Canada would benefit from a shift in attitude away from streaming young people toward universities to instead considering the skilled trades and the education provided by community colleges as a way to improve their economic prospects.

The Confederation Bridge is another example of the importance of crucial infrastructure. The construction of the Confederation Bridge that was completed in 1997 at a cost of $1.3 billion and has provided a clear economic boost to Prince Edward Island by providing a more reliable and high-capacity link between mainland Canda and the Island. It has been particularly important to the tourism and agriculture sectors. It was Premier Joe Ghiz who called for a plebiscite in 1988 that led to the decision to proceed with the construction of the bridge.

Another example of the importance of infrastructure was the construction of the Nova Centre in Halifax. The new convention centre has not only been a boon for the urban core, but has also helped stimulate the development of the core of the city. According to its annual report for 2023–24, the

Halifax convention centre attracted 155 events, of which 40 were national and international (including the Juno Awards), attracting over 95,000 guests from around the world. These events generated more than $70 million for the economy in Nova Scotia. It should be noted that the Nova Centre generated a profit of $3.5 million from its operations in 2023–24.

TOO MANY ECONOMIC DEVELOPMENT AGENCIES

There has been an enormous amount of investment in economic development at the municipal, provincial, and federal levels over the years. The Atlantic Canada Opportunities Agency has grown to have a budget of half a billion dollars and more than six hundred employees, far beyond the size envisioned by Donald Savoie, the father of ACOA. It is likely if you were to add up all the money spent by municipalities, regional development agencies, and various provincial and federal government departments and agencies on economic development efforts, the total would easily exceed $1 billion per year. Yet until the population began to grow recently, there was little evidence that this investment had made any material difference, certainly not in terms of improving overall economic growth in the region or increased employment. There has long been a challenge for these economic development agencies to provide measures of performance to demonstrate a tangible return on investment. There is little doubt that there are too many economic development agencies in the region, many with overlapping and competing responsibilities, without sufficient evidence that they are making an economic difference. The lack of accountability has been a problem for some time.

The Halifax Partnership, the private–public partnership responsible for economic development in Halifax, offers a good model for other economic development agencies in the region. Before its funding is renewed, the board must not only have their strategy endorsed by their major funder (the Halifax Regional Municipality) but must also present metrics of performance that demonstrate the impact of their efforts. This accountability ensures that the focus of staff and the board is outcome oriented. Interestingly, the Halifax Partnership uses a community-wide consultative process in the development of its five-year strategies that helps ensure widespread endorsement of the final strategy.

There is little question that there needs to be a review of both the number and roles of the economic development agencies in Atlantic Canada. The recent creation of Envision as the regional economic development agency for the greater Saint John area follows the example established by the Halifax Partnership, which had previously been adopted by the Cape Breton Partnership and the Pictou County Partnership. As Wendy Luther, the CEO of the Halifax Partnership pointed out in an *Insights* interview, there is a need to better understand the greater good of working together:

> *I want to capture a point you just made about Halifax's place in the region. If Halifax is successful, Atlantic Canada will be successful, and if Atlantic Canada is successful, Halifax is going to be successful. So, we are the economic engine for the region, but we require the whole region—not just Nova Scotia, the whole region—to be successful, and we are allies. We are not competing against Moncton or anywhere else in Atlantic Canada, but we do have the ability to really drive economic growth throughout Atlantic Canada and we intend to take that role very seriously. As one concrete example, the Halifax Partnership sits on the council of the Consider Canada City Alliance. It's the consortium of major municipalities across Canada. We are the only municipality in Atlantic Canada with representation at that national table, but we have Atlantic Canada in mind when we move that forward in terms of strategies.*

This is the type of co-operative attitude that we need in Atlantic Canada. It is really about Atlantic Canadians working together in everyone's best interest.

LOOKING FORWARD

Sharing prosperity needs a strategy and commitment. It will not happen organically. We need to reconsider our economic development model in Atlantic Canada, beginning with a recognition that economic growth is largely driven by urban communities, and urban communities can help support and develop nearby rural communities.

We need more integrated urban economic development agencies like the Halifax Partnership, which is responsible for economic growth, not only within the urban centre, but in suburban and rural communities as well. All thirty urban communities within Atlantic Canada need to have a population and labour force growth strategy. The six major urban centres already do. There needs to be an immigrant attraction and retention strategy for every community of size. Perhaps more importantly, we need to understand that success in one community is success for everyone in the region.

CHAPTER 19

EXPANDING THE DEFINITION OF ECONOMIC DEVELOPMENT

A LOT OF TIME AND RESOURCES HAVE BEEN SPENT ON ECONOMIC DEVELOPment in Atlantic Canada, with mixed results at best. In the 1970s, '80s, and '90s, economic development organizations in Atlantic Canada spent most of their time and effort trying to attract national and international firms to set up here and to help exporters already in the region expand their sales into outside markets. In the years since, there has been an expanded focus on fostering new start-up companies and boosting innovation.

How do we define economic development—not as something passive but something active? How do we define proactive efforts by government, local communities, and other stakeholders to foster a prosperous and sustainable economy? If you were to ask people involved in economic development, you might hear such things as:

"Our job is to provide funding for small and medium-sized companies."

"Our job is to convince national and international firms to invest here."

"Our job is to market and promote our community."

"We do economic development. Other departments do workforce development."

We need to broaden our definition of economic development. Successful economic development is now (and likely always was) about properly identifying the roadblocks to business investment and then clearing those roadblocks. It is no longer about seeking investment, but creating the conditions that attract investment. This is the exact model that Envision Saint John is employing.

This definition matters now more than ever. The roadblocks to a sustained level of business investment now include a lack of workers, a lack of places for new workers to live, not enough daycare spaces and child-care workers to ensure that everyone who wants to work can join the labour market, and many other issues that fall well outside the traditional activities of economic development organizations.

Our 2021 *Insights* discussion with Paulette Hicks, at that time the CEO of Envision Saint John, encompasses the new direction of economic development that is under way in the region, with the focus on ensuring that the market conditions are in place to support economic growth. Envision Saint John was the newly amalgamated regional economic development agency established to serve four municipalities within the greater Saint John area. Hicks outlined Envision's early goals and approach:

> *It is a new model. There are a lot of expectations on where we are going and what we are trying to achieve. Through the work of the board and this team, we've put a stake in the ground, and it is our ten-year outcome to grow this region by twenty-five thousand residents. We are looking to increase the property- or the municipal tax base, because municipalities want a return on their investment. They want to see that they are growing their base in their respective municipalities.*
>
> *We have put a stake in the ground that we will continue to grow and reposition and strengthen our regional brand as a place to live, a place to work, a place to study, and a place to invest. What is the role of the agency as it relates to our strategic priorities? Growth readiness in order to grow. In order to attract and retain we've got to be ready. We've got to be able to tick all those boxes and that we have a responsibility in this region to identify where the areas of opportunity are. So that whether it's housing or whether it's doctors that are needed, we need to make sure that we've got all the amenities in order to have a sticky talent acquisition pipeline.*

The growing recognition by economic development agencies like Envision of creating the conditions to attract talent and investment is an important change in thinking.

ENSURING A TALENT PIPELINE

Thirty years ago, there were too many people and not enough jobs across Atlantic Canada. Although the reality was more nuanced, it is true the region was turning out a lot of young people who ultimately left the region. That has changed dramatically in recent years. Figure 19-1 shows average annual net interprovincial migration to and from Nova Scotia by time frame going back to the early 1980s. In the recession of the early 1980s, Nova Scotia attracted more people from other provinces than it lost, but between the late 1980s and 2015, the region suffered a significant net loss of people to other provinces. The 2002–08 time frame featured the largest net outward migration with a net loss of nearly nineteen hundred people per year.

Since 2016, the migration flow has been decidedly positive with an average of 5,600 more people moving in than moving out over the six-year period to

2024. This does not include direct immigration or non-permanent residents.[26] It will be vitally important for the region to ensure there are enough workers to meet demand in the coming years. If businesses do not believe the talent will be available in the future, they could curtail investment in the region.

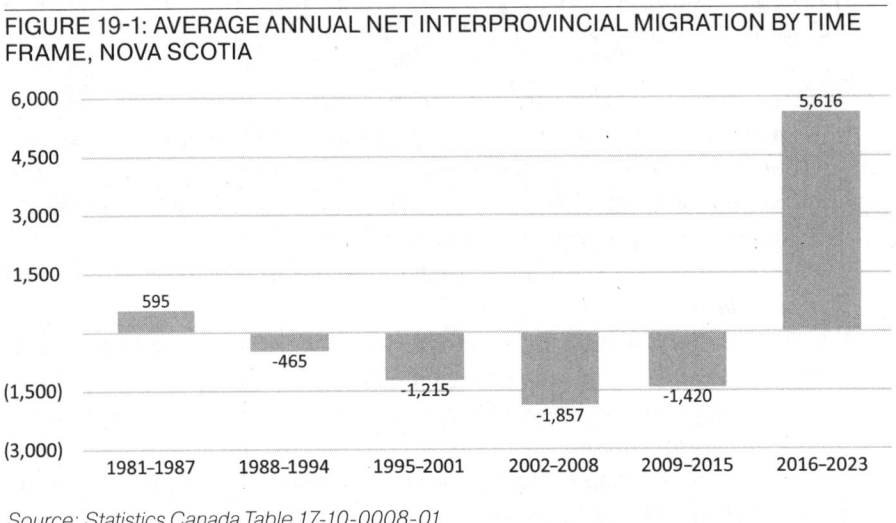

FIGURE 19-1: AVERAGE ANNUAL NET INTERPROVINCIAL MIGRATION BY TIME FRAME, NOVA SCOTIA

Source: Statistics Canada Table 17-10-0008-01

The availability of workers represents a bigger challenge in Atlantic Canada as it has an older workforce and a larger share heading toward retirement. It will be critical for the region's universities and colleges to help ensure there is enough talent to meet workforce demand in the years ahead. It will not be the role of economic development organizations to do the training, but they will need to shine a spotlight on the demand and the direct relationship between the talent pipeline and business investment.

The good news is that post-secondary education institutions are responding. In a recent *Insights* podcast, UNB's president and vice-chancellor, Paul Mazerolle, detailed the work being done at the university to boost enrollment in critical occupations such as health care, engineering, and computer science. The university is also expanding its role as a conduit for international talent and is looking to boost enrollment from outside Canada from 25 to 30 percent. The recent cap on international students is hoped to be a temporary measure.

The region's colleges are also stepping up. The seven public institutions delivering college programming in Atlantic Canada have over sixty thousand full- and part-time students annually at forty campuses across the region. They are evolving their curricula to meet the needs of the new workforce. As an example, the College of the North Atlantic in Newfoundland and

Labrador offers a wind turbine technician program, among others related to the growing renewable-energy sector in the region. The New Brunswick Community College has expanded its cybersecurity programs to support the growth of this sector in the province. In Nova Scotia, the community college network is expanding its ocean-related programming to support the growth of the ocean economy.

REMOVING ROADBLOCKS

Atlantic Canada will need to attract tens of thousands of people to the region over the next twenty years to ensure there are enough workers to support a growing economy. In the past four years, the region has added more population than at any time in history. This has put significant strain on the housing market, health care, education, and other local services. It will be important to build capacity across the region to support sustained population growth, particularly among the working-age population.

THE CHILD CARE EXAMPLE

One good example is child care. Many of the people moving in are under the age of thirty-five. In fact, according to Statistics Canada, there were more people aged twenty-five to thirty-four living in Atlantic Canada in 2021 than back in 2005. The population in that age group is expanding at a rate of nearly 2 percent per year. Access to high-quality early childhood education and child care services is an important consideration when people in this age group are considering where to locate. Figure 19-2 shows the ratio of child care workers in each province per one thousand persons under ten years old. Because of its generous daycare subsidy regime and other factors, Quebec has the most workers in these occupations of any province. Prince Edward Island and New Brunswick have an above-average ratio of child care workers to young children. However, it is important to point out that nearly 2,700 workers in the occupation categories of early childhood educators and assistants and home child care providers are aged fifty-five and older and will be retiring in the near future. The expansion of subsidized daycare will also lead to expanded demand for these services.

This is not just important as a quality-of-life consideration. A lack of child care workers can directly impact the workforce participation of women and men.

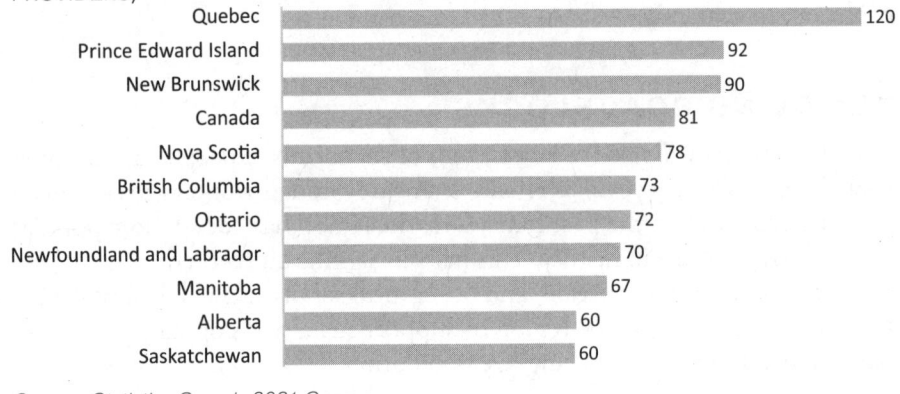

FIGURE 19-2: CHILD CARE WORKERS PER 1,000 PEOPLE AGED 0–9 BY PROVINCE, 2021
(INCLUDES EARLY CHILDHOOD EDUCATORS AND ASSISTANTS AND HOME CHILD CARE PROVIDERS)

Province	Workers
Quebec	120
Prince Edward Island	92
New Brunswick	90
Canada	81
Nova Scotia	78
British Columbia	73
Ontario	72
Newfoundland and Labrador	70
Manitoba	67
Alberta	60
Saskatchewan	60

Source: Statistics Canada 2021 Census

THE CRITICAL NEED FOR HOUSING

Having enough housing options at costs aligned with household income is a particular challenge in much of rural Atlantic Canada, where the number of houses built on an annual basis has dropped by 60–90 percent compared to the 1960s and 1970s. Jean-Claude Savoie, the founder of Groupe Savoie in Saint-Quentin in northwestern New Brunswick, decided to build housing for the company's workers just as many other large employers have done in rural areas. Without housing, the nascent population growth we are seeing in much of rural Atlantic Canada will be stifled.

One of the top challenges related to home-building is the lack of workers in the residential construction sector, particularly in skilled trades. This is an issue across the country, but it is particularly acute in Atlantic Canada. Because the region went for a long period with virtually no population growth, annual housing starts were relatively limited compared to places in Canada where the population was growing. When the regional population started to increase, the size of the residential construction sector workforce did keep pace.

In the early 2000s the residential construction workforce in Atlantic Canada was just under 9 percent of the total across the country. By 2023, only 6 percent of the national residential construction workforce was employed in Atlantic Canada, a relative decline of nearly 30 percent.

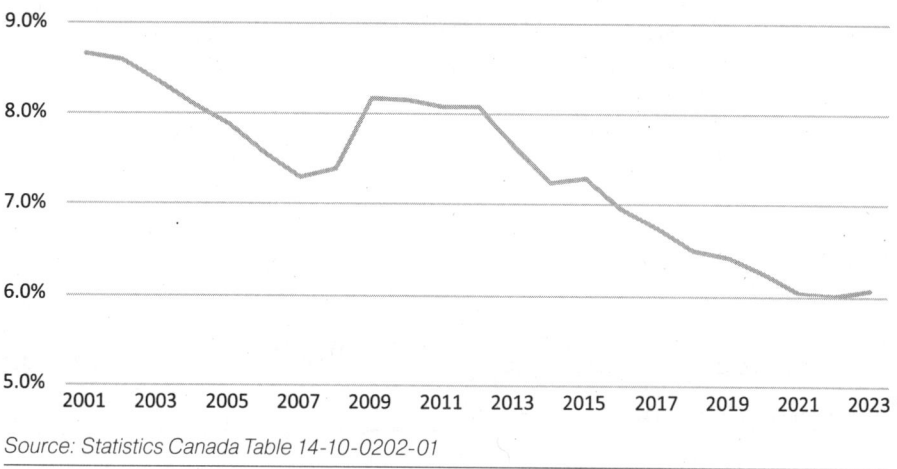

FIGURE 19-3: ATLANTIC CANADA'S RESIDENTIAL CONSTRUCTION SECTOR WORKFORCE RELATIVE TO THE NATIONAL WORKFORCE (% OF NATIONAL EMPLOYMENT IN THE RESIDENTIAL CONSTRUCTION SECTOR)

Source: Statistics Canada Table 14-10-0202-01

Provincial governments have responded. The number of people in skilled trades apprenticeship programs has increased significantly across the region. Further, there are now efforts under way to attract more skilled tradespersons from around the world. In an *Insights* podcast, Dan Mills, the deputy minister of Post-Secondary Education, Training, and Labour in New Brunswick talked about the province's goal of bringing in at least one thousand tradespeople per year from other countries, along with efforts to expand the local talent pool.

Nova Scotia has responded with a number of incentives to encourage more tradespeople to move to the province. In addition to a variety of incentives to encourage young people into trades training, the provincial government has eliminated the provincial income tax owed on the first $50,000 of income earned by workers under the age of thirty in eligible skilled trades.

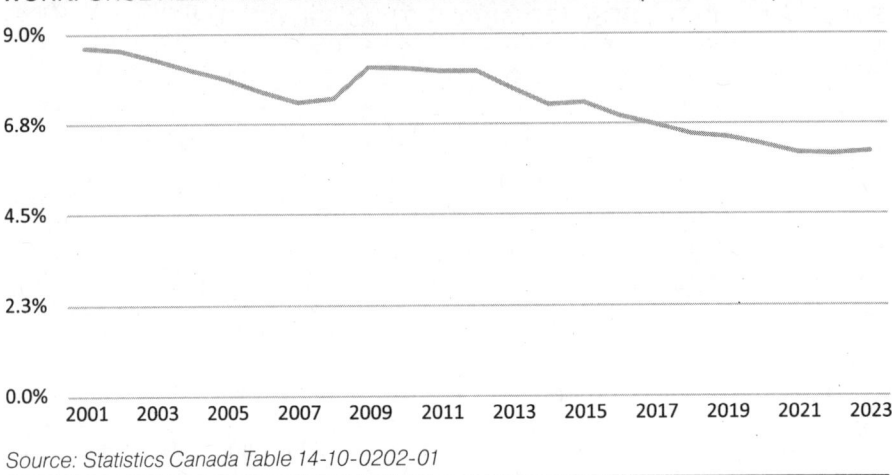

FIGURE 19-4: ATLANTIC CANADA'S RESIDENTIAL CONSTRUCTION SECTOR WORKFORCE RELATIVE TO THE NATIONAL WORKFORCE (2002 = 1.00)

Source: Statistics Canada Table 14-10-0202-01

IMMIGRANT SETTLEMENT SERVICES

The long-term retention of immigrants will be very important to the region's prosperity in the years ahead. Research suggests that newcomers who have strong early-stage settlement support are more likely to stay in an area long-term than those that do not.[27] The federal government, through the Department of Immigration, Refugees and Citizenship Canada (IRCC) primarily funds formal immigrant settlement services through agencies such as Immigrant Services Association of Nova Scotia (ISANS) and the Multicultural Agency of the Greater Moncton Area (MAGMA). In recent years there has been a substantial increase in the number of newcomers arriving in the region who are not eligible for IRCC-funded settlement support services (international students, temporary workers, and asylum seekers, for example). Provincial and local governments, along with other community stakeholders, should work with these agencies and other partners to ensure that all newcomers have access to support services.

A HIGH QUALITY OF LIFE

Now more than ever it is vitally important for communities large and small across Atlantic Canada to focus on their quality of life. It is not enough just to have available jobs and entrepreneurial opportunities; people are more mobile now than ever before. Communities must have high-quality green spaces (parks, trails, etc.), access to local services, good-quality health care and education services, and low crime rates.

Access to a good mix of local services is especially essential in smaller communities across the region. People will not want to drive beyond thirty to forty-five minutes to access basic services that should be available in nearby communities, assuming there is enough of a population base to justify the service.

A COMPETITIVE BUSINESS ENVIRONMENT

Ultimately, we should want Atlantic Canada to be a place where companies can make a good return on their investment. There are many ways the government has an influence on the competitiveness of jurisdictions. Chapter 22 looks at the importance of having a competitive tax environment. In addition to taxes, provincial and municipal governments should focus on creating a positive business environment in areas such as access to land for development, reducing red tape, and ensuring environmental and business development regulations are fair, transparent, and competitive with other jurisdictions.

MEASUREMENT FOR ECONOMIC DEVELOPMENT AGENCIES

There are numerous economic development agencies across Atlantic Canada at the federal, provincial, and municipal levels. Often there are overlapping mandates. At least $1 billion is spent on economic development in the region with a relatively unknown return on that investment. We have called for greater accountability for economic development and the need for meaningful metrics to measure the impact of those economic development measures. Unfortunately, few economic development agencies have such metrics. The Halifax Partnership is an example of an economic development agency that has always had performance measures. This has been largely driven by a mostly private-sector board of directors.

Wendy Luther, the president and CEO of the Halifax Partnership told us during an Insights podcast in 2023:

> *The key priorities are to stand up and resource the economic strategy. Don, you mentioned at the outset the importance of metrics and accountability. We have a scorecard for our business plan each year that we present to our board at every single Halifax Partnership board meeting. We also present that up through the Community Planning and Economic Development standing committee of regional Council and the mayor to show how we're progressing on the goals that we set in advance of the economic strategy being approved.*

> *We did receive approval on our scorecard that is based on this plan for this fiscal year. So top priorities are exactly as you see here in bringing those actions to life, and we have specific metrics that line up with all of them. We're seeking our private-sector, public-sector, and post-secondary partners' input on what is the most efficient and effective way to get from action to the measurement that we look to see.*

The Partnership releases its *Halifax Index* each year to update the community about its impact. The Partnership has four key goals with metrics: GDP growth, population growth, labour-force growth, and community well-being. Their recent economic strategy targets growing GDP to $25 billion, growing the population of Halifax to 525,000, and growing the labour force to 310,000 by 2027. Improving well-being of the community, while being measured by public opinion research, does not yet have a defined goal and is perhaps the most difficult to measure or directly impact.

THE FUTURE

There is no expectation that economic development organizations should be actively involved in addressing all these challenges. But these organizations are best positioned to educate government, the post-secondary sector, the community, and other stakeholders as to how these challenges impede economic growth.

PART THREE

A PRESCRIPTION FOR FUTURE PROSPERITY

CHAPTER 20
THE ROLE OF ECONOMIC HUBS

ECONOMIC CLUSTERS FOCUS ON INDUSTRIES THAT HOLD POTENTIAL FOR growth in the region and on the proper approach to developing those clusters. This chapter looks at the importance of urban economic hubs in fostering long-term economic development in the region.

Economic development in Canada has been largely driven by the growth of urban centres across the country. More than 80 percent of the population in Canada lives in urban communities. This is not the case in Atlantic Canada, where there are twice as many people living in rural communities as compared to elsewhere in the county.

Urban communities provide critical mass in terms of the needed infrastructure and labour to enable economic development. Population growth is essential for economic prosperity. Population growth is largely limited to urban communities in the developed world and the best way to protect rural communities is to have growing nearby urban communities able to attract people and capital.

Don Mills: The concept of economic hubs is not new. I have been promoting this concept for Atlantic Canada for more than a decade. My interest in this approach began when I was the first chair of the board of the then newly amalgamated Halifax Chamber of Commerce back in the mid-1990s. I was the last president of the Halifax Board of Trade and worked with the Dartmouth Chamber of Commerce and the Bedford and Sackville Boards of Trade to create a single business voice for the greater Halifax area. One of the first initiatives of the new Chamber of Commerce was to advocate for a single economic development agency to replace the four economic departments and end the counterproductive competition between the four municipalities at the time. That effort was successful, leading to the creation of the Greater Halifax Partnership (now simply the Halifax Partnership) which had an independent, mostly private-sector–led board. That consolidation of economic development efforts saved the municipalities millions of dollars.

After the amalgamation of the four municipalities, the Greater Halifax Partnership was endorsed by the new council, based on a five-year strategy presented at the time. The new entity had the distinction of not only being funded by the three levels of government, but by the private sector. I led the first campaign to successfully raise $1 million from the private sector; they were subsequently classified as investors in the partnership. More than a hundred companies continue to contribute annually to the Partnership's work. I later joined their board and went on to become chair.

It was then that I recognized the power of the new economic development model and how it could be applied elsewhere across the region. Since that time there have been several other regional economic agencies modelled after the Halifax Partnership, including the Cape Breton Partnership, Envision Saint John, Economic Development Southeast NB, and the recently announced Advantage St. John's.

The Halifax Partnership established a collaborative strategic development process looking at all parts of the municipality: urban, suburban, and rural. It developed measurable metrics for funders to properly evaluate its success. Based on this experience, I began to actively advocate for an economic hub strategy using Halifax as an example, presenting the concept to all the provincial governments and frequently speaking publicly about the strategy. While there was some interest by the provincial governments, there seemed to be a reluctance to adopt the strategy for some unfounded concerns that the rural population would see the strategy as having a negative consequence on them. The opposite is true. The strategic development of economic hubs in nearby urban centres would in fact enhance the lives of those in rural communities by increasing both economic opportunities and government services within an easy commute.

To be clear, economic hubs have been and will continue to develop organically. But what if they became a formal strategy by governments in the region? What if governments aligned and enhanced their public service delivery by focussing on these hubs? What if economic development agencies were aligned to market zones rather than individual communities like what has been done in Halifax?

POPULATION GROWTH DRIVES ECONOMIC PROSPERITY

Atlantic Canada has led the country in unemployment and trailed the nation in economic growth for much of the last fifty years or so. The structural challenge associated with having twice as many people living in rural communities, as compared to the rest of the country, without sufficient full-time work and an overreliance on seasonal work is a key reason for the chronically weak economic performance for all of the region except Prince Edward Island, where economic performance has been near the national average in terms of economic growth for the last decade. Prince Edward Island's strong economic performance can be largely attributed to a steadily growing population.

Having more than twice as many people living in rural communities increases the costs of service delivery for both the public and private sectors. As an example, the promise by governments to provide high-speed internet to 100 percent of the population is much more costly in Atlantic Canada due to the distribution of the population. Given that high-speed rural internet service must be subsidized by all users, the proportion of those available to subsidize these costs is smaller across the four Atlantic provinces relative to the rest of the country. Another example is the cost associated with the delivery of health care and the challenge of trying to keep small rural hospitals open.

ECONOMIC PROSPERITY CONCENTRATED

In Atlantic Canada, six dominant urban communities account for the majority of economic activity across the region: Halifax, Charlottetown, Saint John, Moncton, Fredericton, and St. John's. Yet, there are many more urban centres in Atlantic Canada that could provide for a greater distribution across the region if their assets were better utilized for economic development, if government policy supported the development of these hubs, and if economic development agencies were properly aligned to the economic zones around these hubs.

In total, there are thirty communities that meet the criteria set by StatsCan to be defined as urban communities, that is, communities with populations of at least five thousand people. Each of these communities is an economic hub already, providing critical health and post-secondary education infrastructure, as well as employment opportunities and other amenities for nearby rural communities. What is needed is a more formal approach to turn these economic centres into planned economic zones with specific strategies and performance metrics to harness and grow the unique assets of each of these communities.

These thirty urban communities all have common assets. Each has a significant hospital and a post-secondary institution. Each is a destination for shopping and business services to surrounding rural communities. Each has employment opportunities within a short commute from these nearby rural communities. Each provides cultural and entertainment activities for those living near these centres.

Halifax is perhaps the best example of what is possible. Halifax is a destination for work and play for all those living within an hour of the city. For people living in nearby rural communities, it provides the amenities of a city with a rural lifestyle, all within a reasonable commute.

In the mid-1990s, the Greater Halifax Partnership was formed as the economic development agency for the previous four municipalities, including the former County of Halifax. For perspective, the Halifax Regional

Municipality is larger in geographic size than the province of Prince Edward Island. Despite this geographic challenge, the Halifax Partnership (its current name) developed a strategy focussed on the growth of the whole municipality. Having a single economic development agency focussed on what could be called the Halifax Economic Zone has been highly successful. This same approach is now emerging in other parts of the region, with Envision Saint John now focussed on the greater Saint John area, the Cape Breton Partnership focussed on the greater Sydney area, the newly established Advantage St. John's focussed on the greater St. John's area and Economic Development Southeast NB focussed on the greater Moncton area. Each of these economic development agencies is focussed on strategies that take advantage of the unique assets within its economic zone. This is the way forward for the rest of the region.

WILLINGNESS TO COMMUTE

Don Mills: When I was still running my market research company, I conducted proprietary primary research to determine the public's definition of a reasonable commute for a number of activities like seeing a doctor, going to a pharmacy, going to a hospital, travelling to a job, and going to a bank, among a variety of activities researched. Importantly, I found that those living in rural communities are largely unwilling to move to access better job opportunities. I discovered that, for critical activities like work and medical care, the majority of the rural population felt that up to 65 kilometres was a reasonable distance to travel. I then used this distance to create notional economic hubs for each of the four provinces to determine what percentage of the population could be served within a reasonable commute. A 65-kilometre radius equates to about a forty-five–minute drive from the outer edges.

This willingness to commute provides an opportunity to reconsider not only how public services are delivered but how economic development is conducted across the region through an economic hub strategy. More importantly, such a strategy is the best way to ensure that economic prosperity is more equally shared beyond the six major urban markets in Atlantic Canada.

NOVA SCOTIA'S ECONOMIC HUB STRATEGY

In Nova Scotia, there are nine zones that could serve 97 percent of the population within a 65-kilometre commute (based on the 2021 Census). As the following map illustrates, there is considerable overlap in coverage by the urban hubs, meaning that many rural residents have access to more than one hub for their urban needs. The economic hub for the Strait area is anchored by two urban centres, both of which have populations of fewer than five thousand: Antigonish and Port Hawkesbury.

FIGURE 20-1: POPULATION WITHIN 65 KM OF AN URBAN CENTRE, NOVA SCOTIA

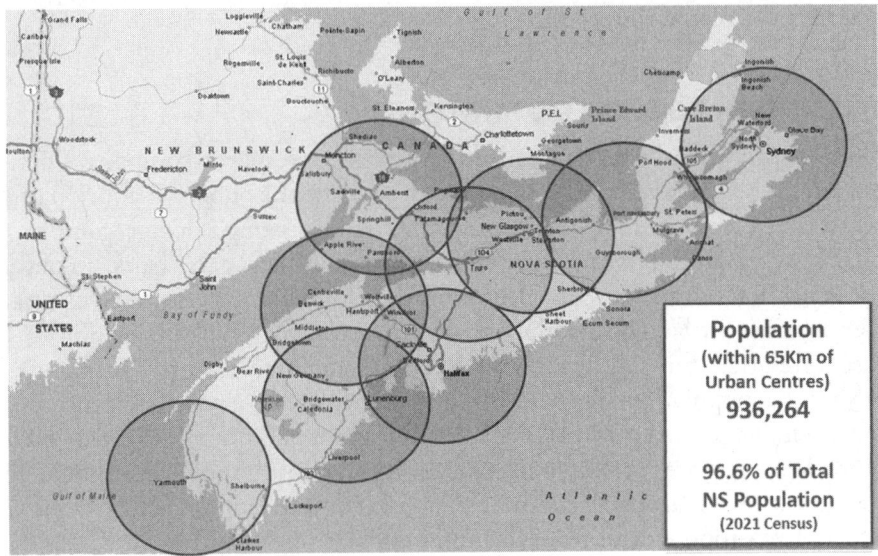

Population (within 65Km of Urban Centres)
936,264

96.6% of Total NS Population (2021 Census)

Source: Narrative Research

NEW BRUNSWICK'S ECONOMIC HUB STRATEGY

In New Brunswick, there are seven possible economic hubs, including Saint John, Moncton/Dieppe, Fredericton, Miramichi, Campbellton, Bathurst, and Edmundston. These seven economic hubs currently serve nearly 90 percent of the population in the province within a 65-kilometre commute (based on the 2021 Census). As in Nova Scotia, many rural communities have access to more than one hub for economic purposes.

FIGURE 20-2: POPULATION WITHIN 65 KM OF AN URBAN CENTRE, NEW BRUNSWICK

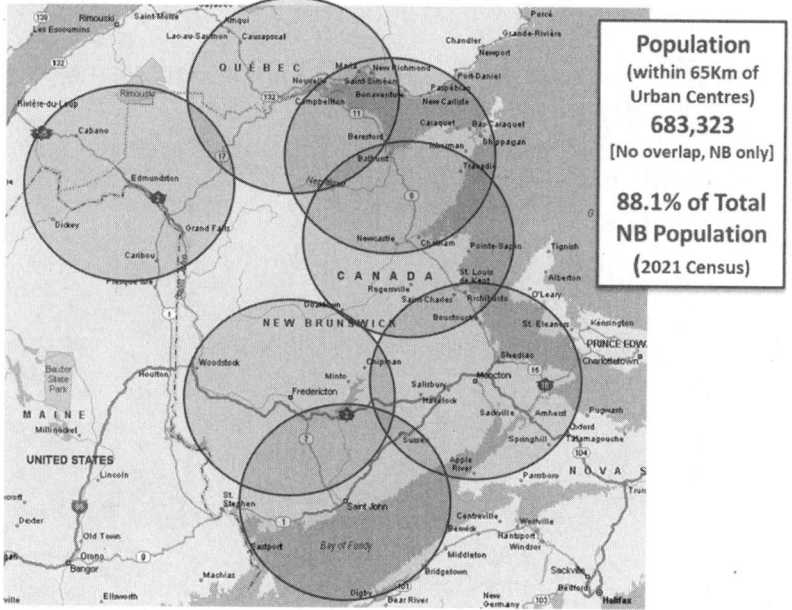

Source: Narrative Research

NEWFOUNDLAND AND LABRADOR'S ECONOMIC HUB STRATEGY

The economic strategy in Newfoundland and Labrador is a little more complicated due to the sheer size of the province and its many small communities. Fortunately, most of the population is along the Trans-Canada Highway between Port aux Basques and St. John's. Newfoundland and Labrador has more urban communities with populations of at least five thousand than the rest of the region. There are twelve urban hubs in the province, including two in Labrador. Despite the vast geography of the province, these hubs still serve nearly 90 percent of the population within a 65-kilometre commute (based on the 2021 Census). As the map below illustrates, a significant number of those rural communities have a choice in which hub they use for their urban needs.

FIGURE 20-3: POPULATION WITHIN 65 KM OF AN URBAN CENTRE, NEWFOUNDLAND AND LABRADOR

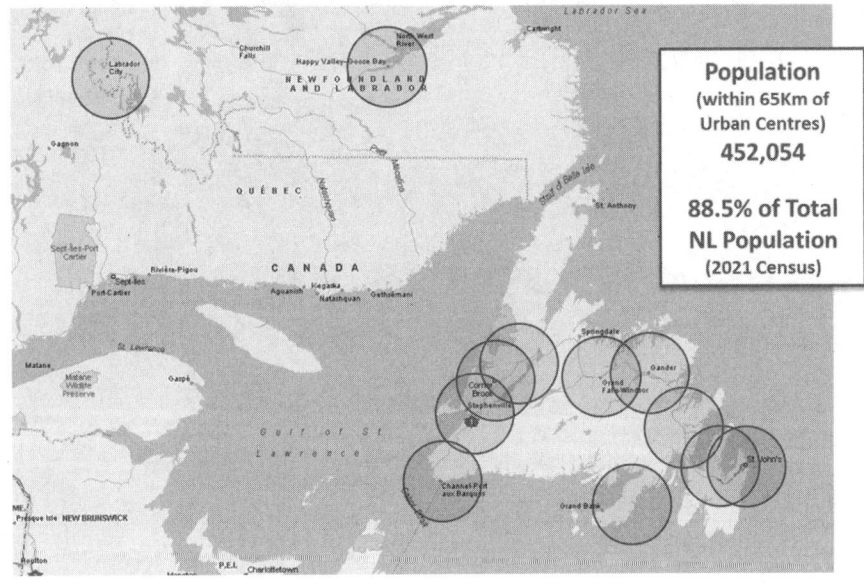

Source: Narrative Research

PRINCE EDWARD ISLAND'S HUB STRATEGY

Prince Edward Island has both a small geography and a small (but rapidly growing) population. In fact, the Island is smaller geographically than the Halifax Regional Municipality. There is a clear advantage in having a much smaller geography and there is much less disadvantage to living in smaller rural communities because everything is nearby on the Island. There are two clear economic hubs: Summerside and Charlottetown. Between these two hubs, 98 percent of the population is within a 65-kilometre commute with a significant proportion of the population living between Summerside and Charlottetown.

FIGURE 20-4: POPULATION WITHIN 65 KM OF AN URBAN CENTRE, PRINCE EDWARD ISLAND

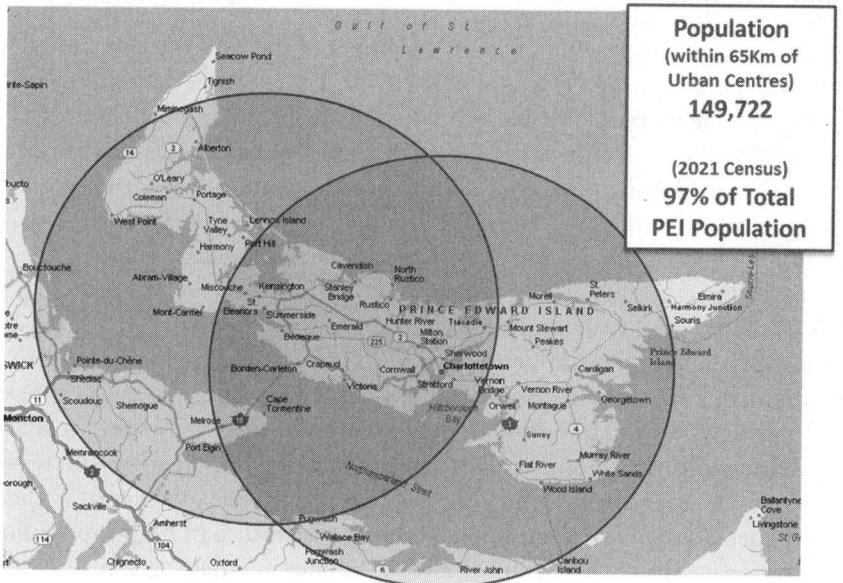

Source: Narrative Research

THE ROLE OF ECONOMIC HUBS **175**

A QUESTION OF EXPECTATIONS

For too long, Atlantic Canadians have been conditioned to believe that they have the right to live anywhere they wish and to expect the same level of public services and economic opportunities, or to be subsidized in that expectation. This expectation has been fostered by government policies at both the provincial and federal levels for decades. It is simply not possible to have primary health care facilities in smaller rural communities. Many smaller communities had their local schools closed due to declining enrollments. The cost of these policies has led to chronic difficulty balancing provincial budgets and ever-increasing public debt (except in New Brunswick). It has led to an over-dependence on transfer payments from other Canadians to maintain public service levels. It has led to a culture of entitlement and resistance to change. EI has become an income supplement program and a way of life for generations of workers in the region rather than a short-term insurance program. How else can we explain the unwillingness of a segment of the workforce to work longer than the period needed to qualify for EI, even when work is locally available? It might at least partially explain why Atlantic Canada continues to have more than twice as many people living in rural areas as the rest of the country.

Atlantic Canada does not have the same commuting experience as those living in other parts of the country, although there are plenty of people driving an hour or more each day for work across Atlantic Canada. There is a need to set new expectations in terms of access to public services. Is it better, if you live in the tri-county area of Nova Scotia, to drive to Yarmouth for specialized medical care than to drive to Halifax? If you live in northeastern New Brunswick, is it better to drive to Miramichi for specialized medical care than to Moncton? What if government policy was to concentrate its service delivery models on a limited number of economic hubs and find ways to increase or enhance those services to limit the need to travel to the larger centres? Clearly, some specialized treatment needs to be concentrated in higher-population communities. But what about dialysis, diagnostic imaging, routine cancer care? All provinces in Atlantic Canada have regional hospitals. What can be done to leverage those regional hospitals to bring more care closer to those living nearby?

It is difficult to have economic prosperity without population growth. The vast majority of population growth occurs in urban communities. The thirty urban communities in Atlantic Canada should all have population growth strategies as part of their economic strategies. Each of these communities needs to have an economic development agency aligned with the market it serves. Key to the success of these economic hubs is the creation of a regional economic plan, similar to the ones created for Greater Moncton and Halifax (municipalities serving both rural and urban residents). The development of strategies specific to each economic hub zone, based on the assets and opportunities within that hub region, is critical. The alignment of regional economic development agencies to these economic zones is also critical. Part of the regional economic plan must include the development of a population growth strategy that includes the attraction and retention of immigrants.

Politicians need to realize the best way to support their rural constituents is by increasing their access to services and economic opportunity within a reasonable commute so there is no reason to give up their rural lifestyle. In fact, having prosperous economic hubs will likely increase the number of people who live in the nearby rural communities close to an economic hub.

This is the new promise that politicians can make to the population with such an economic hub strategy. As a citizen, you have the right to live wherever you wish and expect the same level of public services and job opportunities, as long as you are prepared to commute a reasonable distance for such purposes.

CHAPTER 21
THE IMPORTANCE OF ECONOMIC CLUSTERS

THE CONCEPT OF AN INDUSTRY CLUSTER WAS INTRODUCED AND POPULARIZED by Michael Porter in his 1990 book, *The Competitive Advantage of Nations*. An industry cluster represents a high concentration of economic activity in a specific sector leading to the expansion of other related support industries. Over time, economic clusters are better positioned to attract investment and grow.

ATLANTIC CANADA'S ECONOMIC CLUSTERS

Atlantic Canada has a number of industries that could be considered economic clusters. Across the region, there is a high concentration of fishing activity and that has led to hundreds of companies in the supply chain specializing in everything from fishing boat repair to fishnet manufacturing to aquaculture feed. Post-secondary education providers are turning out talent to meet the specialized needs of this industry. Research organizations, including the federal Department of Fisheries and Oceans, spend millions of dollars each year on fish-related research. Information technology companies develop software and other tools to support the fishing sector.

Depending on the province and urban centre, there are a number of economic clusters. In the Halifax region, shipbuilding, defense services, and universities all generate relatively more economic activity than most other urban centres across the country. Newfoundland and Labrador have significant oil and gas, mining, and fishing clusters. Prince Edward Island has the highest concentration of economic activity related to food production in the country. The Charlottetown region has a dominant biosciences cluster. New Brunswick generates more economic activity from forest products than any other province in Canada. The Moncton region has the most dominant business–support services sector, with seven times as much employment as the country overall. Saint John has a significant energy production cluster with oil refining, liquified natural gas importation, and multiple electricity generation facilities. In Saint John, NB, there is a growing opportunity to develop a health cluster.

Canada's Ocean Supercluster is a federally supported effort to take advantage of Canada's proximity to ocean resources. No region is better positioned to take advantage of this opportunity than Atlantic Canada. In a 2024 *Insights* episode, Kendra MacDonald, CEO of Canada's Ocean Supercluster, outlined the opportunity under its "Ambition 2035" initiative to grow the sector in Canada to $220 billion by 2035. The plan is truly ambitious, calling for the ocean-based energy sector to grow its output from $9 billion in 2019 to $100 billion in 2035. Seafood and aquaculture are expected to grow from $8 billion to $25 billion by 2035.

Ocean technology is another growth engine in the plan; it's expected to generate $13 billion in economic value by 2035. In a 2023 *Insights* episode, Melanie Nadeau, the CEO of COVE (Centre for Ocean Ventures and Entrepreneurship) in Halifax, discussed the role of her organization in helping to commercialize new marine technologies.

DEVELOPING SUPPLY CHAINS

One of the important benefits of economic clusters is that they have enough scale to develop local supply chains. However, Atlantic Canada has relatively small urban centres, meaning the region could be missing out on urban-centred activities related to professional services, research, finance, and more. Having more developed supply chains in the region helps insulate the cluster from economic disruption. In general, the more supply chain activity that goes to firms in other jurisdictions, the more vulnerable the local cluster could be from a competitiveness perspective.

As one example of potential supply chain opportunity, consider the oil and gas sector in Newfoundland and Labrador. A review of the industry's supply chain spending on various services shows that much of this spending occurs in other provinces such as Ontario, Alberta, and Quebec. Figure 21-1 shows the spending on information technology goods and services by province across the country. After more than two decades of the oil and gas industry in Newfoundland and Labrador, only 8 percent of the industry's $117 million spending on information technology products and services goes to firms in the province. Could more of the IT-related supply chain activity go to Newfoundland and Labrador–based firms? For all industry clusters in Atlantic Canada, economic development organizations should be seeking to build deeper supply chains.

FIGURE 21-1: BREAKDOWN OF NEWFOUNDLAND AND LABRADOR'S OFFSHORE OIL AND GAS INDUSTRY SPENDING ON INFORMATION TECHNOLOGY GOODS AND SERVICES BY PROVINCE (% OF TOTAL)

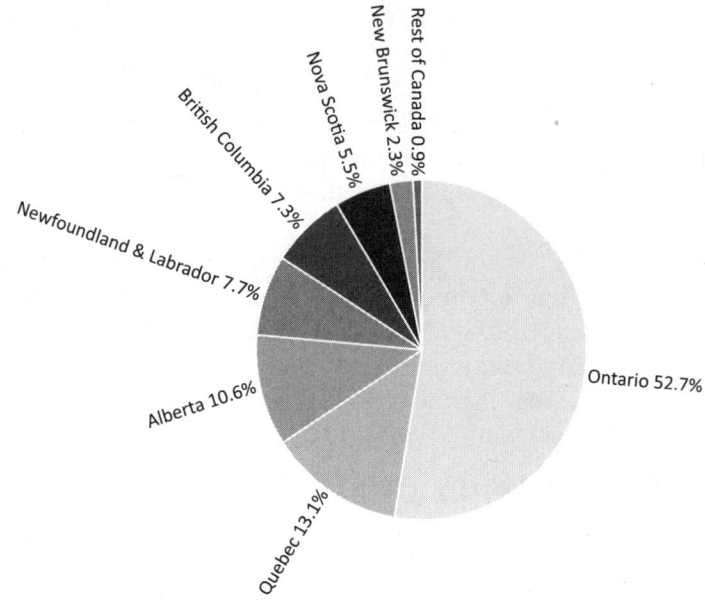

NOTE: FOR 2019. INCLUDES OIL AND GAS EXTRACTION AND OIL AND GAS ENGINEERING CONSTRUCTION.

INCLUDES THE COMBINED SPENDING IN FOUR SECTORS: COMPUTER SYSTEMS DESIGN AND RELATED SERVICES, GENERAL PURPOSE SOFTWARE, CUSTOM SOFTWARE DESIGN, AND DEVELOPMENT SERVICES AND DATA PROCESSING, HOSTING, AND RELATED SERVICES.

Source: Statistics Canada

CLUSTER-FOCUSSED EDUCATION AND TRAINING

When an industry has a relatively high concentration of firms and employment, the education and training sector builds its capacity to support the industry. For example, New Brunswick has a significant training capacity in the area of forestry professionals. Prince Edward Island's post-secondary education system has many programs that support the workforce needs of the food economy. The University of Prince Edward Island offers a number of courses that support the food economy on the Island, including the Food and Nutrition program in the Faculty of Science. The Atlantic Veterinary College is one of only five veterinary colleges in Canada and the only one in Atlantic Canada. Holland College's Culinary Institute of Canada is an important part of the Island's talent pipeline.

RESEARCH AND DEVELOPMENT

Another important attribute of successful economic clusters is the alignment of R & D activity. Governments have aligned investment in R & D to targeted industries in the past and this should continue into the future.

GOVERNMENT AND COMMUNITY SUPPORT

Governments across Atlantic Canada provide support to economic development in a variety of ways, including support for start-up company incubators and accelerators, investment in research, promotion of new investment in targeted industries, and financial support programs. This support should be particularly focussed on the region's important economic clusters and potential new industries.

LOOKING TO THE FUTURE

Strong cluster effects can help make an industry more competitive. As the region looks to the future and new industry opportunities there should be a focus on ensuring a broad ecosystem of activity is in place. In addition to suppliers, this includes education and training, research, industry associations, and other value-added activities.

CHAPTER 22

A MORE COMPETITIVE TAX ENVIRONMENT

BENJAMIN FRANKLIN IS CREDITED WITH SAYING THERE ARE ONLY TWO CERTAINties in life: death and taxes. When it comes to taxes, Atlantic Canada is at a distinct disadvantage and governments should find ways to become more competitive to attract the region's share of investment capital and people wishing to live and work here.

Atlantic Canada did not become the highest tax jurisdiction overnight. It took decades of economic underperformance. It took decades of slow or stagnant population growth. It took decades of slower-than-average job growth than the rest of the country. The fact is that, without a growing taxpayer base, the burden of increasing public-sector spending falls on essentially the same group of taxpayers. In addition, the region has a proportionately smaller private sector relative to the rest of the country, resulting in a lower corporate tax base to share the tax burden.

Niels Veldhuis, CEO of the Fraser Institute, outlined the challenges facing Atlantic Canada on our *Insights* podcast in 2022, shortly after the Atlantic Institute for Market Studies merged with his institute:

> *Our goal in Atlantic Canada is the same as our goal for Canada as a whole. Let's make the region the most prosperous region in Canada, and let's make Canada the most prosperous country in the world. Let's have the highest standard of living. And one of the goals for us right now in Atlantic Canada is for the region to catch up with the rest of Canada.*
>
> *The first study we did post-merger was* Catching up with Canada: A Prosperity Agenda for Atlantic Canada, *and there are some unfortunate gaps. If you just look at GDP, the size of our economy on a per-person basis, the gap between Atlantic Canada and the rest of Canada is almost $10,000 per person. If you look at household income, it's $4,500 per household. That's the gap. If you think about how much $4,500 can purchase in terms of standard of living, it's very significant, and you can say the same thing about the employment rate in Atlantic Canada, which is materially lower than the rest of Canada. So one of our goals is to create debate in Atlantic*

Canada to get rid of that gap. Let's have Atlantic Canada catch up with Canada. But I would say let's go one step further: let's see if we can't make Atlantic Canada the most prosperous place in Canada.

We agree with that aspiration.

TAXING ATLANTIC CANADIANS

The top sources of revenue for governments in the three Maritime provinces are personal income tax, harmonized sales tax (HST), and corporate income tax.[28] For example, in Nova Scotia, personal income tax represents 30 percent of all provincial government taxes raised. HST brings in another 20 percent, followed by corporate income tax at 5 percent, and other source revenue at 6 percent. Federal transfer payments account for nearly 40 percent of all provincial government revenue.

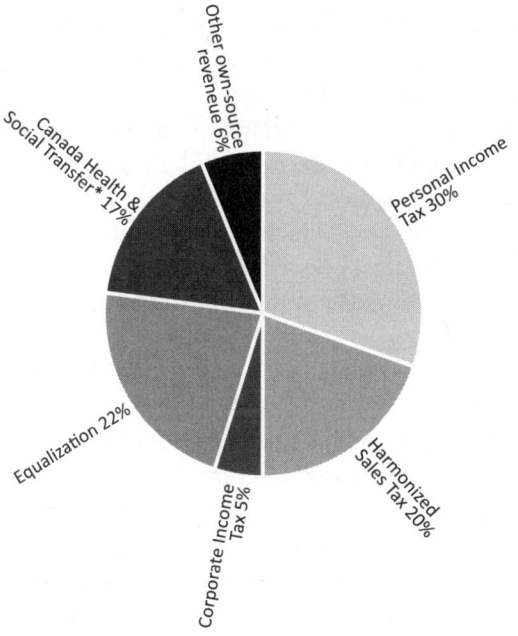

FIGURE 22-1: BREAKDOWN OF REVENUE BY SOURCE, 2021–2022, GOVERNMENT OF NOVA SCOTIA

*INCLUDES A SMALL AMOUNT FROM THE OFFSHORE ACCORD

Source: Government of Nova Scotia, Main Estimates 2023–2023

THE TAX BURDEN

Atlantic Canadians pay the highest provincial sales tax rate, at 10 percent (the federal portion is an additional 5 percent). By contrast, the provincial sales tax rate is 0 in Alberta, 6 percent in Saskatchewan, 7 percent in Manitoba and 8 percent in Ontario. The good news is that, at the time of writing, there appeared to be some interest in lowering consumption taxes in both Nova Scotia and New Brunswick.

Depending on the income bracket, taxpayers in Atlantic Canada can face a much higher income tax rate. For those reporting income of $75,000 per year, Nova Scotia has the highest average income tax rate in the country, followed by Prince Edward Island.[29]

Property tax rates can be considerably higher in Atlantic Canada, but this is offset by lower average property assessment values.

Fuel taxes in Atlantic Canada are also relatively high, and households in the region rely more on their vehicles for transportation given the higher percentage of those living in rural communities.

CANADA IS A HIGH TAX JURISDICTION

Canadians are heavily taxed in general. The Fraser Institute estimated in 2022 that the average Canadian family of two or more people pays 43 percent of total income in one form of taxes or the other. In addition to sales, income, property, and fuel taxes, Atlantic Canadians face other taxes and levies, including deed transfer taxes, capital gains, dividends, and interest earned taxes. There are business taxes and payroll taxes. Now there is the added burden of the carbon tax, which was particularly challenging for those using oil to heat their homes. Nova Scotia and Prince Edward Island have the highest share of households among the ten provinces using heating oil.

HIGHEST MARGINAL TAX RATES

It is challenging to compare income taxes by province because each province has different income categories and different tax rates for similar income categories. For the highest federal tax category (over $200,000), the rate is a hefty 33 percent. For anyone making over $200,000 in Nova Scotia, the combined marginal income rate is now 54 percent, the second highest in Canada behind only Quebec (55.8 percent). The comparable numbers in New Brunswick are 53.3 percent, 51.3 percent in Newfoundland and Labrador, and 51.4 percent in Prince Edward Island.

The highest marginal tax rate kicks in at significantly lower income levels in Atlantic Canada. The highest rates start at a little less than $100,000 on the Island, while the highest rates start at nearly $190,000 in Newfoundland and Labrador. The lowest combined tax rates for individuals making over

$200,000 in Canada are in Alberta (48 percent with the highest rate kicking in above $300,000) and Saskatchewan (47.5 percent where the highest rate starts at $235,000).

LOWEST BASIC PERSONAL EXEMPTIONS

The level at which income taxes start to be levied is lower in Atlantic Canada. The average personal exemption in Canada is $14,398. The average basic personal exemption in Atlantic Canada is $10,088, more than 40 percent lower than the Canadian average. There is also significant variance within the region, with Nova Scotia having the dubious honour of the lowest personal exemption in the country ($8,481), while the Island has the highest exemption in the region ($11,250). Up until only very recently, Nova Scotia and PEI do not automatically index their tax rates to protect from inflation. In early 2025 the Island adjusted its tax rates and Nova Scotia announced its intention to index its tax rates against inflation in 2025.

WHAT ABOUT THE CANADIAN CONSTITUTION?

Is it "fair" for certain provinces to extract relatively more tax revenue from residents than others? One of the most important reasons Canada has such a high quality of life across the country has been a national commitment to ensuring that good-quality public services are available in all provinces and regions at reasonably comparable tax rates. In fact, subsection 36(2) of the Canadian Constitution specifically states: "Parliament and the government of Canada are committed to the principle of making equalization payments to ensure that provincial governments have sufficient revenues to provide reasonably comparable levels of public services at reasonably comparable levels of taxation."

A lot of the conversation these days in Canada is focussed on the "reasonably comparable levels of public services," but the "reasonably comparable levels of taxation" are equally important. If one or more provinces have a much higher tax burden it will hurt population growth, entrepreneurship, and overall economic growth.

THE NEED FOR MORE HIGH-INCOME EARNERS

One of the problems in Atlantic Canada is having a lower number of high-income earners than other provinces. Newfoundland and Labrador has been changing this somewhat in recent years, but the three Maritime provinces rank eighth, ninth, and tenth among the provinces for the share of taxpayers reporting $200,000 or more in annual income on their tax returns (figure 22-2).

To put this into perspective, if New Brunswick had the same share of taxpayers earning $200,000 or more, it would increase the number by 2.6 times and would add enough tax revenue to substantially reduce the need for federal equalization payments.

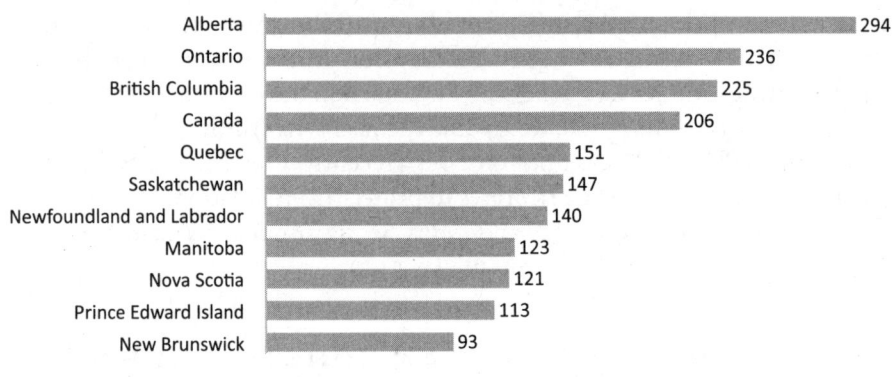

FIGURE 22-2: NUMBER OF TAXPAYERS REPORTING $200,000+ ANNUAL INCOME (PER 10,000 TOTAL TAXPAYERS), 2021

Alberta	294
Ontario	236
British Columbia	225
Canada	206
Quebec	151
Saskatchewan	147
Newfoundland and Labrador	140
Manitoba	123
Nova Scotia	121
Prince Edward Island	113
New Brunswick	93

Source: Statistics Canada Table 11-10-0055-01

There is another important reason to encourage more high-income earners to live in Atlantic Canada. As shown in table 22-1, high-income earners pay a large share of all provincial income taxes each year. The top 5 percent of all taxpayers in Ontario contribute 45 percent of all income tax revenue in that province. The top 1 percent, 26 percent. However, in Atlantic Canada, high-income earners contribute a much lower share, and those in lower income cohorts pay a much higher share than those in Ontario.

TABLE 22-1: TOTAL INCOME TAXES PAID BY INCOME GROUP, 2020*

	Atlantic Canada	Ontario
Top 1 percent income group	11%	26%
Top 5 percent income group	27%	45%
Top 10 percent income group	39%	58%
Bottom 90 percent income group	61%	42%
Bottom 50 percent income group	10%	6%

*FEDERAL AND PROVINCIAL COMBINED
Source: Statistics Canada Table 11-10-0055-01

Who earns high income in Canada? A review of income by occupation and other attributes shows that the top income earners in Canada tend to be business owners, senior managers, and specialized high-value occupations such as physicians. Higher personal income tax rates make it harder to recruit top talent and encourage business ownership.

COMPETITIVE CORPORATE INCOME TAX RATES

Atlantic Canada needs to have a competitive corporate income tax rate across Atlantic Canada to ensure that companies will invest in the region. As of 2023, the provincial corporate income tax rate in New Brunswick and Nova Scotia is 14 percent, in Newfoundland and Labrador it's 15 percent, and in Prince Edward Island it's 16 percent, compared to 10 and 11.5 percent in Ontario. A four percentage-point difference between Ontario and Nova Scotia for manufacturing companies may not seem like a lot, but in reality, it is a large difference. If a manufacturing company in Nova Scotia generated $5 million in net profit before tax, they would be required to pay $700,000 in provincial income tax. In Ontario, the amount would be $500,000. To put it another way, the company would pay 40 percent more in Nova Scotia than in Ontario.

There is another interesting reality about the Canadian tax system that supports the case for equalizing corporate income tax rates in Atlantic Canada with Ontario in particular.

Relative to GDP, in 2021–22 the Ontario government collected 2.6 times as much corporate income tax as the Nova Scotia government and 2.3 times as much as the New Brunswick government. This, despite the fact that Nova Scotia and New Brunswick have much higher corporate income tax rates for medium- and large-sized companies. A review of previous years shows a similar pattern. This underscores the challenge of having a small private sector in Atlantic Canada relative to the rest of the country.

A part of this differential is likely due to the smaller private sector in Nova Scotia and New Brunswick and because there are more head offices in Ontario, but it is difficult to attribute such a wide variation to these factors alone. It is distinctly possible that companies with operations in Atlantic Canada and in the rest of Canada and beyond are reporting higher profits in Ontario to take advantage of the lower provincial tax rate. For companies that have customers and operations in multiple provinces, the calculation of provincial property taxes owed is based on a formula that takes into account operations and markets in each province, and the amounts are not insignificant. If the New Brunswick government brought in corporate income taxes that were the same as those in Ontario, relative to GDP, it would have added over $600 million to provincial tax coffers in 2021–22. In Nova Scotia, this would have added $850 million.

GROWING ORGANIC TAX REVENUES

There are basically two ways to increase tax revenues: 1) raise tax rates, or 2) grow the economy and boost taxes raised organically without the need to raise tax rates. A larger private-sector economy should induce more tax revenue. The four provincial governments should target annual private-sector economic growth of 2 to 3 percent per year (real GDP growth) to ensure a growing tax base to be able to sustainably fund public services.

PROVINCIAL GOVERNMENT FISCAL MANAGEMENT

With the exception of New Brunswick, the Atlantic provincial governments continue to accumulate debt through deficit budget financing. There is a need to return to balanced budgets and this will require restrained spending by all levels of government—not necessarily less spending, but spending in line with economic growth to decrease the pressures on taxpayers. Living within our means must become a mantra for governments (all levels of government, to be clear), which will mean making choices on priorities. Currently, hundreds of millions of tax dollars are needed to service an ever-increasing debt load. Higher interest rates have pushed up government debt servicing costs from new debt and from rolled-over previous debt as it is refinanced at higher rates. Lowering interest rates will slow the growth of debt but will not fix the problem.

DOES A LOWER COST OF LIVING OFFSET HIGHER TAXES?

Some people argue that, while the total tax burden of higher-income individuals and households is more substantial in Atlantic Canada, the lower overall cost of living means they still have more disposable income here compared to elsewhere. There was at one time some truth to this idea, particularly in the area of housing and shelter costs, but the rapid rise of the cost of housing in this region is rapidly eroding any benefit.

A COMPETITIVE TAX REGIME

At a time when the population within Canada is more mobile than ever, and when newcomers have choice about where to live, it is important for Atlantic Canada to have a reasonably competitive tax regime for households. The same applies to businesses. We need to ensure the difference in tax rates is not a significant barrier to living or operating a business in the region.

In the 2021 Census, Statistics Canada reported the average employment income of people who moved out of Atlantic Canada between 2016 and 2021 compared to those who had moved in over the same period. Across all four provinces the people moving out reported higher employment income, on average, than those moving in. Those moving out of Newfoundland and Labrador reported a 24 percent higher income than those moving in.[30] This is only one data point for a period of time, but it reinforces the importance of ensuring we are not losing high-income earners or businesses because of uncompetitive tax rates.

THE YEARS AHEAD

Atlantic Canada has economic momentum, which is being driven by unprecedented population growth, especially within the Maritime provinces. Declining unemployment rates during a period of significant population growth means more tax-paying jobs are being created, which should provide the basis for more competitive tax rates and the sharing of tax burden. There is a need for more prudent fiscal management. Perhaps it is time for provincial governments to return to a zero-based budgeting process to examine all its expenditures and determine the value for those expenditures. (Zero-based budgeting is a process where each item in a budget has to be justified starting with zero budget.) The region should use New Brunswick as a model for fiscal management to reduce the growing need for more taxes to fund debt. It is time for our politicians to help make this region more attractive for investors and talent and, in the case of Nova Scotia and PEI, index their tax rates to protect against bracket creep. With a growing tax base from population growth, it's also time for the whole region to increase the basic exemption to the national average. Let's not lose this opportunity to become more tax competitive.

THE LESSON FROM SASKATCHEWAN

In our 2021 *Insights* podcast with the CEO of the Fraser Institute, Niels Veldhuis used the province of Saskatchewan as an example of what is possible. In the 1990s, Saskatchewan faced the same fiscal challenges as most of Atlantic Canada, with high debt levels, budget deficits, and significant out-migration. Veldhuis said there are important lessons to be learned from Saskatchewan's fiscal challenges:

> Saskatchewan almost also went bankrupt in the early 1990s. They had difficulty selling their bonds. Roy Romanow's NDP government was elected in 1991 and had to deal with this very serious fiscal situation. Janice MacKinnon was finance minister at the time, and she put forth a plan to change the direction of the province.
>
> The first thing they did was attack the fiscal side. This was a government that was almost bankrupt. They had obviously a real problem: massive debt,

massive deficits. They went through a really serious review of government. How do you make government smarter? How do peel off things that are best done in the private sector? How do you consolidate? How do you become more efficient? Lo and behold, they went through quite a significant reduction in government, spending 12 percent less over the course of two years and they balanced their books in three years. The NDP government created a fiscal surplus. They were then able to say, "Well, let's have a look at our tax system. Let's make our province more competitive."

In 2005, they had a personal income tax review and fundamentally changed the nature of their tax system. And then they went through a business tax review as well and fundamentally reduced business taxes.

You had government—an NDP government, which has typically been big-spend high-tax government—fundamentally changed into more efficient government, with balanced budgets, creating surpluses, reducing income taxes on investment. They made Saskatchewan a much better place to invest and fundamentally changed the trajectory of Saskatchewan.

Important lessons indeed—and perhaps a blueprint for Atlantic Canada.

THE PATH FORWARD

The four Atlantic provinces should work with each other to harmonize corporate income tax rates across the region and work with the federal government to determine the fairness of the distribution of provincial income tax payments for companies operating in multiple provinces. They also need to ensure that income tax rates and policies for higher income earners are not a disincentive to locate in the region. And the provincial governments should target annual private-sector economic growth of 2 to 3 percent per year (real GDP growth) to ensure a growing tax base to be able to sustainably fund public services.

CHAPTER 23

DEVELOPING THE EXPORT ECONOMY

THE VISION FOR THIS BOOK IS TO LAY OUT A ROAD MAP FOR HOW ATLANTIC Canada can prosper in the years ahead. Sustaining and growing the region's exports will be critically important to this vision. Without a strong export economy, it will be difficult to grow the tax base to sustainably fund public services across the region.

THE RISE OF IMPORTS

As a jurisdiction with a relatively small population base, Atlantic Canada imports the majority of its goods consumed by households, businesses, and institutions (and a large share of its services). In the eighteenth and nineteenth centuries, most of what was consumed in the region was produced locally, but during the decades after Confederation and into the early twentieth century, Atlantic Canada could import goods that were produced more cheaply elsewhere and could export locally produced goods for which the region had a comparative advantage.

In recent decades, trade liberalized even faster with the introduction of agreements such as the North American Free Trade Agreement (NAFTA),[31] and that led to even more reliance on imports. By 2022, the region imported over $84 billion in goods and services from other provinces and countries, an amount equivalent to approximately $35,000 for every person living in the four provinces.[32]

REGIONAL IMPORTS

Table 23-1 shows Nova Scotia's top imports. In 2020, the province imported $2.8 billion worth of food and beverage products, or approximately $6,500 per household that year. That was offset by $3.3 billion worth of food-related exports, mainly fish and seafood. Nova Scotia imported $1.6 billion worth of cars, SUVs, trucks, and other vehicles and parts to support the sector, and another $1.3 billion worth of transportation fuels. Information technology (software, data housing, and IT services) was another sector with substantial imports of $877 million, although much of that was offset with $720 million worth of IT-related exports. Nova Scotia imported a lot of rubber, but that was transformed by Michelin into tires, which was the second most important export in 2020. The province imports a lot of wood and paper products, computers, and medicines, as well as services such office and business administration services and architectural, engineering, and related services. It offsets some of the imports by exporting products and services such as food (fish, apples, blueberries, cheese, frozen foods), financial services, IT products and services, and wood and paper products.

TABLE 23-1: TOP IMPORTS AND EXPORTS BY VALUE, NOVA SCOTIA, 2020

Top imports		Top exports	
Food and beverages (incl. fish)	$2.8 billion	Food and beverages (incl. fish)	$3.3 billion
Vehicles and parts	$1.6 billion	Tires	$1.1 billion
Gasoline and other transportation fuels	$1.3 billion	Financial and insurance services	$720 million
Software, data hosting, and IT services	$877 million	Software, data hosting, and IT services	$712 million
Wood and paper products	$763 million	Wood and paper products	$635 million
Computers and electronics	$722 million	Tourism-related**	$484 million
Pharmaceutical and medicinal products	$646 million	Office and business administration	$453 million
Office and business administration	$592 million	Plastic products	$441 million
Rubber and rubber compounds and mixtures*	$416 million	Aircraft engines and parts	$372 million
Clothing and footwear	$385 million	Tuition (post-secondary education)	$358 million
Architectural, engineering, and related services	$342 million	Water freight transportation services	$303 million

*IMPORTED FOR USE IN THE PRODUCTION OF VEHICLE TIRES. IN 2020, THE VALUE OF TIRE EXPORTS FROM NOVA SCOTIA WAS $1.1 BILLION.

**DATA FOR 2019 AS 2020 WAS INFLUENCED BY THE PANDEMIC. INCLUDES ACCOMMODATIONS, FOOD SERVICES, AND OTHER RELATED ACTIVITY.

Source: Statistics Canada Table 12-10-0101-01

WHAT ARE SERVICES EXPORTS?

Asked to describe exports from Atlantic Canada, many people would suggest commodities such as wood or fish, or manufactured products such as vehicles or televisions. Services are also a very important part of Atlantic Canada's exports. For example, in 2020 Prince Edward Island exported $1.35 billion worth of services to other provinces and countries, almost as much as its goods exports ($1.88 billion). These exports included post-secondary education, administrative services, and information technology services. The province's largest export sector from a services perspective is tourism. In 2019, the province exported over $300 million worth of tourism-related services such as accommodations services, food services, and amusement services.[33]

New Brunswick relies on services-based exports, including administrative services, IT services, and tourism. Nova Scotia companies export a high number of professional services, including legal services, engineering, and management, scientific, and technical consulting services.

INTERPROVINCIAL TRADE VERSUS INTERNATIONAL TRADE

A common misconception is that most of Atlantic Canada's exports leave the country and are consumed in the United States and elsewhere in the world. The truth is that interprovincial exports can be as important. In 2022, Statistics Canada reported that Prince Edward Island and Nova Scotia exported more to other provinces than to other countries (goods and services combined). New Brunswick exported more to other countries, mainly due to the oil refinery. Newfoundland and Labrador's largest export, crude oil, is exported to other countries. Excluding that one industry, the province exports more to other provinces than countries.

The region also relies more heavily on imports from other provinces, with a few exceptions such as the international crude oil imported into Saint John for processing at the Irving refinery. In 2022, Prince Edward Island imported $3.3 billion worth of goods and services from other provinces and only $2 billion from other countries. Nova Scotia imported $15.1 billion worth of goods and services from other provinces and the same, $15.1 billion, from other countries.[34]

THE LARGEST TRADE DEFICITS IN THE COUNTRY

As shown in table 23-2, the three Maritime provinces have the largest annual trade deficits when compared to the other provinces. Newfoundland and Labrador is different because it exports a large amount of crude oil from offshore production. Without crude oil exports, the province would have had the second largest trade deficit among the ten provinces in 2022 (just behind Nova Scotia).

TABLE 23-2: ANNUAL TRADE DEFICIT/SURPLUS BY PROVINCE AND YEAR, PER CAPITA

	Newfoundland and Labrador	Prince Edward Island	Nova Scotia	New Brunswick
Imports ($B)	$17.4	$5.3	$30.2	$30.8
Exports ($B)	$15.0	$3.7	$16.2	$22.5
Trade balance (exports per $1.00 imports)	$0.86	$0.69	$0.54	$0.73
Provincial rank (out of 10)	4	9	10	8
% change in the trade balance (2002–22)	-31%	-6%	-29%	-28%

CHAINED (2017) DOLLARS
Source: Statistics Canada Table 36-10-0222-01

WHY SHOULD WE CARE ABOUT THE TRADE DEFICIT?

Most of the economic value associated with imports, including tax revenue, occurs where the product or service is produced. The production of vehicles, televisions, packaged foods, and entertainment services in Ontario, and subsequently consumed in Nova Scotia, generates far more economic value in the producing province. A large trade deficit means the province is generating less economic value relative to total output (the total amount spent on goods and services throughout the year). This can mean less employment and income and fewer profits and taxes compared to jurisdictions with a stronger trade position.

THE RELATIONSHIP BETWEEN EXPORTS AND ECONOMIC GROWTH

New Brunswick, as one example, imported $30.8 billion worth of goods and services and exported $22.5 billion in 2022.[35] That $8.3 billion trade "deficit" means lost GDP and tax revenues for the government. Table 23-3 shows the relationship for each of the four provinces.

TABLE 23-3: RELATIONSHIP BETWEEN EXPORTS AND ECONOMIC GROWTH

Jurisdiction	Relationship between exports and economic growth
New Brunswick	Over the forty-year period between 1982 and 2022, when annual real GDP growth averaged less than 1 percent or was negative, the value of exports declined by an average of 2 percent per year, but when real GDP growth exceeded 2 percent, the value of exports increased by 2.5 times faster. Between 1993 and 2006, real GDP increased by an average of 2.6 percent per year. This was the longest sustained period of economic growth in New Brunswick's recent history. Over this period the value of exports increased by an average of 4.2 percent per year.
Prince Edward Island	Over the forty-year period between 1982 and 2022, when annual real GDP growth averaged 2 percent or higher, the value of exports increased by an average of 5 percent per year, but when real GDP growth was below 2 percent, the value of exports increased by only 1 percent per year. The longest sustained period of economic growth in the province's recent history was 1994 to 2005, when real GDP increased by an average of 3.3 percent per year. The value of exports from the province during that period averaged 5 percent per year.
Nova Scotia	Over the forty-year period between 1982 and 2022, on an annual basis when the value of exports was decreasing, real GDP growth averaged below 2 percent. When GDP growth was higher than 2 percent, the value of exports increased by 6 percent per year. Between 1997 and 2002, real GDP increased by an average of 3.9 percent per year. The value of exports increased by over 6 percent per year.
Newfoundland and Labrador	Over the forty-year period between 1982 and 2022, when annual real GDP growth averaged 2 percent or higher, the value of exports increased by an average of 8 percent per year, but when real GDP growth was below 2 percent, the value of exports decreased by an average of 4 percent per year. Because of the introduction of the offshore oil and gas industry, the relationship between GDP growth and exports has been even more pronounced. Between 1998 and 2003, real GDP expanded by an average of 6.9 percent per year. The value of exports increased by an average of 13 percent per year.

Source: Derived using Statistics Canada Table 36-10-0222-01; all figures based on chained (2017) dollars.

In New Brunswick, the value of exports relative to GDP was on an upward trajectory until the turn of the century and then started a slow decline. In 2003, the value of exports was equivalent to 89 percent of GDP. By 2022, it had declined to 71 percent.[36] In Newfoundland and Labrador, the ratio of exports to GDP peaked in 2008 and in Nova Scotia, 2004. Nova Scotia has seen the sharpest decline in the relative value of exports, which dropped to only 33 percent in 2022.

Prince Edward Island is the only province in Atlantic Canada where the value of exports relative to GDP has not been in decline, but the figure has hovered at around 48 to 50 percent of GDP since 2015.

HOW TO FOSTER A STRONG EXPORT ECONOMY

We have interviewed the CEOs of many of the top exporters from Atlantic Canada on the *Insights* podcast, including those from forest products companies such as J. D. Irving, Ltd. and Groupe Savoie; fishing and aquaculture firms such as Cooke Inc.; manufacturers such as Michelin, and many IT companies focussed on export markets. We have seen a consistent theme among these firms: Atlantic Canada needs to ensure it has a strong value proposition for exporting companies. These companies compete in global markets for business and will continue to invest in Atlantic Canada if there is a strong talent pool, competitive business costs, and other factors. Verafin, for example, is a Newfoundland and Labrador–based financial technology company that is selling its services internationally and creating export revenues for the province.

BIOVECTRA is a Prince Edward Island–based pharmaceutical manufacturer that exports its drugs internationally. It is part of the PEI BioAlliance that currently generates $600 million in mostly export revenues, making that sector the third most important from a GDP perspective. Oliver Technow, the CEO of BIOVECTRA, spoke to us in 2021 about building a global company from Prince Edward Island:

> Usually when I think about our organization and its people, what comes to mind is relentless problem-solving. I keep saying this whenever I have an opportunity, but I think it's really accurate and it's grounded in the sense of belonging, the sense of community. So, we are here in Prince Edward Island, in Nova Scotia. We are an Atlantic Canada organization, and we are out here to show everyone that innovation and first-class global technology can be done here in the region.
>
> It goes back to our origins. It's strongly connected to where we are and how we operate, and the adversity the organization had to overcome over the years. With the recent announcement [to build a state-of-the art vaccine production facility] putting us clearly on the Canadian map, this is a very different trajectory we're on. But make no mistake. BIOVECTRA and the technology that we stand for is based on microbial fermentation. We are one of the top five companies in the world doing it. It is truly a value proposition of global dimensions. A lot of conversation over the last couple of years has centred around the importances of having anchor companies in Canada. If BIOVECTRA, with its size, scale, and global relevance is not considered a true Canadian anchor company, then I have a hard time making sense of that definition. So, we consider ourselves a key part of the domestic ecosystem in biomanufacturing, and as such, certainly an anchor company for this sector.

Historically, Atlantic Canada benefitted from natural resources such as minerals, oil, natural gas, forest products, fish, and agricultural products such as potatoes, blueberries, apples, and maple syrup, which were all in demand around the world. These products made up the bulk of all exports. In the past twenty to thirty years, the region has seen an increase in service-focussed exports such as business services (hotel reservations centres and banking call centres, for example) and information technology services. Tourism has also been an important export sector (meaning money from other jurisdictions flows into the region).

The development of economic clusters and the importance of entrepreneurs are both key to developing export industries. For this section, here are some important themes to consider when looking to foster increased exports.

TABLE 23-4: THEMES TO CONSIDER WHEN LOOKING TO FOSTER INCREASED EXPORTS

Theme	Considerations
Natural resources should continue to be a source of exports for generations to come	The region's traditional industries such as fish/seafood, agricultural products, and forest products will continue to bring billions of dollars' worth of export revenue into this region each year, provided the business case remains strong. If they cannot find workers, if energy and other operating costs accelerate faster than in other regions, or if some other challenge makes it harder to generate profits from these exports, companies may start moving investment out of the region. There are new natural resource–based opportunities such as green hydrogen, critical minerals, and new agricultural opportunities, but these will all need public support and First Nations participation.
Exporters compete globally	One of the most important considerations for policy-makers and the public at large is that Atlantic Canada's exporters compete with companies elsewhere in Canada, the US, and around the world. A company that might be considered "large" in the context of Atlantic Canada might be a small player in that industry worldwide. Governments, education providers, and other organizations that influence the business environment for exporters need to understand this reality. If our exporters cannot compete and make a good return on their investment in Atlantic Canada, they will not be here for long.
Jurisdictions with the talent pipeline will attract business investment	Until recently, companies looking to establish a new manufacturing plant, warehouse, or other export-focussed operation ranked operating costs, taxes, and incentives as the most important criteria for deciding where to locate. In recent years, access to talent has risen to the top of the list of important criteria. This includes both the ability to recruit initially and the ability of a community to demonstrate it has a strong talent pipeline for the future.
Productivity is key	The region's export industries must push to become more productive in the face of increasing national and international competition. Even for commodity sectors such as fish, timber, and minerals, low productivity sectors cut into profit margins and could risk future investment.

CHAPTER 24

THE GREEN ECONOMY AND NEW ENERGY ALTERNATIVES

BASED ON NUMEROUS *INSIGHTS* PODCASTS IN WHICH WE HAVE ADDRESSED topics like tidal power, green hydrogen, nuclear power, and small modular reactors (SMRs), it seems clear that Atlantic Canada is on the verge of becoming an energy powerhouse in Canada. This conclusion is supported by a recent report by Peter Nicholson for the Public Policy Forum entitled *Catching the Wind: How Atlantic Canada Can Become an Energy Superpower.*

TRANSITIONING TO A GREEN ECONOMY

The need to move away from the dependency on fossil fuels to generate electricity and heat homes is perhaps most urgent in Nova Scotia, which has a high dependency on coal to generate electricity (52 percent) and the highest number of homes heated by oil. New Brunswick also depends on coal for electricity generation, although not to the same extent as Nova Scotia. New Brunswick has nuclear power; the Point Lepreau Nuclear Generating Station has a CANDU 6 reactor that generates a gross output of 680 megawatts (MW), which supplies between 40 and 65 percent of the province's electricity. In Newfoundland and Labrador the vast majority of electricity is generated by hydro, although the development of Muskrat Falls has placed the province in considerable debt and put pressure on power rates in the province. Prince Edward Island is reliant on NB Power's Point Lepreau, where the province has a 15 percent ownership interest, for 60 percent of its electricity needs.

NUCLEAR POWER

Nuclear power currently accounts for about 15 percent of Canada's electricity, according to the World Nuclear Association. Nuclear power has always been a controversial topic in Canada, with ongoing widespread opposition to its use across the country. Most of the opposition is related to concerns about safety.

Yet the safety record for nuclear power in Canada has been exceptional and the CANDU reactors used are considered among the safest nuclear designs in the world. Canada's efforts to achieve net zero emissions by 2050 have renewed interest in nuclear power as a low-emission source of electricity. The recent COP28 United Nations Climate Change Conference in Dubai saw a commitment by twenty-two countries, including Canada, to triple nuclear energy capacity by 2050.

As one of only two provinces with nuclear power, New Brunswick has benefitted from rate stability for decades, although the debt burden has been substantial and the most recent refurbishment of the plant cost in excess of $3 billion. Point Lepreau was originally commissioned in 1983, and the refurbishment was completed in the fall of 2012, extending the life of the plant up to 2040. It is not known what will happen to the plant at that time, but in the meantime, NB Power has a $5 billion debt load that must somehow be repaid by ratepayers.

It is worth noting that Nova Scotia has had a legislative prohibition on the construction of nuclear power plants (the Nova Scotia Power Privatization Act of 1992) and a permanent ban on uranium mining in the province since 1981. Nevertheless, the Tim Houston government has included nuclear as a low-emission electricity source in its most recent gas emissions regulations, which signals the province may now be open to the use of nuclear power. In a 2024 *Insights* podcast, Premier Houston signalled his openness to both nuclear power and uranium mining when he stated, "I support both" and pointed to the establishment of the recently created independent system operator that would allow for the consideration of nuclear power in the long term. This is a major change in government policy, which had previously banned both nuclear power and uranium mining.

Peter Gregg, CEO of Nova Scotia Power, put the role of nuclear power in perspective recently on *Insights*:

> I think for Canada, for North America, for the world to achieve the broad decarbonization net zero goals, nuclear energy has to play a role in that. It'll play a significant role. We will look at it as part of our longer-range planning, and now there's going to be a system operator setup that will actually do that longer-range planning; they will look at that and a make a determination. We're not at this point pursuing small modular reactors as part of our strategy. It is not part of the clean power plan to get us to 2030.

He went on to say SMRs may be part of a longer-term plan and that "one of the biggest challenges for nuclear is getting greenfield site approval." Also of note, the government of Prince Edward Island has expressed interest in the use of SMRs on the Island.

SMALL MODULAR REACTORS

One of the ways other provinces may benefit from nuclear power is the development of small modular reactors. SMRs are a class of nuclear fission reactors that are smaller than conventional nuclear reactors, which can be built in one location and then shipped to and commissioned in a different location.

There is a race to develop SMRs around the world. In Canada, New Brunswick, Alberta, Saskatchewan, and Ontario have signed a memorandum of understanding to work collaboratively to develop an SMR industry. Currently, work on SMRs is under way in both Ontario and New Brunswick. In New Brunswick, NB Power is working with two separate companies on their development: ARC Clean Technology Canada and Moltex Energy Canada. In an *Insights* podcast, Bill Labbe, the former CEO of ARC Clean Technology Canada indicated that he expected their SMR to be operational by 2030, with the Moltex version expected shortly after.

Much of the current work on SMRs is in the Saint John area and, if successful, could become a significant export opportunity for New Brunswick. The province is looking at the opportunity to develop an SMR cluster that will create up to seven hundred high-paying jobs and provide a $1 billion increase to the province's GDP and a $120 million contribution to government revenues over the next fifteen years.

SMRs are expected to deliver between 100 and 300 MW of electricity, with 1 MW enough to provide the electricity to power seven hundred homes. For comparison purposes, conventional nuclear plants produce between 600 and 1,500 MW.

It is worth noting that SMRs have been safely used for decades by the military to power nuclear submarines and aircraft carriers. SMRs can be used in both grid and non-grid applications, including the production of hydrogen and ammonia. The Port of Belledune in northeastern New Brunswick has announced plans to use SMRs in its planned transition to a green energy hub that would include the production of hydrogen for export to Europe.

GREEN HYDROGEN

Hydrogen gas has been touted as the fuel of the future, with a fuel source (water) which is abundant, clean, efficient, and renewable. Hydrogen gas is extracted from water by a process known as electrolysis, which involves the use of a high electric current through water to separate the hydrogen and oxygen molecules. However, this electrolysis process is both energy intensive and expensive. To date, the energy used to produce hydrogen has been mainly from natural gas. But hydrogen can be produced from renewable sources like hydropower, wind, and solar, as well as nuclear power, with no greenhouse emissions.

The government of Canada, through its Department of Natural Resources (NRCAN), has developed a comprehensive hydrogen strategy that is a blueprint for the development of the hydrogen industry in Canada, with the goal of having the country become a major exporter of hydrogen and hydrogen technologies.

The war in Ukraine exposed the growing opportunity to provide Europe with a safe and secure source of green, renewable energy. This is particularly of interest to Atlantic Canada, which is geographically closer to Europe than the rest of North America and has deep-water ports. To that end, German Chancellor Olaf Scholz signed an agreement with Canada in August 2022 for the export of green hydrogen to that country. The establishment of the Canada–Germany Hydrogen Alliance has helped kick-start the development of green hydrogen in Atlantic Canada through companies like EverWind Fuels and Bear Head Energy in Nova Scotia and World Energy GH2 in Newfoundland and Labrador. The goal is to create a transatlantic supply chain by 2030, with first deliveries of Canadian green hydrogen by 2025. As Sean Leet, Managing Director and CEO of World Energy GH2 recently told us during an *Insights* podcast, the company expects to begin construction on its infrastructure in 2024, once final environmental approvals have been completed.

There are several green hydrogen projects across the region but the most advanced are EverWind Fuels and Bear Head Energy at the Strait of Canso in Nova Scotia and World Energy GH2 in Stephenville, NL, where entrepreneur John Risley is involved. All three projects have received environmental approvals and are in the design phase of development. World Energy GH2 has signed an agreement to provide Canadian-made hydrogen to Germany. All three intend to use onshore (and eventually offshore) wind turbines to produce their hydrogen and ammonia. If these projects proceed, they will establish Atlantic Canada as a regional hydrogen hub and create a new sustainable industry for the region. The World Energy GH2 project is expected to be built in two phases, beginning with the construction of a 1-gigawatt facility (a million kilowatts) powered by 164 wind turbines, followed by another 2-GW facility that will eventually produce 250,000 metric tons of hydrogen and 1.1 metric tons of ammonia for export. The first phase is expected to cost $6 billion. Sean Leet, CEO of World Energy GH2, provided an overview of the significant economic impact of the first phase of their project in a 2024 *Insights* podcast:

> It's significant; there are going to be twenty-two hundred direct construction jobs—probably four hundred during operations—and the numbers work out to about forty-two hundred indirect jobs. The project will boost provincial GDP by $2.5 billion over the first three years of development, and we expect this to continue as we build out the other sites in the future. It will

> boost the federal GDP by about $3.6 billion over the first three years and the CapEx [capital expenditure] investment will result in approximately $1.3 billion in household spending in local communities across the province during the construction phase. Tax revenues will be more than $800 million, and that's broken down to $70 million for municipalities, about $430 million for the province, and $410 for the federal government. So it's significant by anybody's standards.

The EverWind project in Nova Scotia has plans for an initial 527 MW of capacity, with plans to add up to 650 MW of capacity. EverWind also has a project in progress in Newfoundland. Bear Head Energy has approval for a 2-GW facility. EverWind has plans to begin construction of two onshore wind farms in 2024 in partnership with the Membertou First Nation, which will be the majority shareholder in those wind farms.

There is no doubt that it will be costly to develop a hydrogen energy sector in this region. At the same time, while there appears to be some momentum, there is still lots of uncertainty about green hydrogen. In particular, there remain concerns about the markets for hydrogen. Indeed, John Risley surprised attendees at the CBRE Conference in the fall of 2024 by announcing a pivot by World Energy to data-mining farms that illustrates growing concerns about the ultimate market for hydrogen in the region.

TIDAL POWER

Tidal power has long been a dream in Atlantic Canada and there have been numerous failed attempts to harness the power of the tides in the Bay of Fundy over the years, with Sustainable Marine being the latest marine energy project to fall short in its efforts. Sustainable Marine was in the process of demonstrating the capability of its solution, a surface-based turbine system that was delivering power to the grid, before it declared bankruptcy due to delays and complexities associated with the regulatory process. At the time of its bankruptcy, the company had reportedly invested nearly $40 million of its own capital in the project. In an *Insights* podcast, former CEO Jason Hayman indicated that there was an opportunity to use tidal power to power two million homes, making it an export opportunity for the region. The departure of Sustainable Marine is clearly a setback for the development of tidal power. The regulatory environment needs to be significantly streamlined and clarified before tidal power becomes a realistic alternative for renewable energy in the region.

WIND POWER

One resource that Atlantic Canada has in abundance is wind. A recent report from the Public Policy Forum, *Catching the Wind* authored by Peter Nicholson, made a strong case that the region has the potential of becoming a wind energy superpower. The report makes a strong case for the development of offshore wind, starting with the Scotian Shelf off Nova Scotia and calls for a bold vision to take advantage what it calls "the greatest undertaking in human history"—the global green energy transition. It also suggests that the massive development of wind energy off the coast of Atlantic Canada could significantly contribute to the national decarbonization objective and at the same time create generational prosperity for the region. Nicholson provided an example of the opportunity associated with offshore wind in a 2023 *Insights* podcast:

> *Fortunately, offshore wind has a very high capacity factor. I'll use 15 gigawatts as an example. It's an amount that I describe as one of the scenarios in the report. It's an amount that I believe is entirely feasible to be generated on the Sable Island bank off the Nova Scotia coast. So, 15 gigawatts would provide the electrical needs of roughly six and a half million households. It would be somewhat more than 10 percent of Canada's total current electrical generation. It's a substantial amount; a very substantial amount. To put it another way, it would be almost twice the total electricity consumption of Atlantic Canada currently, and of course if we were to install and produce 15 gigawatts of capacity offshore, we'd obviously be exporting a lot of it. And that's a key point actually. In fact, it's I would say the major theme of my whole report is that this is an enormous export opportunity—and I'm not talking about export to Europe; I'm talking about export of electrons into Quebec, possibly the northeastern US.*

Nicholson not only outlines the potential for offshore wind but also calls for bold action to take advantage of this enormous opportunity. He went on to tell us that the potential of offshore wind in Atlantic Canada holds the same transformational impact as hydro power in Quebec and oil and gas in Alberta. The question is whether or not Atlantic Canada can seize this transformational opportunity that would likely lead our region to becoming a "have" part of Canada. There is little doubt that it would take an enormous amount of capital, and there would be a need for significant incentives to realize the opportunity, but Nicholson believes Atlantic Canada has great potential in this area.

The Nova Scotia government has established a target to license 5 GW of offshore generation capacity by 2030. Canada currently has no offshore wind turbines in operation. Meanwhile, the UK has 30 GW of offshore power coming from the North Sea. The *Catching the Wind* report indicates that the area around Sable Island is an ideal location for offshore wind and could easily accommodate enough turbines to generate 15 GW of electricity, which is twice the total electricity currently consumed in Atlantic Canada annually. There are other sites around Nova Scotia and the Gulf of St. Lawrence off Newfoundland and Labrador that are potentially ideal locations for offshore wind farms.

At the same time, the development and integration of wind power into the grid is expected to require a vast amount of capital investment. The report concludes that Canada and our region need a "new level of ambition, even audacity" to take advantage of this opportunity and turn the region into an energy superpower. One thing seems abundantly clear: wind represents an unprecedented opportunity for Atlantic Canada and could be a true game changer economically for the region.

SOLAR POWER

Atlantic Canada receives much less sun than the rest of the country. That might explain why commercial applications of solar have been slower to develop in the region. With the cost of solar panels becoming more affordable, the push has been toward the use of solar power in residential applications driven by generous rebates. Commercial use has been limited by the need to have sufficient battery storage to provide a reasonable level of reliability from solar power when the sun doesn't shine. Nova Scotia Power just announced the construction of major storage facilities in sites across the province to support the renewable energy sector in partnership with First Nations and is also piloting a project testing home battery storage with those using solar for residences.

Nonetheless, there is a growing number of commercial solar projects across the region, mostly led by municipalities. One of the earliest was the Digby Neck Wind Farm that was commissioned in 2010, which produces enough energy to power ten thousand homes annually. The City of Summerside developed a solar farm that began generating 21 MW of energy in 2023, or about a quarter of the power needed for the city. The cost of that project was more than $65 million and included nearly fifty thousand solar panels covering eighty acres. In 2023, the Town of Shediac completed a community solar farm that was the first grid-connected solar farm in New Brunswick. The Town of Mahone Bay completed Nova Scotia's largest utility-scale solar facility that produces 4.8 MW of clean energy, while the Town of Berwick operates a 2.4-MW facility.

It is clear that the transition to green energy will take a portfolio approach that includes wind, solar, hydro, and nuclear to reach the net zero targets for Canada by 2050.

CHAPTER 25
SEIZING THE GREEN OPPORTUNITY

ATLANTIC CANADA HAS ARGUABLY THE MOST UNPRECEDENTED ECONOMIC opportunity in its history to date. A transformational opportunity. A once-in-a-lifetime opportunity. It will require a certain boldness of vision to convert this opportunity into reality and a massive investment of capital. While there are opportunities across a variety of sectors, including technology, biosciences, aquaculture, and ocean industries, there is no greater opportunity than green energy. Our region is blessed with the highest tides in the world, leads the country in the development of hydrogen, is the Saudi Arabia of wind resources, and is developing small modular reactors in our region. Seizing the opportunity of green power has the potential of transforming Atlantic Canada into a "have" region on the scale of other resource-rich provinces in western Canada. It will take more than "election cycle"–thinking but the target should be 2050, several elections away. It will take both political and business leadership. As the Ivany Report stated, "It is now or never."

ATLANTIC CANADA AS AN ENERGY SUPERPOWER

The very important and thought-provoking report released in 2023 by the Public Policy Forum, entitled *Catching the Wind: How Atlantic Canada Can Become an Energy Superpower*, makes a compelling case that Atlantic Canada has a transformational opportunity to change its economic future by harnessing the abundant winds in our region. Peter Nicholson, the report's author, is currently the chair of the Canadian Climate Institute but has a long and distinguished career in both the public and private sectors. The Public Policy Forum is the non-partisan organization that has developed the *Atlantic Canada Momentum Index* chronicling the increasing economic momentum with the region. As Peter Nicholson told us in a 2023 *Insights* podcast:

> Atlantic Canada lies adjacent to one of the world's greatest resources of clean energy: the strong winds blowing constantly off our coast. And because offshore wind and Labrador's hydro power are complementary—each serving to make the other more reliable—the combination could go a long way

> to meeting Canada's objective to decarbonize the national energy system. By developing offshore wind energy on a very large scale and expanding transmission capacity into Quebec and Ontario, clean energy could become for Atlantic Canada what fossil energy has been for Alberta. In prospect, it is a project of national scope which would bring unprecedented prosperity to our region.

THE GREEN ENERGY TRANSITION

Nicholson notes that the world is facing the greatest challenge in history in addressing climate change, one that will take both full commitment and effort and enormous capital investments to achieve. The transition to green energy is well under way but has a long way to go. To achieve net zero by 2050, the Canada Energy Regulator (CER) estimates that electricity generation in Canada will have to more than double by 2050. At least half of that increase in annual electricity generation is expected to be supplied by wind. The good news is that Atlantic Canada is one of the best places in Canada, if not the world, to generate electricity from wind, particularly offshore where the winds are stronger and steadier. The offshore potential is important because there is significant resistance to large land-based wind farms.

Currently, wind accounts for about 6 percent of the electricity generated in the world, according to the International Energy Agency (IEA), but is expected to represent nearly a third of all electricity generated by 2050.

THE BENEFITS OF OFFSHORE WIND

There is no energy source that is more climate-friendly than wind. Wind generates about 10 grams of carbon dioxide ($CO2$) per kilowatt hour of electricity generated. A 1-GW facility would produce approximately 45 tonnes of $CO2$ annually, the equivalent of ten gas-powered automobiles, but would be sufficient to supply electricity to almost a third of the homes in Atlantic Canada.

Another benefit of offshore wind is that the wind is usually strongest during the winter when demand for electricity is highest in Canada. Typically, offshore turbines are much larger than onshore turbines and generate more electricity. The offshore wind is also stronger and more reliable than on land and the availability is less intermittent than solar.

ENVIRONMENTAL CONSIDERATIONS

As with all energy sources, there are environmental impacts that need to be considered, including the impacts on marine life and birds, marine transportation, and the fishery. As the Nicholson report notes, the giant offshore turbines are typically located at least a kilometre apart, providing space for marine transportation and fishing vessels. It is worth noting that there has been a long history of offshore wind farms in the North Sea that have had a limited and moderate impact on the environment and marine life. There is also an important difference between offshore wind farms that are near shore and visible from land, like the two recently announced near the Strait of Canso, and those further offshore which are less likely to impact the inshore fishery where there are justifiable concerns.

THE ECONOMIC OPPORTUNITY

Nicholson's report provides an economic development scenario in which thirty thousand jobs could be created over the several decades to develop the 15 GW of offshore wind power proposed in the report—enough to provide electricity to more than 6 million homes and create a major energy export industry for Atlantic Canada. In his report, Nicholson uses the Sable Island Bank as an example of a shallow seabed that could accommodate more than one thousand wind turbines over its eight thousand square kilometres; this would be capable of generating 15 GW of electricity or more. A development of this size could also help develop a supporting supply-chain ecosystem that might include component manufacturing, logistics support, offshore servicing, and monitoring systems. Perhaps the most important opportunity would be the ability to export wind energy elsewhere, with many of the benefits accruing in the region.

Another important opportunity is the ability to attract manufacturing to Atlantic Canada for companies seeking reliable sources of green energy. The development of hydro in Quebec led to the creation of a significant aluminum sector in the province and other spinoffs. The same opportunity exists in Atlantic Canada.

ONSHORE VERSUS OFFSHORE WIND

As the *Catching the Wind* report points out, electricity produced by onshore wind is currently considerably less expensive to produce than electricity from offshore wind. It is expected that the difference in cost will decrease with time and scale. The main advantages associated with offshore wind are that there are no land-use conflicts (and thus, less public opposition) and more consistent strong winds that are more easily accommodated by the grid. There are increasing numbers of onshore wind farms across the region, including Prince Edward Island's West Cape Wind Farm, with fifty-five turbines that produce enough energy to power twenty-five thousand homes.

As previously mentioned, there are already a number of hydrogen projects under development that intend to initially use onshore wind farms as their energy source to produce their ammonia and hydrogen. For example, Bear

Head Energy recently announced an agreement with the Nova Scotia government for access to public lands to construct up to two hundred onshore wind turbines that would generate 2 GW of electrolyzer capacity. The same is true for EverWind Fuels, which has projects under development in both Nova Scotia and Newfoundland and Labrador. In Nova Scotia, EverWind will need 300 MW of wind energy in its first phase, sufficient to produce 200,000 tonnes of ammonia a year. The company anticipates energy from both onshore and offshore wind farms eventually. World Energy GH2 in western Newfoundland expects to generate 3 GW of renewable energy using hundreds of onshore wind farms. A 2024 *Insights* podcast with Sean Leet, the managing director and CEO of World Energy GH2, indicated he expected that the $6 billion project would begin construction in 2024 and be operational by 2026. Leet told *Insights*:

> *The emerging green hydrogen projects in Atlantic Canada are recognized worldwide amongst the most advanced and largest projects of their kind. There is currently foreign direct investment focus on our region that, quite possibly, will exceed what we have witnessed over the past decades in our valuable offshore sector—a local industry that will remain vitally important to the energy transition for many years to come, providing a strong foundation for us to build upon for developing the next phase of our energy industry.*

POLICY AND REGULATORY SUPPORT

Both the federal government and its provincial counterparts need to commit to offshore wind power. The first step is to ensure a regulatory environment that is clear, transparent, and timely. That includes the licensing process, regulations, and impact assessments. The federal government, which has jurisdictional responsibility for renewable offshore energy development through the Canada Energy Regulator (CER), recently expanded the mandate of the joint federal–provincial management groups (the Canada–Nova Scotia Offshore Energy Board and the Canada–Newfoundland and Labrador Offshore Energy Board), both of which were previously responsible for offshore petroleum, to include the responsibility and authority for offshore wind energy. On paper, this should facilitate the development of the needed regulations on a timely basis, but we will see.

In addition, there will be a need for incentives to attract the kind of capital investment necessary to capitalize on this opportunity. This might include government-backed guarantees of a fixed price for the energy generated (the feed-in tariff) over a number of years. The federal government has made a major commitment to a clean-energy future already with various programs in place to support the development of offshore wind, including the $15 billion

Canada Growth Fund and $20 billion from the Canada Infrastructure Bank to support the development of clean electricity, as well as tax incentive programs such as the Clean Electricity Investment Tax Credit.

A BOLD VISION

Perhaps the biggest challenge to realizing the enormous opportunity presented by our offshore wind resources is the need to seize the opportunity, to have a bold vision of what is possible, and, as Peter Nicholson states in his report, to embrace a certain "audacity" in thinking. Atlantic Canada will need the participation of its energy utilities, not just in upgrading the transmission infrastructure to export wind energy elsewhere, but to invest in a green energy future by becoming involved in the development of offshore wind. It will also require the support and commitment of the federal and provincial governments in the region. The future is now.

Let's be audacious.

CHAPTER 26

EMULATING ENTREPRENEURIAL SUCCESS

OVER THE PAST COUPLE OF YEARS, WE HAVE HAD THE OPPORTUNITY TO TALK with dozens of successful entrepreneurs across the region on the *Insights* podcast. Some of the stories of success stand out and provide examples of what is possible in Atlantic Canada. All of the examples share a "bold" vision of what is possible and clearly underscore the ability of Atlantic Canadian businesses to compete both nationally and internationally. Here are a few interesting examples that can serve as inspiration and models for others to follow.

COOKE INC.: A GLOBAL JUGGERNAUT

Cooke Inc., the parent company of Cooke Aquaculture, has quietly become the largest privately owned seafood company in the world out of Blacks Harbour, NB. Cooke's core purpose is to "cultivate the ocean with care, nourish the world, provide for our families, and build stronger communities." This purpose is especially relevant as most of its operations are in rural communities, providing well-paid, year-round jobs.

Cooke is currently the fifth-largest salmon producing company in the world, behind four publicly traded companies, and its owner and CEO Glenn Cooke has every intention of moving up the list. In a 2023 *Insights* podcast, Cooke provided some insight regarding the company's growth focus and its ambitions:

> We've been fortunate to grow the company, doubling the company every two or three years on our track record, and I think our growth is only limited by how many good people we can find. Cooke is about people, and our capacity to grow is only limited by the capacity of our people that either step up or come aboard. We want to continue to grow it as a family. We believe in investing and growing. We are excited when we create jobs in rural areas around the world. We're excited when we create jobs in the head office in Saint John, New Brunswick, so we can keep investing, and a lot of that's got to be through acquisition because a lot of that resource, whether it's farmed

or wild, is in somebody else's hands. The sky's the limit. We're only number five [in the world] in farmed salmon so there's more room to grow.

Cooke currently has more than 15,000 employees in fifteen countries, generating more than $4 billion in revenue annually. The company has been on an accelerated growth strategy through acquisitions. Since 2016, it has made fifteen acquisitions, including in November 2024, Peru-based Copeinca. The acquisition of Copeinca, which is Peru's largest fishing company, was worth more than $1 billion. The company has spent more than $3.5 billion on acquisitions since 2016.

Cooke is a fully integrated seafood company, utilizing a fleet of more than eight hundred vessels and thirty processing plants around the world, not including the Peru acquisition. The company has its own genetics research, hatcheries, feed plants, harvesting facilities, production plants, and transportation. It is headquartered in Saint John, NB and has about 2,500 employees in the region, mostly in rural communities. Of that number, about 250 are head office jobs.

The company began in Blacks Harbour in 1985 with two fish farming pens and five thousand salmon. The company now produces between 30 and 40 million salmon per year, as well as many other species of fish. Cooke currently harvests and sells 30 percent wild seafood products and 70 percent farmed seafood products. It has been ranked as one of Canada's Best Managed Companies for the last seventeen years.

GROWTH THROUGH ACQUISITION

With fifteen acquisitions since 2016, it is evident what Cooke's growth strategy is. Some of the acquisitions have been enormous, including the acquisition of the Tassal Group, the largest seafood company in Australia, in December 2022 for a reported $1.5 billion. This was the company's largest acquisition to date. At the time of purchase, Tassal had 1,700 employees and revenues approaching $1 billion annually. When asked about the criteria used in his acquisition strategy, Glenn Cooke indicated the most important criteria was to ensure the corporate values and culture of the target company aligned with those of Cooke.

REGULATORY CONSTRAINTS

Despite the company's rapid growth in recent years, Cooke has struggled to expand its business in its home market. It is clear that Cooke still considers Atlantic Canada to be a market of opportunity to expand the aquaculture sector, although its investment in the region has been relatively modest in recent years. Unfortunately, the company's plans to expand in the region are being severely constrained by the regulatory process within the region, especially Nova Scotia, which the company considers to be the most difficult jurisdiction in which to receive approval for new sites. In looking at the number of applications currently under review by the province of Nova Scotia, many by First Nations, it is apparent that the process is not particularly quick, with some applications still waiting for approvals more than seven years after having been submitted. This is perhaps the reason Cooke has looked elsewhere to expand its business. As Glenn Cooke made clear in our conversation with him, his company fully commits to protecting the environment, but he questions the lack of speed in the process to approve new sites. In Norway, pre-approved sites for aquaculture are released each year and are available for lease through a competitive bidding process.

FUTURE PLANS

Cooke Inc. is the world's largest privately owned seafood company but ranks fifth in size behind four larger public companies. There is no indication that the company's explosive growth is near completion. Glenn Cooke, when asked about the future of the company, indicated his interest in continuing to move up the list of the world's largest seafood companies. That is a bold vision—some might even say audacious—for a company from Blacks Harbour, NB.

KILLAM APARTMENT REIT: A REAL ESTATE POWERHOUSE

Few Atlantic Canadians know much about Killam Apartment REIT (more commonly known as Killam Properties) unless they rent one of the company's apartments. Yet Killam, headquartered in Halifax, has quietly become one of Canada's largest residential multi-family property owners, with 275 properties and more than twenty-five thousand units in seven provinces across the country. And it all started with the company's first acquisition in 2002.

EARLY YEARS

Killam was incorporated in May 2000 (and became a publicly traded real estate investment company later that same year) by founding president and CEO Philip Fraser, and Rob Richardson, a founding director and shareholder and now executive vice-president of the company. Killam's initial investment of $10 million was in 2002 and included 149 units in three buildings. It took only five years for the company to achieve $500 million in assets. It became a real estate investment trust (REIT) in 2016.

In the ensuing years, aggressive growth has led to annual revenues of $330 million and Killam's property portfolio today totals $5 billion. Over the last decade, the company has averaged $185 million in new investments annually.

Killam self-manages its assets, preferring to be closer to its residents to better build a sense of community in its properties. The company has moved from solely employing an acquisition strategy to a combined strategy of acquisition and constructing its own buildings, and now has $700 million worth of buildings that it has built itself.

HEAD OFFICE JOBS

Atlantic Canada has proportionately fewer head offices in the region than elsewhere in Canada. As we know, companies with head offices provide incremental economic value to the communities where they are located through their higher paying jobs to support their business activities elsewhere.

Killam Properties is headquartered in Halifax in the same building on Kempt Road where it started in 2000. Currently, Killam has over seven hundred full-time employees, with an additional fifty to seventy-five seasonal positions. Of those jobs, eighty-five are head office jobs.

THE REIT MARKET

In Canada, the Income Tax Act of 1986 established the foundation for the REIT market, with the first established in 1993. REITs, which are publicly traded companies that own, operate, or finance real estate, are required to pay 90 percent of their annual taxable income to their unitholders as monthly distributions. This means that earnings are taxed in the hands of their investors and not at the corporate level. As such, REITs offer investors both steady and some of the highest yields in the stock market. REITs are impacted by interest rates and inflation and sometimes challenged in jurisdictions with rent caps such as Nova Scotia currently.

Canadian Apartment Properties (CAPREIT) is Canada's largest REIT, with real estate holdings worth $17 billion and more than forty-five thousand housing units in Canada. By comparison, Killam's real estate holdings are worth $5 billion, and the company has twenty-five thousand housing units. There are currently about forty-five REITS listed on the TSX. Killam is currently ranked eleventh as a REIT by cap size overall (cap size refers to the market capitalization of a company based on the value of its outstanding shares), and among those in the apartment market, Killam is ranked third.

MARKET REACH

Killam has been an aggressive market consolidator over the years, especially within Atlantic Canada. There are other consolidators in the market, including Boardwalk out West and CAPREIT in Ontario. The company now has a presence in seven provinces: the four Atlantic provinces, Ontario, Alberta, and British Columbia.

Over a period of twenty years, Killam has grown to nineteen thousand apartment units and nearly six thousand manufactured homes. In addition, the company has 6 percent of its holdings in commercial real estate—about a million square feet of space. In 2021, it purchased the Charlottetown Mall (rebranded as Royalty Crossing) with Tim Banks, a well-known PEI entrepreneur.

Killam is the largest landlord in Atlantic Canada with six thousand units in Nova Scotia, forty-five hundred units in New Brunswick, one thousand in Newfoundland and Labrador and one thousand units in Prince Edward Island.

CHALLENGES OF THE HOUSING MARKET

In a recent *Insights* podcast, Phil Fraser discussed the challenges associated with the housing market today, especially in terms of dealing with rising operating costs and higher interest rates. He acknowledged that higher interest rates had impacted the company's growth strategy but expects a return to normal as rates begin to subside. Fraser told *Insights*:

> The biggest stumbling block today, before getting out the door and starting the building cycle, is at the municipal level, and, as much as they say they want development, the process to get an actual building permit to put a shovel into the ground is complicated and time-consuming. The number of roadblocks in every municipality across the country is long and hard. It is just something that I don't see changing overnight.

Killam has been actively involved in reducing its energy expenses through the use of solar power and geothermal heating and cooling plants. It has a goal to self-generate 10 percent of its energy by 2025. Fraser indicated that the annual operating cost per unit had increased from $2,000 to $7,000 over the past twenty years, with realty taxes the single biggest driver of that increase.

The cost of building is another challenge. In the early years, Killam could purchase an apartment building for $20,000 to $50,000 per door (unit). According to Fraser, the cost to build a unit today is approaching $500,000. He estimates that there is a need in Canada to build 3–5 million housing units over the next decade or so. It will take about $100 billion to build 200,000 units, so the overall costs to meet housing demand over the next decade will be in the trillions.

Fraser believes that municipalities are the biggest barrier to increasing housing supply because their permitting processes are too complicated and take too long. He also mentioned that taxes on housing construction were too high, accounting for 20 percent of the cost of construction, and advocated for the need to reduce those costs. The recent decision by the federal government to remove its portion of the HST on the construction of rental buildings is helpful, as are Nova Scotia's and Prince Edward Island's decisions to do the same.

AFFORDABILITY

Fraser indicated that Killam had a near-100 percent occupancy currently, with waiting lists in many buildings. The company's turnover rate in 2022 was 22 percent and is expected to be below 20 percent in 2023 (down from 33 percent in the early years).

Interestingly, despite the numbers reported in the media that the rent for many apartments in the region's cities is now above $2,000 per month, the current average cost at Killam of their 19,000 units is $1,318, with 75 percent of its units under $1,500. Statistics Canada reported the average rent for a two-bedroom apartment in Halifax during 2023 was $1,626 per month.[37]

Killam works with the non-profit sector, especially those in mental health, and has had long-term affordability commitments on eleven hundred of its units since the very beginning, where these units are offered at below market rates for the non-profit organizations the company has agreements with. Fraser feels that the responsibility for affordable housing lies, at least in part, with the private sector, while the problem of housing for the homeless is a public-sector or societal responsibility. He is encouraged by the federal government's housing strategy that has earmarked $82 billion to address housing affordability.

LOOKING AHEAD

Despite the current high-interest environment over the past couple of years, Killam expects to continue to expand its holdings and is committed to increasing the supply of new housing to respond to increasing population growth across the region. In the meantime, Killam will continue to be a growing presence in the housing market, both regionally and nationally and will serve as a model for other companies in the region wishing to compete outside this region.

THE BIOVECTRA ANNOUNCEMENT: A GAME CHANGER

You may recall the early days of the pandemic when Canada struggled to obtain the vaccine doses it needed to protect the population. That was because, over the years, the domestic manufacturing capability for producing pharmaceuticals had been diminished as the country moved to import these medicines from countries with lower production costs, following the Mulroney government's strategy to privatize and sell off some of the country's domestic manufacturing capacity, especially Connaught Labs. During the pandemic, the federal government, to its credit, recognized the need to repatriate our capacity to produce our own medicines domestically and was quite quick to address this issue. The government has committed to rebuilding Canada's biomanufacturing and life sciences sector. That is a good thing.

The federal government had already announced that more vaccines and therapeutics will be produced in Canada in partnerships with Sanofi Canada, Moderna, and Novavax, and more recently Merck Canada. The 2021 announcement by the federal government and PEI-based BIOVECTRA to establish new vaccine manufacturing facilities in Charlottetown, PEI, and Windsor, NS, is part of this repatriation strategy. This is a game changer for Canada for sure, but a potentially bigger game changer for the bioscience sector in Atlantic Canada.

The bioscience sector is becoming significant in Atlantic Canada, accounting for about four thousand jobs, revenues of $655 million from two hundred companies, and fifty research organizations. Much of that activity is currently, and surprisingly for some, located in Prince Edward Island, which accounts for more than half of all revenues and employment in the sector.

HISTORICALLY DISADVANTAGED

Since Confederation, as Donald Savoie has articulated so well in his book *Looking for Bootstraps*, national policies have favoured central Canada to the detriment of other regions of the country, including Atlantic Canada. National policies have led to the concentration of much of Canada's manufacturing might in Quebec and Ontario. The 2023 completion of BIOVECTRA's $90 million biomanufacturing centre is perhaps one of the few times our region has been given serious consideration for being part of a national policy. (The national shipbuilding strategy was the other policy that favoured this region in recent years.)

BIOVECTRA WELL POSITIONED

How did a relatively unknown company based in tiny Prince Edward Island position itself to become part of Canada's domestic supply chain for pharmaceutical production? It may surprise many that BIOVECTRA was founded in 1970 by Regis Duffy as Diagnostic Chemicals Limited (DCL) in the basement of then Saint Dunstan's University. Duffy was the dean of science and was looking for a way to employ some of his students during the summer so he set up a small company to produce bioagents. Over the years, the company evolved to become what is known in the pharmaceutical industry as a CDMO, or a company that provides design and manufacturing services to pharmaceutical companies. Technow told us about the advantages of being a CDMO during an *Insights* podcast, shortly after the announcement of the plans to build a new manufacturing plant to produce mRNA vaccines:

> In the pharmaceutical world, CDMO stands for contract development and manufacturing organizations. You've got to look at organizations like BIOVECTRA as trusted partners of all pharmaceutical and biotech companies. We help to scale up and develop what I would call the most precious assets of pharmaceutical companies. Pharmaceutical companies often do that themselves with their own dedicated manufacturing sites, but the pharmaceutical companies more and more turn to organizations like ours and partner up and hand over their assets to us to scale them up and make sure that they can successfully launch products and manufacture products as they need. We are the ones who have very flexible platforms. We can actually switch manufacturing platforms relatively efficiently, which of course is one of the key aspects of the entire CDMO business.

The company is an important part of the Island's biosciences sector and currently employs about 550 people in a sector has more than 2,200 employees on the Island and has export revenues of nearly $600 million in 2023. Interestingly, Regis Duffy was the first chair of the board for the PEI BioAlliance, the industry association led by Executive Director Rory Francis.

Francis told us that the announcement "represents national recognition of the credibility and sophistication of the companies in the region and will open the door to national and international attraction of brainpower, investment, and new technology."

The BioAlliance has been instrumental in the creation of CASTL (Canadian Alliance for Skills and Training in Life Sciences), which was established to develop a pipeline of talent needed to grow the bioscience sector not only in PEI, but across Canada. CASTL is based in PEI and is the first partnership of its kind between industry, academia, and government to address the future skills needs of the Canadian life sciences sector, with a focus on biopharmaceutical manufacturing jobs.

THE PLAN

In a 2021 *Insights* podcast, BIOVECTRA's CEO, Oliver Technow, outlined his company's plan and ambition. Technow is an experienced international pharmaceutical executive. Originally from Germany, he worked in both Europe and the United States before landing in PEI in 2015. He is a good example of both the kind of talent that can be attracted to Atlantic Canada and the kind of talent needed to propel our region to a new level of prosperity.

The expansion of BIOVECTRA's facilities in Charlottetown and Windsor is anticipated to create an additional 125 new high-paying jobs. Recently, the company reached the 700-employee level. The new manufacturing facilities have the capacity to provide 160 million mRNA vaccine doses annually—more than enough to supply Canada and other export markets.

THE FUTURE FOR BIOSCIENCES IN ATLANTIC CANADA

According to Technow, the announcement to produce mRNA vaccines in Atlantic Canada is a potential game changer for the region, which will draw more attention to this part of Canada and create "limitless possibilities for growth as our global clients announce significant and new investments."

The importance of having a strong industry association such as the PEI BioAlliance cannot be understated in terms of the success that PEI has had in creating a successful bioscience cluster on the Island. It serves as a blueprint for the rest of the region in creating similar clusters in other parts of Atlantic Canada. The recent BIOVECTRA announcement provides a near-term opportunity for the PEI BioAlliance to leverage the profile created.

There is also an opportunity for greater interprovincial collaboration in the bioscience sector. There is little question that the region is better off working together than separately to develop a thriving bioscience sector. The Atlantic Canada Bio Industries Alliance is a pan-Atlantic bioscience industry association, leveraging the work of provincial associations, including the PEI BioAlliance, BioNova in Nova Scotia, BioNB, and techNL. This alliance is more informal than formal and has no organizational structure currently to support its efforts. The Alliance provides an umbrella for the region's bioscience companies to attend the annual Global Bio Conference, which acts as the annual gathering event for the Canadian bioscience industry.

The Alliance is collectively undertaking a regional economic impact study this year (pending funding) to help delineate the size and scope of the sector in Atlantic Canada. But there is also an opportunity for the Alliance to create a regional HR strategy to address the supply of a skilled workforce to satisfy the increasing demand. This will require more collaboration with the post-secondary sector within the region.

Currently, BioNova hosts the largest health and life science conference in the region called BioPort. There is likely an opportunity to expand this conference regionally and hold it in other venues in Atlantic Canada. A broader regional conference would encourage more collaboration and support commercialization opportunities for those in the sector.

There is little doubt that the opening of BIOVECTRA's new

manufacturing facility is a game changer for the bioscience sector in the region. As Technow states, "The new biomanufacturing facility catapults us into an entirely new level of possibilities." The question is, how can the region take advantage of this moment?

THE KING OF SUPPLEMENTS IN CANADA

Supplements as a product category is big business. Many Canadians take a supplement of some sort for nutritional or health reasons, whether a probiotic, omega-3, or a multivitamin. The market in Canada is estimated to be worth more than $1.5 billion and is expected to grow by a compounded annual rate of 6 percent between now and 2030.

SUPPLEMENT MARKET

Supplements are widely available in Canada through a variety of channels, including big box retailers like Costco and Walmart, grocery stores, pharmacies, and online through sites like Amazon. There are also specialized retail outlets that sell only supplements. The two biggest retail chains in Canada are Popeye's Supplements and Supplement King. Interestingly, Supplement King is headquartered in Nova Scotia.

There have been ongoing concerns related to product safety and efficacy for supplements over the years. Few clinical trials exist to back up product claims. In Canada, a natural product number (NPN) indicating that the product has been approved by Health Canada and is safe, works as described, and is of high quality is now required. Supplement King carries only products with this designation. In addition, the company endeavours to carry as many Canadian-made products as possible, with the majority of its products currently being produced in Canada.

THE SUPPLEMENT KING

Supplement King was founded in 2004 by Nova Scotian Roger King, originally from Rothesay, NB. The company was started while King was attending Saint Mary's University as a source of student income. His interest in supplements was driven initially by his involvement in weightlifting. It led to the opening of a small mall kiosk and then the opening of his first retail outlet in 2006.

Recently, King opened his one hundredth retail store in British Columbia, and he opens, on average, two new outlets per month. The chain has revenue of more than $100 million according to King, who was reluctant to provide an exact revenue number as a privately held company. Supplement King employs a thousand people across the country and has a head-office staff of twenty in

Dartmouth who primarily provide centralized financial and accounting support and marketing services, as well as managing the chain's merchandising and online sales program and product distribution.

King has been recognized for his business success by being named to *Atlantic Business*'s Top 50 CEO Hall of Fame as an Ernst & Young Entrepreneur of the Year in Atlantic Canada and as the Halifax Chamber's Businessperson of the Year.

MARKETING STRATEGY

In a 2024 *Insights* podcast, King talked about how he developed his marketing strategy:

> I had quickly realized being located next to a fitness centre was going to be an important part of any type of growth. I also realized that my customer was not who I expected him or her to be. I thought that I would see athletes and fitness enthusiasts. In reality, I saw a mostly corporate crowd that were looking to try to lead a healthier life but very unsure of how to do so. I quickly also realized that this crowd was much less price-sensitive than traditional supplement consumers at the time, and if they were going to get some result and a little bit of bang for their buck, they were pretty happy to pay for it.
>
> Our biggest competitor at the time was Popeye's Supplements Canada and their marketing and their direction was towards the bodybuilding and athlete crowd. We decided to take all of our marketing and store fixturing and branding in a very mainstream fitness-goals–based direction, so everything that we do in our business is about the fitness goal when somebody walks through our doors and how do we help them achieve this.

One of his biggest challenges in growing the business was sourcing product manufacturers and establishing vendor relationships with manufacturers of supplements. Having now reached scale for his operations, Supplement King is able to negotiate better price and volume discounts for his retail chain. With each additional retail store that King opens, his ability to secure improved pricing and volume discounts increases.

GROWTH STRATEGY

The rapid growth of Supplement King over a relatively short period of time has been driven by the decision to license his brand to others. King's licensing strategy is focussed on finding people interested in owning multi-retail stores. This helps secure the success of his expansion plans as most new outlets are being managed by experienced and successful operators. In fact, King told us that eight out of ten new openings are with existing licensees. It also has the added advantage of dealing with fewer licensees and having stronger relationships with those licensees as a result. It currently requires an investment of about $400,000 to become a Supplement King licensee, which includes the costs of fitting up the retail outlet.

The selection process for potential new retail stores is also key to the company's success and growth. Supplement King prefers to locate their retail stores in close proximity to major health and fitness facilities to be nearer to a key customer base for the chain—those interested in sports nutrition and health.

King has ambitious plans for growth; he expects to double the number of retail stores to two hundred within the next three and a half to four years, with twenty-six new stores scheduled for the current year alone. If he succeeds with this growth plan, he is likely to establish Supplement King as the leading specialized supplement retailer in Canada. At the time of writing, Popeye's Supplements and Supplement King have about the same number of outlets. One thing that is driving the aggressive expansion plan for the company is population growth across the country.

Supplement King is the official supplement retailer for both the CFL and the CHL. When asked about possible expansion into the US, King indicated that the company is considering that market, but unlikely to enter the US until it has achieved it current expansion goals in Canada.

Another key to the company's success is the product knowledge of its staff. The company places great emphasis on the training of its front-line staff to build confidence and long-term relationships with its customer base. King also places a strong emphasis on building a corporate culture that focusses on helping Canadians achieve their fitness goals.

It is interesting to note that one market the company has yet to penetrate is Quebec. In our *Insights* discussion, King acknowledged the challenge of entering a mainly francophone market, and said the company is looking at that market and expects to eventually have a presence.

LOOKING AHEAD

Supplement King is a rare example of an Atlantic Canadian–based company achieving success nationally as a retailer. With the possible exception of Sobeys, there are few national retailers that have originated and been based within the region. Many have had success expanding beyond the region, including Irving Oil. What is encouraging about Supplement King is that the company's success nationally demonstrates it is possible to achieve such success while headquartered in Atlantic Canada. But it does require a certain ambition that we need more of within the region.

CHAPTER 27
FIRST NATIONS IN REGIONAL ECONOMIC DEVELOPMENT

ATLANTIC CANADA'S FIRST NATIONS ARE BECOMING AN ECONOMIC DEVELOPment engine in the region. According to the census, there were 136,000 persons of Indigenous origin living in the four Atlantic provinces as of 2021, or approximately 6 percent of the regional population. There is a significant difference in the size of the Indigenous populations by province. Measured by share of the total, Newfoundland and Labrador has the third largest Indigenous population in the country as a percentage of the population. As of 2021, there were over 52,000 Indigenous people living in Nova Scotia, 33,300 in New Brunswick, 46,545 in Newfoundland and Labrador, and 3,400 in Prince Edward Island.

FIGURE 27-1: INDIGENOUS POPULATION AS A PERCENTAGE OF TOTAL POPULATION, 2021

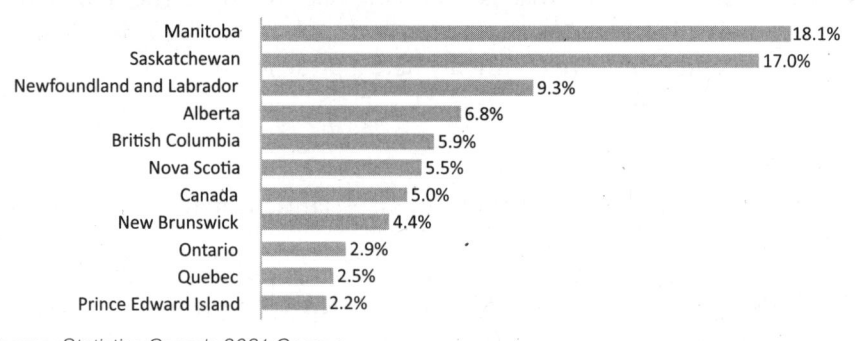

Region	%
Manitoba	18.1%
Saskatchewan	17.0%
Newfoundland and Labrador	9.3%
Alberta	6.8%
British Columbia	5.9%
Nova Scotia	5.5%
Canada	5.0%
New Brunswick	4.4%
Ontario	2.9%
Quebec	2.5%
Prince Edward Island	2.2%

Source: Statistics Canada 2021 Census

The growth in the Indigenous population has been significant in recent years. Between 2011 and 2021, in Nova Scotia the population rose by 55 percent, in Prince Edward Island by 52 percent, in New Brunswick by 47 percent, and across Newfoundland and Labrador by 30 percent. As shown in figure 27-2, the Indigenous population in Atlantic Canada is growing faster here than across the country overall.

FIGURE 27-2: PERCENTAGE CHANGE IN THE INDIGENOUS POPULATION, 2011–2021

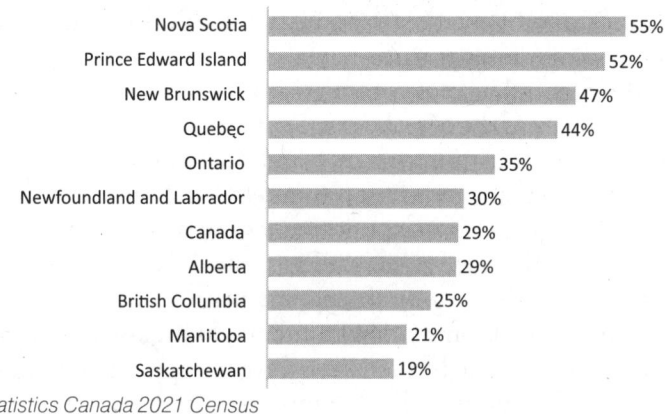

Source: Statistics Canada 2021 Census

The Indigenous population in Atlantic Canada is much younger than the non-Indigenous population, with 47 percent under the age of thirty-five, as compared to 36 percent among the non-Indigenous population.

FIGURE 27-3: AGE BREAKDOWN, NON-INDIGENOUS AND INDIGENOUS POPULATIONS, 2021

	Non-Indigenous	Indigenous	Index (non-Indigenous = 1.00)
0 to 14 years	14%	20%	1.45
15 to 24 years	11%	14%	1.37
25 to 34 years	11%	13%	1.14
35 to 44 years	12%	12%	0.98
45 to 54 years	13%	13%	1.00
55 to 64 years	16%	14%	0.84
65 years and over	22%	13%	0.60

Source: Statistics Canada 2021 Census

Although the economic outcomes for the Indigenous population have been improving in recent years, average incomes, workforce participation, and other statistics continue to show gaps compared to the non-Indigenous population.

THE FIRST NATIONS ECONOMIC RENAISSANCE

Across Atlantic Canada, the First Nations are taking a leadership role when it comes to economic development.

Among the first Indigenous communities to embrace a robust economic development agenda was the Membertou First Nation in Nova Scotia. Led by a visionary leader for nearly forty years, Chief Terrance Paul, the community has been investing in many industries from retail and services to fishing and energy. In 2023, the Membertou government generated $80 million from its investments. This money was reinvested into the community in the form of housing, services, and future growth opportunities.

The Qalipu First Nation in Newfoundland and Labrador is partnering with many companies related to the new green energy industry emerging in the province. Not content with just a simple royalty stream, the sixty-seven traditional Mi'kmaq communities that make up the Qalipu Nation are taking equity stakes in the projects, setting up or buying suppliers, and advancing workforce development efforts to ensure that the entire Band can take advantage of the next generation of industry in the province.

After decades of working all over the world, brothers Terry and Jim Richardson came back to New Brunswick to lead an economic development renaissance for the Oinpegitjoig (Pabineau) First Nation. Chief Terry and Councillor Jim are working with the community to attract commercial investment and other opportunities. They are a leading partner in the development of a new green energy park at the Port of Belledune that potentially represents the largest industrial investment ever in northeastern New Brunswick. Working with the North Shore Mi'kmaq Tribal Council, this Indigenous population is well-positioned to be a key beneficiary of this opportunity.

There are many initiatives across Atlantic Canada where First Nations communities and Indigenous entrepreneurs are partnering to mutual benefit. In New Brunswick, a recently announced project near Sussex will see the First Nations of Amlamgog, Natoaganeg (Eel Ground), Oinpegitjoig (Pabineau), Esgenoôpetitj (Burnt Church), Tjipõgtõtjg (Bouctouche), L'nui Menikuk (Indian Island), Ugpi'ganjig (Eel River Bar), and Metepenagiag (Red Bank) partner with the private Nova Scotia company Natural Forces to build new wind energy infrastructure near Sussex. As equity owners, the First Nations will receive an ongoing revenue stream to help fund public services in their communities.

First Nations in Nova Scotia and beyond are now major partners in the regional fishery. Led by Membertou Chief Terry Paul, a consortium of First Nations communities and Premium Brands Holdings purchased Clearwater Seafoods in 2020 for $1 billion. Clearwater is the largest shellfish production company in North America, and it has been generating record profits since the sale.[38]

The growing involvement of First Nations in natural resource development is being driven by progressive leadership within Indigenous communities and improving governance models, especially in terms of having separate economic development organizations with their own board of directors.

A CONTINUED PARTNERSHIP

As the region looks to the future, continued partnerships between Indigenous and non-Indigenous communities will help ensure regional prosperity. Particularly in resource development and other uses of the region's vast land area, First Nations will continue to be at the fore of new opportunities. This will lead to more timely development of our natural resources and a stronger social license to undertake resource development. It will also lead to greater self-sufficiency for First Nations by developing own-source revenue streams that can be reinvested into their communities. It is the critical economic part of the reconciliation process with Indigenous communities. It is a clear win-win scenario.

CHAPTER 28
THE RISK OF BACKSLIDING

A SUSTAINED ECONOMIC GROWTH AGENDA FOR ATLANTIC CANADA REQUIRES continuing support from all three levels of government and from key institutions, the business community, and the general public. Pressures to curb immigration, reduce investment in natural resource–based industries, or divert the focus away from economic development are real risks to the region's future prosperity.

FEDERAL GOVERNMENT BACKSLIDING

The federal government has been an important enabler of the recent population growth in Atlantic Canada through the better alignment of immigrant attraction to workforce demand, the boosting of immigrant targets for the region, the increase in international students, and other initiatives. In addition to immigration, the federal government has supported a number of important economic development–related activities in the region, including the Ocean Supercluster initiative and the provision of new funding for housing.

The recently announced cap on immigration and the reduction on the number of foreign students is concerning and potentially damaging to the economic momentum that the region has been experiencing. Despite growing calls across Canada among certain public policy experts, politicians, and others to curtail the number of immigrants, temporary workers, and international students coming to Canada, there is a need for sustainable (orderly) population growth strategies that allow our economies in Atlantic Canada to grow at a national growth rate. A more nuanced approach to the numbers of immigrants and foreign students is warranted to better reflect the needs and ability of individual provinces to absorb these newcomers. Otherwise, smaller provinces like those in Atlantic Canada will continue to fall economically behind the larger provinces in Canada.

We have seen an increase in the number of permanent residents settling in Canada each year because there has been a rising demand for more immigrants to meet workforce demand and to address entrepreneurial opportunities. Historically, most immigrants have settled in the largest urban centres, and now we are seeing immigrants flow into all regions of Canada, including smaller urban centres and even rural regions. Table 28-1 shows that the largest increases in the past five years have been in places like Moncton, Edmundston, Summerside, and Gander. Edmundston now has an immigration rate similar to that of Edmonton, AB, and London, ON. Bathurst, NB, and Kentville, NS, have higher immigration rates than Montréal, QC.

TABLE 28-1: IMMIGRATION RATE PER 10,000 POPULATION BY YEAR AND SELECTED URBAN CENTRE, FOR CMA AND CA AREAS

	2018	2023	% change		2018	2023	% change
Moncton, NB	94	280	+198%	Edmundston, NB	25	190	+661%
Summerside, PE	54	268	+396%	Saint John, NB	64	128	+100%
Charlottetown, PE	230	256	+11%	Kentville, NS	27	109	+305%
Toronto, ON	168	200	+19%	Bathurst, NB	24	99	+313%
Vancouver, BC	133	185	+39%	Montréal, QC	100	85	-15%
Halifax, NS	118	172	+46%	Corner Brook, NL	26	80	+210%
St. John's, NL	48	163	+239%	Campbellton, NB	8	94	+1080%
Gander, NL	18	157	+771%	Truro, NS	20	73	+263%
Fredericton, NB	137	149	+9%	Cape Breton, NS	21	65	+210%

JANUARY THROUGH OCTOBER 2023
Source: IRCC

The Ontario Ministry of Finance provides population projections for the province out to 2046. In its most recent projection, the reference case calls for a 30 percent increase in immigrants to that province by 2034 and a 40 percent increase by 2046. In the high population growth projection, the province is expecting 50 percent growth in the number of immigrants settling in the province within a decade. If the federal government did not increase the annual permanent resident admissions to Canada, and Ontario was to achieve its vision for high population growth, within a decade that province alone would need to attract 58 percent of all new permanent residents each year by 2033, up from 44 percent now.

One of the country's foremost thinkers on regional economic development, Donald Savoie, has written extensively about the fact that when the interests of the large urban centres or provinces in Canada clash with the interests of the smaller places, the larger places tend to win out. To put it another way, as Savoie says, "the big dogs always eat first." This is an important consideration for Atlantic Canada. Ontario has the most population and the most voters. If the federal government restrains the growth in permanent resident admissions, which province is most likely to be harmed: vote-rich Ontario or New Brunswick?

If the mayors of Toronto, Vancouver, Calgary, and the other largest urban centres are prepared to cut their immigration, temporary worker, and international student numbers significantly, then it is possible there could be a reduction to the national inflow. It would be a mistake for the federal government to cut the immigration flow into Canada if it hurts the small and mid-sized urban centres and rural areas across the country. Given the demographic situation in these areas, they need immigration more than the largest urban centres do.

In addition, Atlantic Canada's universities and colleges are attracting international students, many of whom are playing an important role in the workforce while studying and after graduation through the expanded use of the post-graduate work permit program. A broad-based cut in the flow of international students could also harm the regional economy.

Immigrants are playing a key role in the economic renewal of Atlantic Canada. The immigrant workforce has increased substantially, nearly doubling in Prince Edward Island between November 2017 and November 2023, 80 percent higher in Nova Scotia and 76 percent higher in New Brunswick. Without new immigrants, the regional economy would have struggled in the past few years.

Obviously, we need good policies when it comes to the attraction of international students. The 2024 reduction in the number of foreign students was likely a prudent short-term measure in light of the housing shortages. However, as universities move to increase student housing, these reductions need to be lifted and considered on a province-by-province basis. We should be looking strategically at the post-secondary education sector as a talent pipeline for industries with workforce demand and not just a source of revenue for colleges and universities. The federal government should set national immigration targets based on provincial aspirations and not establish a top-down politically motivated target. If New Brunswick or Nova Scotia wants to grow its population by 1.5 percent per year and has the capacity to absorb that rate of population growth, it should be supported by the federal government's immigration policies.

THE FEDERAL GOVERNMENT AND ECONOMIC DEVELOPMENT

The federal government has significant influence over economic development in Atlantic Canada. This influence is felt in many ways, from the permitting of aquaculture and mining projects through to direct financial support for strategic industries. New green industries' federal tax credit programs will be key to the development of green hydrogen and other industries reliant on non-emitting electricity generation. Direct federal financial support, such as the tens of millions of dollars provided to Michelin in Nova Scotia, shows some willingness to treat Atlantic Canada fairly as the federal government pours tens of billions of dollars in subsidies to the auto sector in Ontario and Quebec.

Atlantic Canada's export economy is starting to struggle. The federal government, through its many economic development agencies, should commit to working with the Atlantic provinces to boost export activity in the coming years.

PROVINCIAL GOVERNMENT BACKSLIDING

The provincial governments across Atlantic Canada also need to remain committed to economic development and population growth. This will require ambitious population growth targets, a robust economic development agency, and targeted investments to support growth in areas such as housing, health care, and education.

Some people will call for government to put the brakes on the progress that has been made in recent years. They will call for a lower population growth rate and for turning inward to take care of our current population.

This would be a mistake. We need to seize the momentum in the region now that we are finally setting the foundation for a long-term, sustained economic growth trajectory in Atlantic Canada.

MUNICIPAL GOVERNMENT BACKSLIDING

Local governments also need to be committed to growth across Atlantic Canada. Only a few short years ago many mayors and councils expected a long period of population decline and were struggling with the implications of that decline. Many municipalities are now growing again.

Among the 830 census subdivisions (municipalities and rural areas) across the four Atlantic provinces, 63 percent were facing population decline before 2019. Since then, two-thirds of municipalities across Atlantic Canada, large and small, have witnessed growth in their populations.[39]

But this growth brings its own challenges. The number of unhoused people has been rising, not only in the largest cities but also in places like Pictou and Truro, NS. Crime rates are rising. Housing costs are increasing in most municipalities at historically unprecedented rates.

It will be important for local municipal governments to commit to supporting a growth agenda by ramping up capacity to support housing development, investing in support systems such as immigrant settlement services, and investing in economic development.

KEY INSTITUTIONS

Many of the region's important institutions, including universities and colleges, hospitals, philanthropic organizations, and industry and professional associations were expecting a long period of population stagnation and weak economic growth. They were not investing in the infrastructure to support long term growth. In the case of industry and professional associations, they were not focussed on a significant expansion of their workforces.

That has all changed in the past few years. We need more accountants, engineers, nurses, doctors, construction workers, hairstylists, veterinarians, and even lawyers. The region's industry and professional associations must respond and push to expand their respective workforces. We are already seeing this with many professional groups such as chartered professional accountants (CPAs) in New Brunswick.

Our universities and colleges should be focussed on turning out the talent needed to meet expanded workforce demand. In general, our institutions need to invest for growth.

BUSINESS COMMUNITY

We need strong leadership from the region's Chambers of Commerce, business councils, and industry associations. They need to clearly embrace a growth agenda for Atlantic Canada and encourage the right environment for growth. In addition to advocating for the right policy environment and workforce development, the business community needs to invest for the future. Atlantic Canada's long-term economic growth will require substantial business investment, which, relative to GDP, has been waning in recent years.

GENERAL PUBLIC

Due to an aging population, the general public does not have as much interest in economic development in 2023 as it would have had in 1973 or 1993. There are now more retired people or those heading toward retirement in the next ten to fifteen years than the entire population aged fifteen to forty-nine. The median age across the region in the early 1970s was twenty-four. Now in many rural areas the median age is over fifty. Obviously, the focus and priorities of those aged twenty-four are considerably different than those in their fifties.

A sustained campaign by both government and industry explaining the importance of population and economic growth will be required to gain the necessary public support in the years ahead, led by the provincial governments in the region and supported by the private sector. What kind of province do we want to leave for future generations? One with a weak economic foundation that struggles to properly fund public services and public infrastructure? One with provincial governments constantly running to Ottawa looking for more money to meet the constitutional requirement to offer Canadians decent quality public services?

CHAPTER 29

MEASURING ECONOMIC MOMENTUM

ATLANTIC CANADA IS FINALLY BEING NOTICED AT A NATIONAL LEVEL. GIVEN THE growing optimism across the region, driven largely by robust population growth, attention must be given to maintaining momentum and ensuring continued economic progress as a priority. There are a number of considerations to ensure continued economic momentum across Atlantic Canada. The ability to track our economic progress is one such consideration. Another is measuring the level of investment in the region from elsewhere.

THE *ATLANTIC CANADA MOMENTUM INDEX*

The Ottawa-based Public Policy Forum, founded in 1987, is an independent, non-partisan, and non-profit organization led, until December 2024, by Ed Greenspon, a former editor of the *Globe and Mail*. The PPF recently released its inaugural *Atlantic Canada Momentum Index* report to measure the economic progress in our region. This is part of the PPF's Atlantic Initiative to build a "sustainable, technology-based knowledge economy to increase living standards for all Atlantic Canadians." Cathy Bennett, business entrepreneur and the former finance minister in Newfoundland and Labrador, and Laurel Broten, now the CEO of Invest in Canada and the former CEO of Nova Scotia Business Inc. (now Invest Nova Scotia), are members of its board of directors.

Greenspon has a connection to the region, as his family arrived in Canada at Pier 21 in 1929. He was a guest on our *Insights* podcast shortly after the release of the PPF's *Momentum Index* and talked about how the success of the Atlantic Bubble during the pandemic initially drew the attention of his organization to the region and led them to further investigate what was happening here. This ultimately led to the development of the *Atlantic Canada Momentum Index*, as part of its Atlantic Initiative (PPF.com), in March 2023.

Greenspon is bullish on the region's economic future. "Today's Atlantic Canada has momentum unlike anything I have seen in my four decades as a friend from away. The iron is hot; it is time to strike by continuing to grow population, attracting and developing talent, and lowering regional barriers to the movement of people, goods, and capital. It is Atlantic Canada's time to lead. The Public Policy Forum is ready to help out."

It is perhaps important to note that it is rare for a national think tank like the PPF to focus any attention on Atlantic Canada—a tangible signal that real change is in the air in our region, although to be fair the merger of the Atlantic Institute for Market Studies with the Fraser Institute in 2019 has also led to an increase of public policy research in the region. As a PPF release said, "The East Coast of Canada is experiencing a moment. Now it is critical to define what the opportunity will be, and how the region can capitalize on it." It is also critical to ensure that public policies are aligned with what is needed to take advantage of this momentum, especially policies related to the regulatory processes. The recent withdrawal of tidal power company Sustainable Marine due to regulatory issues is an example of a momentum killer.

ECONOMIC MEASURES

The *Momentum Index* is based on twenty economic and social measures under five separate categories, including quality of life, human capital, the macro economy, the labour market, and innovation and investment. The measures were developed in collaboration with the Centre for the Study of Living Standards (CSLS)—a non-profit, national organization that researches trends in productivity, living standards, and economic well-being—and a group of regional advisors. CSLS is led by New Brunswick–born founder and executive director Andrew Sharpe.

The first *Atlantic Canada Momentum Index* determined that the region "definitely" was enjoying a moment of real momentum. These measures compared the period from 2008 to 2015 with the post-2015 period; the results showed significant progress and growing momentum for these five indicators within the region. Note that the *Index* is not actually an index, as all measures are weighted equally, and it should be evident that some factors are significantly more important to the future of the region than others. Nonetheless, the PPF has done a good job of identifying those areas where improvements have been made and those that require more work.

The stated objective of the report was twofold: to report on the indicators and "use the data to shape reinforcing public policy choices" and to "alert the rest of Canada and even residents of Atlantic Canada" to the changing prospects in the region.

Among the most important improvements for the region noted is the narrowing gap in nominal GDP per capita. In 1961, nominal GDP per capita in Atlantic Canada was only 59 percent of the national average. The nominal GDP per capita had risen to 87 percent of the national average as of 2021.

Nominal GDP is a measure of the total value (calculated using current prices) of all goods and services produced in a country during a specific period of time.

In addition to measures like population growth, the *Index* includes other human capital factors like immigration retention rates, which have steadily increased in recent years. In a comparison with the rest of Canada, Atlantic Canada has improved on fourteen of the twenty factors measured over the study period, with Prince Edward Island leading the way with improvement on seventeen factors.

TABLE 29-1: THE ATLANTIC CANADA MOMENTUM INDEX (AVERAGE ANNUAL RATE OF CHANGE)

		2008–2015	2015–2022/23	Difference in Growth Rate (% Points)
Macro economy	Real GDP	0.10	1.14	1.04
	Real GDP per capita	-0.11	0.20	0.31
	Real exports	-1.93	-0.44	1.49
	Population	0.21	1.20	0.99
	Median age	0.94	-0.06	-1.01
Human capital	Immigration	10.43	13.21	2.78
	Immigrant retention rate	0.50	0.31	-0.19
	Proportion of youth not in emplyment, education, or training (NEET)	-0.47	-0.92	-0.46
	Proportion of population with tertiary education	2.03	2.84	0.81
Labour market performance	Employment rate	0.13	0.68	0.55
	Employment income	0.44	-0.07	-0.51
	Labour productivity	-0.82	0.49	1.32
	Labour force participation of women with children under age six	0.52	0.22	-0.31
Innovation and investment	Business enterprise in-house expenditure on research and development (BERD)	2.48	0.04	4.55
	Non-residential investment	5.02	-5.87	-10.89
	Non-emitting energy	0.62	0.13	-0.48
	Investment in renewal energy	37.85	-15.02	-52.87
	Greenhouse gas emissions	-2.80	-2.83	-0.03

		2008–2015	2015–2022/23	Difference in Growth Rate (% Points)
Quality of life	Gini coefficient	0.29	-0.84	-1.14
	Housing starts	-5.76	6.95	12.71
	Housing affordability	-0.51		4.75
	Poverty rate	-1.68	-4.35	-2.67
	Access to family physician	-0.37	-1.02	-0.65
	Life satisfaction	-0.24	-0.94	-0.70
	Community belonging	0.14	-0.95	-1.09

*NOTE: A NEGATIVE CHANGE IN THE RATE OF CHANGE OF THE VARIABLES MEDIAN AGE, THE GINI COEFFICIENT, GHG EMISSIONS, HOUSING AFFORDABILITY, POVERTY RATE, AND PROPORTION OF NEET BETWEEN THE TWO PERIODS IS INDICATIVE OF POSITIVE MOMENTUM. FOR ALL OTHER VARIABLES, POSITIVE MOMENTUM IS ASSOCIATED WITH A POSITIVE CHANGE.

Source: Adjusting the Sails. 2024 Atlantic Canada Momentum Index. *Public Policy Forum*, September 2024.

One area of weakness that has been improving for the region is business R & D spending, which still represents only 35 percent of the national average. Another encouraging measure is related to housing starts, which increased at an average annual rate of 6.95 percent between 2015 and 2023. One measure of concern in the *Index* relates to access to a family physician, which indicates improvement in accessibility nationally but not within Atlantic Canada.

MOMENTUM NOT EQUALLY SHARED

As the *Momentum Index* underscored, performance against the measures is somewhat uneven by province within Atlantic Canada. Prince Edward Island has exhibited the most progress in the region, advancing on seventeen of the twenty measures, followed closely by Nova Scotia, with its advancement of sixteen measures. Newfoundland and Labrador had seen progress on only eleven measures, while deteriorating on the remaining nine.

A TIME FOR OPTIMISM

For the first time in living memory, there is a real sense of positive change and economic momentum with the region. It is not, at this point, consistent across the region or within each of the four Atlantic provinces, and the challenge will be to ensure that the progress is more equally shared across all parts of the region. Nonetheless, there are growing signs that the rest of the country has been awakened to the opportunities and quality-of-life advantages that are available within the region. Having the attention of national organizations like the Public Policy Forum lends credence to the economic progress being made and should contribute to growing confidence in the future of Atlantic Canada.

CHAPTER 30

10 WAYS TO MAINTAIN THE MOMENTUM

WE HAVE WITNESSED OVER A RELATIVELY SHORT PERIOD AN ECONOMIC RENAISsance in Atlantic Canada that is being driven by unprecedented population growth. This population growth has generated significant economic activity, especially in the housing sector. We are now building schools, not closing them, as the number of students explodes. We have growing evidence of a more entrepreneurial environment well supported by the various accelerator and incubator programs around the region. Some of the growing entrepreneurism in the region is driven by immigrants who have demonstrated a high tolerance for risk through their decision to immigrate to Canada in the first place. There is more interest in the region from the investment community than ever. There are a growing number of regionally based private equity and venture capital companies.

The question remains: how do we maintain this momentum? We have early evidence of a shift in attitudes and growing confidence in the future of Atlantic Canada. People outside the region are looking at Atlantic Canada in a new light and with renewed interest. We need to have a bold vision of what is possible. This is true for both our private-sector leaders and our political leaders. We need the courage to make the changes necessary to continue the momentum we have already achieved. Obviously, there are many other ideas that would support momentum, but here are the ten that we believe would make the most difference.

1. DEVELOP AN ECONOMIC HUB STRATEGY FOR ECONOMIC DEVELOPMENT

One way to ensure prosperity for all is to change the way service delivery and economic development is done in the region. The fact that Atlantic Canada is more than twice as rural proportionately than the rest of the country means that our rural communities need to be better supported in terms of access to key services and economic opportunities. There are thirty urban centres (with populations of five thousand or more) across Atlantic Canada that serve more than 90 percent of the population within a reasonable commuting time. Attracting jobs to rural communities has always been challenging and will continue to be challenging, especially since many of the jobs in rural areas are resource-based and often seasonal. Rural communities lack the critical infrastructure and human resources to attract the capital investments needed to create year-round, full-time jobs.

What these thirty urban centres have in common is that they all have key infrastructure like post-secondary institutions and hospitals, along with critical population mass to attract jobs. They are all destinations for retail, professional, and other services for nearby rural communities. They are all employment centres for these same nearby rural communities.

Rural communities, due to their small populations, lack access to key public services like education and health care. The closure of rural schools due to a lack of students has been commonplace. Too many rural hospitals struggle with staffing to keep their emergency rooms open. Nova Scotia currently has forty hospitals. It may surprise some to learn that, until quite recently, there were thirty-eight emergency departments in Nova Scotia with all but seven working on a 24/7 schedule. A number of these more rural emergency departments have been recently converted to urgent care centres with more limited schedules. Repurposing some of these rural hospitals to long-term care and their emergency departments to urgent care centres makes sense, especially if the major emergency care centres are being expanded, as is the case with the South Shore Regional Hospital in Nova Scotia.

In New Brunswick, the government repurposed six hospitals in the province in 2020, turning 120 acute-care beds into long-term care beds and closing emergency rooms overnight. New Brunswick currently has thirty-six hospitals. In Newfoundland and Labrador, there are thirty-three emergency departments serving a population half the size of Nova Scotia's.

Across the region, many of the specialty treatment services like cancer care or dialysis are centralized in the major urban centres. Is it possible to have more specialized health-care services available across the region by developing more comprehensive regional hospitals with more on-site specialties? The services of the regional hospitals in each of these economic hubs could be expanded to better serve people closer to where they reside and could reduce their need to go to larger centres for specialized treatments.

Another question that needs to be addressed is: what is the most appropriate number of emergency departments to serve the needs of the population given the restraints on human capital? Also, can some hospitals be repurposed, as both New Brunswick and Nova Scotia have done? New Brunswick currently has thirty-six hospitals. In Nova Scotia, some emergency departments in rural communities are being repurposed as urgent care centres to take the pressure off emergency departments. This approach has been widely taken elsewhere, especially in the US.

Karen Oldfield, the Interim CEO of Nova Scotia Health, reaffirmed this change in strategy in a 2023 *Insights* interview: "A serious emergency, like a heart attack or a stroke, requires attention right here, right now, while the urgent care centre is a way to get people care without them having to sit in an emergency room for hours. We are also identifying communities where, for whatever reason, they may not have the human resources to actually staff an emergency department fully."

Economic development needs to be done on a regional, market-based basis. The best example in Atlantic Canada is Halifax, which serves a geography greater in size that of Prince Edward Island. Every day workers commute from as far away as Bridgewater, the Annapolis Valley, Truro, and the Eastern Shore for jobs in the city. The city provides centralized health and educational services for those living outside the urban core. The advantage for those living in rural communities is that they can enjoy the benefits of rural living with all the amenities and services of a nearby urban centre.

There is a need to realign economic development efforts to these economic hubs and create more regional economic development agencies. The hub approach to service delivery and economic development is already developing organically in the six largest urban communities but could be accelerated across the region with a more planned approach by provincial governments to adopt and support this approach.

Political leadership and the alignment of public policy will be needed to achieve the full potential of an economic hub strategy. This approach has the greatest possibility of distributing prosperity more equally across the region and would be a political winner for any party who adopts this strategy.

2. ESTABLISH ATLANTIC CANADA AS A COMMON MARKET

The interconnectivity of the four Atlantic provinces is unique among Canadian provinces and economically advantageous. Family and business relationships can make doing business a little easier within this region.

The Council of Atlantic Premiers was formally established in May 2000 to promote Atlantic Canadian interests on national issues and to develop better co-operation among the four provinces. The Council has worked on a number of initiatives, including agreements on apprenticeship, mobility, and harmonization. It worked together on the Atlantic Growth Strategy that led to the Atlantic Immigration Program. It has also worked to develop a regional approach to procurement and regulatory alignment, although there is much more to do in all areas of co-operation. That includes harmonizing licensing and credentials for all professional groups. Despite some progress on a number of files, there is a need for higher urgency in the work of the Council to be able to take advantage of the immense opportunities that are emerging across the region, including green hydrogen energy and offshore wind energy. Another is regulatory reform and standardization across the region.

There are numerous other common market opportunities for the Council to consider and implement. One is a regional investment tax credit that would encourage private-sector investment by Atlantic Canadian investors in any of the other three Atlantic provinces. This could be done on a pilot basis.

The Council is already working to enhance access to broadband across the region. Another glaring problem is the lack of adequate interprovincial air transportation. While there are some flights between Nova Scotia and Newfoundland, there were few others (until the recent entry of Quebec-based PASCAN Aviation), either intra-provincially or between any of the other provinces. If you wish to fly from Halifax to Charlottetown, a thirty-minute flight from Halifax will take nearly five hours, with a stop in Montréal and a cost of more than $700. Until only very recently, there were no flights between Halifax and Sydney, NS. The lack of scheduled air transportation within Atlantic Canada is damaging the ability to do business and must be addressed.

There is also an urgent need for common regulations for the development of offshore wind, which is the region's biggest economic opportunity.

3. STREAMLINE THE REGULATORY PROCESS

The most frequent complaints about the regulatory process relate to the lack of timeliness and clarity around rules for project approvals. There is an opportunity here to standardize regulations across Atlantic Canada. We have many examples where the regulatory process has unduly delayed economic development in the region. The most egregious is the recent demise of Sustainable Marine, which invested more than $40 million to harness the tidal power of the Bay of Fundy, but went bankrupt waiting for regulatory approvals from DFO.

Another example is the time needed for site approvals for fish farming in Atlantic Canada, which can take years. Yet another is the lack of timeliness in approval of a new mine, which averages seventeen years from discovery to production in Nova Scotia according to Sean Kirby, the executive director of the Mining Association of Nova Scotia. The same is true in many municipalities in terms of the approval process for housing construction. Governments at all levels must commit to not only reducing the timelines for project approvals, but also to providing improved clarity of the regulations. There are some regulations that should be standardized across the region, such as those related to offshore wind and aquaculture.

In a September 2024 *Insights* podcast, Donald Savoie discussed his new book *Speaking Truth to Canadians about Their Public Service*. In the book he describes the 320,000-strong federal government workforce as either "plumbers" (those who directly deliver public services) or "poets" (those who work on policies, advise politicians, and do other administrative-related work). Savoie concludes that, in recent decades, the workforce has shifted from more plumbers to far more poets. He says, "We have reached the point where over 60 percent of federal public servants now work in policy advisory, coordination, oversight, and back-office functions—the bulk of them in the NCR [National Capital Region], dealing with other federal public servants rather than delivering services to other Canadians." He says provincial governments have also increased the number of poets in recent years. Savoie believes that the inability to get big things done in a timely fashion in Canada is directly related to this growth. To address the big challenges ahead (such as decarbonizing the economy) will require a leaner and more focussed public service.

4. CONCENTRATE ON THE BLUE ECONOMY

One of the region's biggest assets is the ocean that surrounds us. Fishing, aquaculture, mineral exploration, and offshore wind all represent opportunities for economic growth. Canada's Ocean Supercluster is focussed on developing our ocean resources, including ocean technologies. Canada's ocean economy currently employs more than 350,000 Canadians and is worth $39 billion to our GDP; this is expected to double by 2030. A 2024 *Insights* interview with Kendra MacDonald, CEO of Canada's Ocean Supercluster, talked about Ambition 2035, the sector's ambitious goal to grow the sector to $220 billion by 2035. "The focus of the Ocean Supercluster is on sustainable seafood, marine transportation, energy, and tourism. Atlantic Canada currently represents about a third of the blue economy in Canada but has perhaps the greatest opportunity to grow in Canada," MacDonald told us. As we have seen with the bioscience cluster's success in Prince Edward Island, focussing attention on specific clusters can pay huge dividends. The potential for the Ocean Supercluster in Atlantic Canada is perhaps a game changer for the region.

5. DON'T FORGET ABOUT NATURAL RESOURCES

Atlantic Canadians are particularly resistant to the development of our natural resources (although less so in Newfoundland and Labrador) and have developed well-honed NIMBY attitudes to such development. No mines developed, no forest cut, no natural gas drilled, no fish farms, no wind farms, no tall buildings built in our communities. It seems we all support change, as long as nothing really changes. These attitudes have harmed economic development in our region for far too long. These attitudes have led to our over-dependency on governments in the region as well.

In a world focussed on artificial intelligence and technology development, it is easy to overlook the natural resource sector. With our abundant forests, there is an opportunity for significant growth to support the need for lumber in the housing construction market, which is forecasted to triple by 2030 based on current population growth in the region. The permanent closure of Northern Pulp in Nova Scotia hurt the forestry industry significantly. Recently, Paper Excellence, the owners of Northern Pulp, have signalled their interest in building a new pulp mill in the Liverpool area of the province, and this is already generating resistance. This is in an area that previously lost a pulp mill run by Bowater Mersey.

In a world in search of sustainable protein production, there is an opportunity to significantly increase fish farming (both onshore and offshore) given our immense coastline.

With the world needing to increase the production of critical minerals six-fold to support the goal of net zero by 2050, it is time to unlock access to our mining resources. This includes the mining of uranium in Nova Scotia to support the doubling of nuclear power that twenty-two countries at COP28 just committed to achieving by 2050. The arguments that uranium is unsafe to mine need to be challenged given Saskatchewan's long history of safely mining uranium over many decades.

Interestingly, Premier Houston signalled a change in thinking by his government with regard to both nuclear power and uranium mining in a 2024 *Insights* podcast went he publicly stated, "I am supportive of both…the mining of uranium, significant uranium deposits… that is something that I personally think we need to figure out, but it's another opportunity." Interestingly, the government of Nova Scotia recently tabled legislation that would "remove a barrier to Nova Scotia Power owning a nuclear power generating station, allowing the utility to consider the use of small nuclear reactors in the future".

One important opportunity is natural gas. There is currently only one producing well in Atlantic Canada and that is the McCully Field near Sussex, NB, operated by Headwater Exploration. There are significant gas reserves off the coast of Newfoundland and Labrador that have been confirmed but not yet developed.

Phil Knoll, the former CEO of Corridor Gas (now Headwater Exploration) told us on *Insights* in 2024 that the use of natural gas will not likely peak until 2040 or later because it will be needed in the transition to green energy. He indicated that the natural gas reserves near Sussex, NB, represent billions of dollars in revenue for the province of New Brunswick if fully developed, adding:

> New Brunswick has a significant natural gas resource in their shale. The Sussex field alone is estimated to have sixty TCFs [trillion cubic feet] of gas and there are other shale formations in New Brunswick that could have

> similar amounts. That's a very large number. It's hard to put into context. It wouldn't be amongst the biggest potential shale gas fields in North America, but it's a very significant one. It could supply the needs of Nova Scotia and New Brunswick for decades if it was developed, but there are challenges to significantly develop those resources in New Brunswick.

He also pointed out on that podcast that Atlantic Canada imports about $400 million of natural gas that mainly serves an industrial customer base, and all these imports could be replaced by our own natural gas. This point was recently confirmed in an *Insights* podcast with Gilles Volpé, the president of NB Gas. Volpé noted that the total energy provided by natural gas currently used in New Brunswick is equivalent to the energy provided by electricity. It should be pointed out that in December 2024 NB Power announced its plans for a new 400-MW natural gas plant near Moncton to be built by a private company. This will require a source for natural gas.

6. BECOME A GREEN ENERGY SUPERPOWER

Atlantic Canada is poised to become a leader in renewable green energy. There are several green hydrogen projects currently under development in the region, and the first in Canada may be developed in Atlantic Canada. The proposed hydrogen projects will rely on wind power, mostly onshore wind at the moment. These projects will require massive capital investments that will transform the economy across the region.

The *Catching the Wind* report provides a compelling vision for the region to become an energy superpower by harnessing offshore wind, one of the region's most important advantages. As Nicholson points out in his report, Atlantic Canada could become a net exporter of green energy to other jurisdictions outside the region.

In addition, the work that NB Power is doing to develop SMRs with ARC Clean Technology Canada and Moltex opens another opportunity for low-emissions energy. Nova Scotia premier Tim Houston appears to be on board with the use of SMRs by Nova Scotia Power and his government is in the process of passing legislation to allow that possibility. The question is, do we have the vision and audacity as Peter Nicholson has stated to seize this transformational opportunity and become a net exporter of green energy?

In order to fulfill the promise of becoming a green energy superpower, the issues of building transmission infrastructure, confirming markets for export, streamlining the regulatory process, and securing the capital will all have to be addressed.

7. FOCUS ON BOTH ATTRACTION AND RETENTION OF NEWCOMERS

Retention of newcomers has long been a challenge in Atlantic Canada, although there is evidence that retention rates are improving. This is especially the case for those who have been attracted to the region through the Atlantic Immigration Program. These immigrants have a guaranteed job when they arrive, and many of the employers involved in this program make special efforts to assist in the settlement of these newcomers. Atlantic Canada is often described as a friendly place, but is not particularly welcoming to newcomers. It may be that for too long, newcomers were viewed as unwelcome competition for the scarce jobs within the region. Newcomers seek a sense of community and a sense of belonging, and this can really only happen when they are actively included in community circles. This calls for a change in attitudes within the region; perhaps it can begin within our school system.

There is also a need to be more strategic in attracting immigrants by focussing our efforts on building critical mass within specific countries of origin. That in no way should exclude any others interested in immigrating to our region. One of the advantages larger urban areas like Montréal, Toronto, and Vancouver have over most of the rest of the country is the large ethnic communities that provide cultural support to immigrants from those areas. There are examples of communities with critical mass in the region—the Lebanese community in Halifax and the growing Asian community in Charlottetown. Critical mass provides the ability to offer services like churches, grocery stores, and restaurants that cater to their ethnicity. Such communities increase the retention rate of newcomers. But there are some downsides to this strategy, one of which is slowing the integration of newcomers into the population at large.

It would be wise for provincial governments to promote the importance of welcoming newcomers to our region and the positive economic impact that these newcomers can have on our region. This will be increasingly important given the recent unfavourable shift in attitudes toward immigration.

8. BECOME MORE TAX COMPETITIVE

For decades, the lack of population growth at the national level has left the region with a lower capacity to fund public services and has led to the highest taxes in the country. Little or no growth in the number of those employed has meant an increasing tax burden for the relatively static number of taxpayers in the region. That is now finally changing, providing governments with an opportunity to begin lowering taxes to be more in line with other jurisdictions in Canada. The minimum tax deductions for taxpayers are the lowest in Canada, meaning Atlantic Canadians start paying taxes at lower income levels than other Canadians and pay higher rates at higher levels of income.

In the case of Nova Scotia, basic deductions need to be tied to inflation as in the rest of Canada to eliminate "bracket creep," which was finally addressed by the PC government in Nova Scotia in its 2024 provincial budget. All four Atlantic provinces are benefitting from higher revenues tied to population and job growth and need to follow the province of New Brunswick's example, which has taken a more disciplined approach to its fiscal management, including balancing its budget and reducing its provincial debt.

There is also a need to ensure that corporate taxes across the region are competitive with those elsewhere in Canada to assist in attracting capital and investment in Atlantic Canada.

9. INCREASE CAPITAL INVESTMENT

Atlantic Canada trails the rest of the country in terms of capital investment. This needs to change. One small way to change capital investment is to adopt a regional equity tax credit for individuals and companies residing in one of the Atlantic provinces who wish to invest in another province in the region. Companies may need more incentive to invest in their own companies, especially in the adoption of technologies and equipment that will improve their productivity and efficiency. Faster depreciation of those capital investments specifically targeting productivity improvements would likely be helpful. Many large capital investments will be happening in the region over the next decade or so, especially on the green energy transition and the continued development of wind power, which will greatly expand capital investment in the region. But these green energy investments will need to be supported by government tax credits, which need to be put in place sooner rather than later.

10. INCREASE THE FOCUS ON PRODUCTIVITY

Atlantic Canada has the lowest productivity in the country and Canada lags internationally in terms of its productivity. In order to compete, many Atlantic Canadian trade-exposed industries need to boost their productivity. Historically, many industries used lower wages and other operating costs to offset weaker productivity compared to peers in other parts of Canada and beyond. Now, the operating cost advantage in most industries has been reduced and, in some cases, has completely disappeared. These industries will need to boost innovation and productivity to compete in national and international markets. Adoption of new technologies and the use of artificial intelligence should be considered. As an example, Canada's Ocean Supercluster is working to leverage the use of AI for the blue economy and is supporting the adoption of new technology solutions in this sector.

CHAPTER 31
TOWARD PROSPERITY

THIS BOOK HAS BEEN AN ATTEMPT TO CHRONICLE THE RECENT ECONOMIC HIStory of Atlantic Canada and chart a course for a prosperous future. There are a few fundamental requirements for any region to thrive, including export-focussed industries, a strong talent pipeline for the workforce, and an environment that encourages entrepreneurial activity and business investment. It also requires a regulatory environment that has clear rules and timely responses to applications.

The increasing uncertainty associated with a change in the political climate in both Canada and the US will increase the risks to the momentum that we have achieved in the region, especially if the Trump administration proceeds with a significant increase in tariffs. In may force our region and the rest of the country to more aggressively pursue new export markets for our goods and services, which would have long-term benefits and lead to less dependency on the US market.

Atlantic Canada has many strengths, including ample land and natural resources, small but dynamic urban centres, many universities and colleges, and a population that supports immigration. The region has benefitted from many important export-focussed industries, including natural resources such as fish, forest products, agriculture, energy and minerals, manufacturing industries such as rubber products, shipbuilding, and aerospace, as well as knowledge-based industries such as information technology, life sciences, and business services.

As we look to the future, there will be new industries and new opportunities to exploit. Atlantic Canadian businesses are becoming more confident in their ability to compete in a bigger world and the start-up community is growing, with more and more young entrepreneurs focussed on national and even international markets. There are an increasing number of new entrepreneurs, driven in part by highly motivated and ambitious immigrants who are revitalizing the private sector in our region. Old attitudes within the region driven by long-standing dependence on government are slowly changing for the good, with a growing sense of pride and a greater ambition to be self-reliant.

There are many opportunities emerging as a result of the transition under way to achieve net zero by 2050. There are opportunities for our natural resources like mining to source the critical minerals needed to support the electrification of the transportation sector and the use of natural gas in the transition phase that is likely to last decades. Green hydrogen represents another significant opportunity for the region.

Wind power may be Atlantic Canada's greatest opportunity, but as Peter Nicholson underscores in his *Catching the Wind* report, it will require audacious ambition. Nicholson, in his report, is convinced that "offshore wind could be for Atlantic Canada what oil was to Texas or hydro power to Quebec. We are talking here not of something incremental, but monumental."

We believe it is time for Atlantic Canada to aim higher in its ambition and take advantage of the opportunity that has been presented to us. It will require bold thinking and bigger dreams by our business leaders and political leaders.

The emergence of economic opportunities for our First Nations in the development of our natural resources is an important turning point for our regional economy.

A top challenge in recent years has been the shrinking talent pipeline. Until a few years ago, more people were leaving the workforce through retirements than were joining it. Now, because of a surge in immigration and interprovincial migration, the region is rebuilding its talent pipeline and there is a new sense of optimism.

There are still macroeconomic warning signs. Business investment is still lagging the rest of the country and the region's trade deficit is widening. Many important export-focussed industries are not as productive as in other competitor jurisdictions. The region has a serious innovation gap. Further, through our many *Insights* podcast interviews we've learned that there seem to be considerable regulatory and environmental roadblocks in the way of many new industrial opportunities across the region.

Nevertheless, we have never been more personally optimistic about the future of Atlantic Canada. *Toward Prosperity: The Transformation of Atlantic Canada's Economy* provides a roadmap to guide the region's future prosperity. If we can get these things right, the outlook has never been more promising for this region.

Our future is now. Let's not lose our momentum.

ACKNOWLEDGEMENTS

WE WOULD LIKE TO ACKNOWLEDGE THE PEOPLE WHO HAVE SUPPORTED OUR efforts to write this book, beginning with Terrilee Bulger from Nimbus Publishing, who believed that the premise of the book was worth publishing in the first place and, in particular, Angela Mombourquette for her skillful work in editing the book for us. We also want to thank Dan Leger for his assistance and sage advice during the writing process, which greatly improved the final product, as well as the early advice provided by Graham Steele, John DeMont, and Jim Meek.

The book really emerged from our *Insights* podcast and the incredible and uplifting stories that we were hearing around Atlantic Canada about successful businesses and entrepreneurs and about the change in economic opportunities that was happening around the region. The more podcasts we did, the more optimistic we became about the economic future for Atlantic Canada. We are grateful to all those who took the time to share their stories with us on *Insights*, and we wish to especially recognize all those who have been quoted in this book. We continue to tell those stories of success on our podcast.

We would like to thank Narrative Research for providing the opinion research that was used in the book regarding attitudes toward immigration, and Jim Debner, chief statistician, who is responsible for the creation of the economic hub maps referenced in the book. We would also like to thank Thomas Storring, the Director of Economic and Statistics at the Nova Scotia Department of Finance for providing the updated age pyramids used in the book.

Finally, we are grateful to all those who have supported us and encouraged us to write this book, including our families, friends, and business colleagues.

ENDNOTES

1 All workforce data in this section taken from Statistics Canada Table 14-10-0327-01.

2 Ray Ivany, et al., *Now or Never: Report of the Nova Scotia Commission on Building Our New Economy*, 2014, onens.ca/sites/default/files/editor-uploads/now-or-never.pdf.

3 Statistics Canada defines "rural" as those living outside population centres. Population centres are areas that have a population of at least one thousand and no fewer than four hundred people per square kilometre. There can be small population centres as long as there is a high level of population concentration. It should be noted that the definition used for population centres differs from the definitions of a rural community and an urban community, which have been previously referenced in this book. An urban area is defined by Statistics Canada as a community with a population of five thousand or more.

4 Post-secondary education includes both college and university programs.

5 As do many of their spouses/partners.

6 Heather Steel, "Where's the Policy? Immigration to New Brunswick, 1945-1971," *Acadiensis* 35, no. 2, Spring/Printemps 2006: 85–105. erudit.org/en/journals/acadiensis/2006-v35-n2-acadiensis_35_2/acad35_2art05/

7 This is not exclusively an Atlantic Canada challenge. The construction sector workforce is the largest beneficiary of the EI program each year.

8 The year 2019 was used to remove any possible distortions related to the pandemic in 2020 or 2021.

9 Census subdivisions.

10 The exception is much of the population living outside the St. John's region in Newfoundland and Labrador. Nearly 45 percent of the provincial population lives outside the St. John's CMA and the CAs of Bay Roberts, Grand Falls-Windsor, Corner Brook, and Gander.

11 David Campbell, *Making EI Work: For Consistent Economic Growth and the Atlantic Seasonal Workforce*, Ottawa: Public Policy Forum, September 2020, ppforum.ca/publications/making-ei-work-for-consistent-economic-growth-and-the-atlantic-seasonal-workforce/.

12 Statistics Canada.

13 United States Bureau of Economic Analysis.

14 Brazilian Institute of Geography and Statistics (IBGE).

15 The income figures in this section taken from Statistics Canada 2021 Census.

16 Note there are other sources of non-tax revenue, including transfer payments (federal to provincial) and royalty revenues. Source: Statistics Canada Table 10-10-0015-01.

17 The risk associated with Newfoundland and Labrador being reliant on the oil and gas sector is discussed further in chapter 5.

18 Alberta relies less on taxing households because it generates a large share of revenue from non-renewable resource royalties.

19 *NBIF Past, Present and Future: Building on Two Decades of Catalyzing Innovation and Economic Growth in New Brunswick*, Jupia Consultants Inc., April 2024.

20 Average annual capital investment between 2021 and 2023 relative to GDP contribution. Source: Statistics Canada.

21 Statistics Canada, Table 33-10-0304-01, Canadian Business Counts, With Employees, December 2020. doi.org/10.25318/3310030401-eng.

22 Using both Census Tract and Census Dissemination Area data.

23 Canada Mortgage and Housing Corporation. *Housing shortages in Canada: Updating How Much Housing We Need by 2030*. Ottawa, September 2023. cmhc-schl.gc.ca/professionals/housing-markets-data-and-rsearch/housing-research/research-reports/accelerate-supplyhousing-shortages-canada-updating-how-much-we-need-by-2030.

24 CTAS levels I–III (discharged) median (50 percent spent less, in hours). New Brunswick and Newfoundland and Labrador do not submit data to the Canadian Institute for Health Information.

25 As of the 2021 Census.

26 Some interprovincial migrants are immigrants who first settled elsewhere in Canada and then moved to Nova Scotia.

27 As discussed in "The Leaky Bucket: A Study of Immigrant Retention Trends in Canada," Conference Board of Canada, October 2023. forcitizenship.ca/wp-content/uploads/2023/10/print_the_leaky-bucket_2023.pdf.

28 Newfoundland and Labrador receives a large share of its provincial government revenue from offshore oil and gas royalties.

29 Using EY Personal Income Tax Calculator for 2023.

30 This excludes primary immigrants but would include those immigrants who moved to and from Atlantic Canada from other provinces over the five-year period.

31 Now the United States–Mexico-Canada–Agreement (USMCA) which came into force on July 1, 2020.

32 As published by Statistics Canada in Table 36-10-0222-01. Values expressed in chained (2017) dollars.

33 There is data for 2022, but the tourism industry was impacted by the pandemic.

34 This data is shown in chained (2017) dollars.

35 To account for the long time frame, all the data in this section is based on real, inflation-adjusted data.

36 New Brunswick has a higher export-to-GDP ratio mainly because of the oil refinery. However, if the import value of crude was removed, the ratio would drop substantially to less than 50 percent of GDP.

37 Statistics Canada Table 34-10-0133-01.

38 Michael Tutton, "Lobster giant partially owned by Indigenous bands delivering higher sales and profits," The Canadian Press via CTV Atlantic, March 17, 2023. atlantic.ctvnews.ca/lobster-giant-partially-owned-by-indigenous-bands-delivering-higher-sales-and-profits-1.6317579.

39 Share of census subdivisions with a decline in population between 2010 and 2019. Statistics Canada Table 17-10-0142-01.

BIBLIOGRAPHY

"Ambition 2035." St. John's, NL: Canada's Ocean Supercluster, 2023. oceansupercluster.ca/ambition-2035.

Campbell, David. *Making EI Work: For Consistent Economic Growth and the Atlantic Seasonal Workforce.* Ottawa: Public Policy Forum, September 2020. ppforum.ca/publications/making-ei-work-for-consistent-economic-growth-and-the-atlantic-seasonal-workforce/.

Canada Mortgage and Housing Corporation. *Housing Shortages in Canada: Updating How Much Housing We Need by 2030.* Ottawa, September 2023. cmhc-schl.gc.ca/professionals/housing-markets-data-and-research/housing-research/research-reports/accelerate-supply/housing-shortages-canada-updating-how-much-we-need-by-2030.

Eisen, Ben, et al. *Catching up with Canada: A Prosperity Agenda for Atlantic Canada.* Canada: Fraser Institute, 2019. fraserinstitute.org/studies/catching-up-with-canada-prosperity-agenda-for-atlantic-canada.

Foot, David K., and Daniel Stoffman. *Boom, Bust & Echo: How to Profit from the Coming Demographic Shift.* Toronto: Macfarlane Walter & Ross, 1996.

Fuss, Jake and Grady Munro. *Canada's Rising Personal Taxes and Falling Tax Competitiveness,* 2024. Canada: Fraser Institute, 2024. fraserinstitute.org/sites/default/files/canadas-rising-personal-tax-rates-and-falling-tax-competitiveness-2024.pdf.

Immigration, Refugees and Citizenship Canada. Various data. canada.ca/en/immigration-refugees-citizenship.html.

Ivany, Ray, et al. *Now or Never: Report of the Nova Scotia Commission on Building Our New Economy,* 2014. onens.ca/sites/default/files/editor-uploads/now-or-never.pdf.

Jupia Consultants Inc. *NBIF Past, Present and Future: Building on Two Decades of Catalyzing Innovation and Economic Growth in New Brunswick.* April 2024.

Mills, Don, and David Campbell. "Dan Kelly, CEO, CFIB." *Insights* podcast, Saint John: Acadia Broadcasting, March 2024. acadiabroadcasting.ca/dan-kelly-ceo-of-canadian-federation-of-independant-businesses-discusses-small-business-in-canada/.

Mills, Don, and David Campbell. "Dan Mills, Deputy Minister in New Brunswick's Department of Post-Secondary Education, Training and Labour." *Insights* podcast, Saint John: Acadia Broadcasting, September 2023. acadiabroadcasting.ca/discussion-with-minister-arlene-dunn-on-the-growing-population-and-job-vacancies-in-nb/.

Mills, Don, and David Campbell. "Darrel Bricker, Global President for Public Affairs, Ipsos." *Insights* podcast, Saint John: Acadia Broadcasting, July 2021. acadiabroadcasting.ca/podcast-darrell-bricker-on-the-empty-planet-and-what-it-means-for-atlantic-canada/.

Mills, Don, and David Campbell. "Donald Savoie, Professor at l'Université de Moncton." *Insights* podcast, Saint John: Acadia Broadcasting, August 2, 2023. acadiabroadcasting.ca/new-brunswick-scholar-donald-savoie-discusses-his-new-book-canada/.

Mills, Don, and David Campbell. "Dr. Beth Mason, President & CEO, Verschuren Centre." *Insights* podcast, Saint John: Acadia Broadcasting, May 2022. acadiabroadcasting.ca/why-beth-mason-says-cape-breton-is-a-magical-place-with-great-innovative-potential/.

Mills, Don, and David Campbell. "Duncan Williams, CEO of Construction Association of Nova Scotia (CANS)." *Insights* podcast, Saint John: Acadia Broadcasting, June 2023. acadiabroadcasting.ca/duncan-williams-on-the-troubling-numbers-behind-nova-scotias-housing-shortage/.

Mills, Don, and David Campbell. "Jean-Claude Savoie, Founder, Groupe Savoie." *Insights* podcast, Saint John: Acadia Broadcasting, March 2023. acadiabroadcasting.ca/northern-new-brunswicks-titan-of-forestry-jean-claude-savoie/.

Mills, Don, and David Campbell. "Jeff White, CEO, New Brunswick Innovation Foundation." *Insights* podcast, Saint John: Acadia Broadcasting, May 2024. acadiabroadcasting.ca/damon-goodwin-and-jeff-white-on-how-to-improve-innovation-in-new-brunswick/.

Mills, Don, and David Campbell. "Jennifer Watts, Former CEO, Immigrant Services Association of Nova Scotia." *Insights* podcast, Saint John: Acadia Broadcasting, April 2021. hotcountry1035.ca/2021/04/29/jennifer-watts-on-nova-scotias-one-stop-for-immigrant-settlement.

Mills, Don, and David Campbell. "Jim Irving, Co-CEO, J. D. Irving, Limited." *Insights* podcast, Saint John: Acadia Broadcasting, October 2023. acadiabroadcasting.ca/jim-irving-discusses-the-importance-of-the-forestry-sector-for-the-future-of-new-brunswick/.

Mills, Don, and David Campbell. "John Bragg, CEO, Oxford Foods." *Insights* podcast, Saint John: Acadia Broadcasting, May 2021. acadiabroadcasting.ca/a-rare-interview-with-atlantic-canada-business-legend-john-bragg/.

Mills, Don, and David Campbell. "Karen Oldfield, Interim CEO of NS Health Authority." *Insights* podcast, Saint John: Acadia Broadcasting, November 2023. acadiabroadcasting.ca/outsider-karen-oldfield-transforming-healthcare-in-nova-scotia/.

Mills, Don, and David Campbell. "Kathryn Lockhart, CEO, Propel." *Insights* podcast, Saint John: Acadia Broadcasting, February 2022. acadiabroadcasting.ca/the-atlantic-canadian-farm-for-baby-unicorns/.

Mills, Don, and David Campbell. "Kendra MacDonald, CEO of Canada's Ocean Supercluster." *Insights* podcast, Saint John: Acadia Broadcasting, March 2024. acadiabroadcasting.ca/canadas-ocean-supercluster-growing-the-blue-economy-with-kendra-macdonald-ceo-of-osc/.

Mills, Don, and David Campbell. "Lee Bragg, CEO of Eastlink." *Insights* podcast, Saint John: Acadia Broadcasting, November 2021. acadiabroadcasting.ca/lee-bragg-on-the-challenges-of-high-speed-internet-in-rural-atlantic-canada/.

Mills, Don, and David Campbell. "Malcolm Fraser, Former CEO of Innovacorp." *Insights* podcast, Saint John: Acadia Broadcasting, May 2022. acadiabroadcasting.ca/how-innovacorps-unique-approach-helps-startups-become-billion-dollar-companies/.

Mills, Don, and David Campbell. "Melanie Nadeau, CEO, COVE (Centre for Ocean Ventures)." *Insights* podcast, Saint John: Acadia Broadcasting, October 2021. acadiabroadcasting.ca/melanie-nadeau-on-the-rise-of-the-blue-economy/.

Mills, Don, and David Campbell. "Michelle Simms, Former President & CEO of Genesis." *Insights* podcast, Saint John: Acadia Broadcasting, December 2023. acadiabroadcasting.ca/michelle-simms-ceo-of-genesis-discusses-the-tech-boom-in-newfoundland/.

Mills, Don, and David Campbell. "Niels Veldhuis, CEO of the Fraser Institute." *Insights* podcast, Saint John: Acadia Broadcasting, August 2021. acadiabroadcasting.ca/niels-veldhuis-on-making-atlantic-canada-the-countrys-most-prosperous-region/.

Mills, Don, and David Campbell. "Oliver Technow, CEO of BIOVECTRA." *Insights* podcast, Saint John: Acadia Broadcasting, December 2023. acadiabroadcasting.ca/biovectra-is-an-emerging-force-in-pharmaceutical-manufacturing-in-canada/.

Mills, Don, and David Campbell. "Paul Mazerolle, President and Vice-Chancellor of the University of New Brunswick." *Insights* podcast, Saint John: Acadia Broadcasting, November 2022. acadiabroadcasting.ca/paul-mazerolle-on-the-entrepreneurial-spirit-at-unb/.

Mills, Don, and David Campbell. "Paulette Hicks, Former CEO, Envision Saint John." *Insights* podcast, Saint John: Acadia Broadcasting, December 2021. huddle.today/2021/12/09/podcast-new-saint-john-economic-development-agency-has-aggressive-plans/.

Mills, Don, and David Campbell. "Peter Gregg, CEO of Nova Scotia Power." *Insights* podcast, Saint John: Acadia Broadcasting, April 2024. acadiabroadcasting.ca/peter-gregg-ceo-of-nova-scotia-power-and-the-race-to-reach-green-energy-targets/.

Mills, Don, and David Campbell. "Peter Nicholson, Author of *Catching the Wind* for the Public Policy Forum." *Insights* podcast, Saint John: Acadia Broadcasting, November 2023. acadiabroadcasting.ca/peter-nicholson-discusses-how-atlantic-canada-can-be-an-energy-superpower/.

Mills, Don, and David Campbell. "Rhiannon Davies, Co-Founder and Managing Director, Sandpiper Ventures." *Insights* podcast, Saint John: Acadia Broadcasting, March 2023. acadiabroadcasting.ca/podcast-rhiannon-davies-on-why-women-led-companies-are-a-better-investment/.

Mills, Don, and David Campbell. "Richard Saillant, Economist." *Insights* podcast, Saint John: Acadia Broadcasting, July 2023. acadiabroadcasting.ca/economist-richard-saillant-provides-a-tutorial-on-the-federal-equalization-program/.

Mills, Don, and David Campbell. "Rob Normandeau, CEO and Managing Director, Seafort Capital." *Insights* podcast, Saint John: Acadia Broadcasting, February 2024. acadiabroadcasting.ca/ceo-and-managing-director-of-seafort-capital-discusses-when-to-grow-or-sell-your-business/.

Mills, Don, and David Campbell. "Sean Leet, Managing Director and CEO of World Energy GH2." *Insights* podcast, Saint John: Acadia Broadcasting, January 2024. acadiabroadcasting.ca/ceo-of-world-energy-gh2-discusses-their-opportunity-to-lead-in-green-energy-production/.

Mills, Don, and David Campbell. "Tareq Hadhad, Founder and CEO of Peace by Chocolate." *Insights* podcast, Saint John: Acadia Broadcasting, October 2022. acadiabroadcasting.ca/tareq-hadhad-on-his-familys-remarkable-journey-from-syria-to-nova-scotia/.

Mills, Don, and David Campbell. "Wade MacLauchlan, Former Premier of Prince Edward Island." *Insights* podcast, Saint John: Acadia Broadcasting, April 2023. acadiabroadcasting.ca/from-bubble-to-boom-is-atlantic-canada-still-a-have-not-region/.

Mills, Don, and David Campbell. "Wendy Luther, CEO of the Halifax Partnership." *Insights* podcast, Saint John: Acadia Broadcasting, April 2022. acadiabroadcasting.ca/halifax-partnership-serves-as-a-model-for-community-economic-development/.

Moreira, Peter, et al. 2023 *Atlantic Canada Startup Data Report*. Halifax: *Entrevestor*, 2023. entrevestor.com/atlantic-canada-startup-data-2023.

Nicolson, Peter. *Catching the Wind: How Atlantic Canada can become an energy superpower*. Ottawa: Public Policy Forum, 2023. ppforum.ca/publications/wind-energy-atlantic-canada/.

Porter, Michael E. *The Competitive Advantage of Nations*. Los Angeles: The Free Press, 1990.

Savoie, Donald. *Looking For Bootstraps: Economic Development in the Maritimes*. Halifax: Nimbus Publishing, 2017.

Sharpe, Andrew. *The Atlantic Canada Momentum Index*. Ottawa: Public Policy Forum, 2023. ppforum.ca/publications/the-atlantic-canada-momentum-index/.

Statistics Canada. Various data. statcan.gc.ca/en/start.

Tutton, Michael. "Lobster giant partially owned by Indigenous bands delivering higher sales and profits." The Canadian Press via CTV Atlantic. March 17, 2023. atlantic.ctvnews.ca/lobster-giant-partially-owned-by-indigenous-bands-delivering-higher-sales-and-profits-1.6317579.

ABOUT THE AUTHORS

DAVID CAMPBELL is the president of Jupia Consultants Inc., an economic development consulting firm based in New Brunswick. He has more than thirty years' experience working with industry, not-for-profit organizations, and governments across Canada on economic development strategic planning, economic impact analysis, workforce development, and sector development. He was previously Chief Economist with the government of New Brunswick. In that role, he led the development of economic policy and economic development strategy for the provincial government. David is a writer, a co-host of the *Insights* podcast, and a columnist with Postmedia.

DON MILLS is president of Crane Cove Holdings, his family investment firm, and a partner and director with CABCO Communications. He is the co-founder and former owner and CEO of Corporate Research Associates (now Narrative Research), which he sold in late 2018. He remained chair and senior counsel until early 2023. He was a regular columnist with both the Saltwire Network and Brunswick News until the end of 2024. He is currently a columnist with the *MacDonald Notebook* and a frequent media commentator on public affairs issues. He is also the co-host of the *Insights* podcast on the Acadia Broadcasting Network. He remains active as an advocate for change, a keynote speaker, and a consultant in marketing and strategy.